POSITIVE DISCIPLINE
IN THE
SCHOOL and CLASSROOM
⊢— MANUAL —⊣

TERESA LASALA, JODY MCVITTIE AND SUZANNE SMITHA

Based on: *Positive Discipline in the Classroom Teacher's Guide*
Jane Nelsen and Lynn Lott

This revision includes new material and work previously published in *Positive Discipline in the School and Classroom Teachers' Guide: Activities for Students* and *Positive Discipline in the School and Classroom Leaders' Guide: Resources & Activities*.

pda
POSITIVE DISCIPLINE
ASSOCIATION

© 2018 by The Positive Discipline Association
Published by the Positive Discipline Association
Printed in the United States of America

ISBN: 978-0-9860181-3-8

POSITIVE DISCIPLINE IN THE SCHOOL AND CLASSROOM MANUAL
Distribution or reproduction of this manual either in print form or electronically without prior written consent is a violation of copyright law.
© Positive Discipline Association ▪ www.PositiveDiscipline.org

Dedicated to the community of committed educators
working to build respectful schools,
classrooms, and communities.

───────

"A teacher with proper respect for each child, who treats him with dignity and friendliness, may induce him to accept the order and regulations necessary for any social function. On the other hand, the educator must also have respect for himself and not yield where firmness is needed."

Dreikurs, Rudolf. *Psychology in the Classroom, 2nd Edition.* Harper & Row, New York 1968 p. 61.

Additional Books and Materials Available in the Positive Discipline Series Supporting Schools, Educators and Students

Positive Discipline in the Classroom, 4th edition
Jane Nelsen, Lynn Lott and H. Stephen Glenn

> This book is part of the materials for the Positive Discipline in the Classroom workshop. It gives a deeper background into Positive Discipline strategies that foster cooperation, problem-solving skills, and mutual respect in the classroom. Full of stories, it helps you understand why Positive Discipline works!

Positive Discipline: A Teacher's A-Z Guide, Revised and Expanded 2nd Edition
Jane Nelsen, Roslyn Duffy, Linda Escobar, Kate Ortolano, and Deborah Owen-Sohocki

> Especially helpful for teachers and intervention teams, this book provides an alphabetical list of challenging behaviors with tips for understanding the problems, useful suggestions, and ways to plan ahead to prevent future problems. It is a useful reference when you want help with a particular problem.

Positive Discipline Tools for Teachers: 52 Tools for Classroom Management (A set of cards)
Jane Nelsen and Kelly Gfroerer

> This handy deck of cards uses encouraging methods for you and for your students. The "text" side of each card provides quick, easy steps for implementation. The cards are an excellent resource for brainstorming during intervention meetings.

Positive Discipline Tools for Teachers: Effective Classroom Management for Social, Emotional, and Academic Success
Jane Nelsen and Kelly Gfroerer

> Expanding on the tool cards, this book is filled with respectful, solution-oriented approaches to ensure a cooperative and productive classroom. It includes up to date research along with teacher testimonials and stories from around the world.

Positive Discipline for Children with Special Needs
Jane Nelsen, Steven Foster, and Arlene Raphael

> Looking beyond diagnostic labels, believing in the potential of each child, helping children integrate socially and cope with frustrations all receive special emphasis in this book, along with belonging, contribution and more.

Positive Discipline for Early Childhood Educators
Jane Nelsen, Cheryl Erwin, and Steven Foster

> Designed for early childhood educators, teachers and caregivers, this manual helps adults apply the principles and tools of Positive Discipline to their work with groups of children ages birth to six years.

Building Classroom Community DVD: Classroom Meetings and Self-Regulation

> This video captures the power of the Class Meeting in two elementary classrooms and also gives teacher and administrator validation for the effectiveness of Positive Discipline in their school.

And finally, we highly recommend reading:

Positive Discipline
Jane Nelsen

> This is the classic guide to helping children develop self-discipline, responsibility, cooperation and problem-solving skills. This is a "gold-standard reference" for any adults working with children. It is a helpful resource for all interpersonal relationships.

These and many more resources for parents are available at positivediscipline.com. Many are available in Spanish, Arabic, French, Mandarin, and other languages.

Table of Contents

Acknowledgments   13
Foreword   14

Introduction 15

The Theory Behind Positive Discipline   16

Trauma-Informed Practices   16

Character Development   17

Social Emotional Learning (SEL)   17

Social Emotional Learning (SEL): Social Skills Make a Difference   18

Implementing the Positive Discipline Social-Emotional Curriculum   19

School-wide Positive Discipline   20

Putting it Together: The Analogy of the Jumbled School House   21

How to Use This Manual 23

Where do you start with the curriculum?   23

Moving it forward   24

How long will it take to implement Positive Discipline?   25

Keeping Parents in the Loop   25

What is Positive Discipline at [School]?   26

Positive Discipline Stories   27

A kindergarten class meeting   27

A middle school story   27

Positive Discipline solving recess problems   28

Positive Discipline in Iceland   29

House of Positive Discipline in the Classroom   30

Essential Skills for a Positive Discipline Classroom: Preparing the Ground 31

The big idea: Preparing the Ground   31

The circle   31

Why preparing the ground is important   31

What else are students learning?   32

Recommended order for teaching Preparing the ground   32

Agreements and Guidelines for the Classroom 35

Concept: Creating agreed-upon guidelines   35

Why agreed-upon guidelines are important   35

    What else are students learning?   35

    Recommended order for teaching *agreements and guidelines*   36

    Teaching is not enough   36

Beginning the Almost Perfect School Year (BAPSY)   37

We Decided: Guidelines for our Classroom   40

Creating Routines for the Classroom ... 41

    Concept: Routines   41

    Why routines are important   41

    What else are students learning?   41

    Recommended process for teachers to teach *routines*   41

    The 5 R's of Routines   42

Teaching Routines   43

Teaching Routines: How Do We Line Up?   45

Meaningful Work ... 47

    Concept: Meaningful work   47

    Why meaningful work is important   47

    What else are students learning?   47

    Activities   47

Classroom Jobs   49

School-wide Jobs   50

    School-wide jobs: Whole classroom   50

    School-wide jobs: Individual students   50

    Job descriptions and "hiring"   50

Examples of individual student jobs   51

Sample Job Description   52

Sample School Job Application   53

Sample Job Interview Guide   54

School-wide Jobs – Sample Letter to Parents   55

Self-regulation ... 57

    Concept: Self-regulation (Self-control)   57

    Why self-regulation is important   57

    Developing self-regulation and self-control   57

    What else are students learning?   58

    Recommended order for teaching *self-regulation*   58

The Brain in the Hand   60

Positive Time Out & Creating the Space   63

More Activities for Self-calming and Self-awareness   65

Glad, Mad, Sad, or Scared: The Wheel of Feelings   69

    Examples of Feeling Words   71

Feeling Faces Quilt 72

Feeling Faces 73

More Activities for Emotional Awareness 74

Communication Skills 75

Concept: Communication skills 75

Why communication skills are important 75

Recommended order for teaching communication skills 75

Bugs and Wishes 77

I-Messages 79

Listening 1: Effective and Ineffective Listening 81

Listening 2: Effective and Ineffective Group Listening 82

Mutual Respect 83

Concept: Mutual respect 83

Why mutual respect is important 83

What else are students learning? 83

Recommended order for teaching mutual respect 83

Charlie 85

Respect for Self and Others 86

Building Cooperation. 87

Concept: Building cooperation 87

Why cooperation is important 87

What else are students learning? 88

Recommended order for teaching building cooperation 88

Exploring Power: Building Cooperation 89

Cooperative Juggling 91

Rope Activity 93

Moving the Ball 94

Crossing the Line 96

Arm Wrestling 97

Mistakes and How to Repair Them. 99

Concept: Mistakes and how to repair them 99

Why learning about mistakes and repair is important 99

What else are students learning? 99

Recommended order for teaching Mistakes and How to Repair Them *99*

Mistakes: Making vs. Being for Younger Students 101

Mistakes: Making vs. Being for Older Students 102

Mistakes Messages 103

The R's of Recovery from Mistakes 104

Apologizing: How to Do It 106

    Apology of Action: Repairing Relationships   107

    Apologizing: How to Accept an Apology or Repair   109

    Apologizing: How to Ask for a Repair   111

Encouragement 113

    Concept: Encouragement   113

    Why learning about encouragement is important for students   114

    What else are students learning?   114

Encouragement Activities   115

Respecting Differences 117

    Concept: Respecting differences   117

    Why respecting differences is important   117

    What else are students learning?   117

    Recommended order for teaching *respecting differences*   118

Animal Kingdom   119

Experiencing Differences   125

You Decided   126

Buy-In for Class Meetings 127

    Concept: Buy-in   127

    Why buy-in is important   127

    What else are students learning?   127

    Recommended order for teaching *buy-in* for class meetings   127

Exploring Power: Win/Win   129

Introducing the Class Meeting   130

Why Have Class Meetings?   131

Middle School/High School Buy-In   133

8 Essential Skills for Effective Class Meetings: Laying the Foundation 135

    The big idea: Class Meeting Essential Skills   135

    Why the essential skills are important   135

    What else are students learning?   136

    Recommended order for teaching the *8 Essential Skills for Class Meetings*   136

Forming a Circle 139

    Concept: Forming a circle   139

    Why forming a circle is important   139

    How class meetings use the circle   139

    What else are students learning?   139

    Recommended order for teaching *forming a circle*   139

Forming A Circle - Quickly, Quietly, Safely   141

Practicing Compliments and Appreciations. 143
    Concept: Giving and receiving compliments and appreciations   143

    Why compliments and appreciations are important   143

    How class meetings use compliments and appreciations   143

    What else are students learning?   143

    Recommended order for teaching compliments and appreciations   144

Compliments and Appreciations 1: Introducing the Format and Process of Giving and Receiving   146

Compliments and Appreciations 2: Sharing Compliments   148

Compliments and Appreciations 3: Give, Get or Pass   150

Respecting Differences. 151
    Concept: Respecting differences   151

    Why respecting differences important   151

    What else are students learning?   151

    Recommended order for teaching these respecting differences   152

It's Not Fair!   153

Rhythm Band Warm-Up   154

Step into My Shoes   155

Communication Skills. 159
    Concept: Communication skills   159

    Why communication skills are important   159

    What else are students learning?   159

    How class meetings enhance communication skills   159

    Recommended order for teaching communication skills   160

    Recommended review lesson for communication skills   160

Focusing on Solutions. 161
    Concept: Focusing on solutions   161

    Why focusing on solutions is important   161

    How class meetings encourage focusing on solutions   161

    What else are students learning?   162

    Recommended order for teaching focusing on solutions   162

Four Problem Solving Suggestions   163

Wheel of Choice   165

Wheel of Choice Sample   166

Wheel of Choice Sample   167

Solution Table   168

Solutions vs. Logical Consequences   170

Solutions and Curiosity Questions, not Blame   172

The Helpful, not Hurtful Monitor   174

Brainstorming and Role-playing 177
    Concept: Brainstorming and role-playing   177
    Why brainstorming and role-playing are important   177
    How class meetings teach role-playing and brainstorming   178
    What else are students learning?   178
    Recommended order for teaching *brainstorming and role-playing*   178

Paper Clip Activity   179

Brainstorming   180

Role-playing   181

Role-playing and Brainstorming: Working with Guest Teachers (Substitutes)   182

Using the Class Meeting Format and Agenda 183
    Concept: The Class Meeting Format and Agenda   183
    Why the class meeting format and using an agenda are important   185
    Recommended order for teaching *the class meeting format and using the agenda*:   185

Positive Discipline Class Meetings Overview   187

Introducing the Class Meeting Format   188

We Decided: Guidelines for Class Meetings   189

Our Class Meeting Agenda   190

Introducing the Class Meeting Format – Group Problems   195

Class Meeting Agenda Using Individual Problems   197

Understanding and Using the Four Mistaken Goals 199
    Concept: Understanding and using the four mistaken goals (the belief behind the behavior)   199
    Why the belief behind the behavior is important   199
    How class meetings teach the belief behind the behavior   199
    What else are students learning?   199
    Recommended order for teaching *understanding and using the mistaken goals*   200

Introduction to The Four Reasons People Do What They Do   201

The Mistaken Goal Chart   202

Mistaken Goals and Us   204

Encouragement Using Mistaken Goals   205

Positive Discipline Principles 207
A Brief Introduction to the Thought of Alfred Adler   210

Dimensions of Kindness and Firmness   210

Two Opposing Schools of Thought on Human Behavior   211

Positive Discipline: Big Ideas   212
    The Courage to be Imperfect   212
    Recovery from a Mistake   212
    Respect   212
    Results of Punishment   212

Positive Discipline: Your Perspective is Important The Development of Self-Control   213
Applying Positive Discipline: A Scaffolded Approach   214

Handouts for Workshop 215

The Brain in the Hand   217
The Class Meeting   218
Class Meeting Closers: Leave 'em Laughing   219
Curiosity Questions: "What" and "How"   220
De-escalation Tips: Rx for the Flipped Lid   221
Helpful Hints for Empowering vs. Enabling Handout   222
Empowering/Enabling Statements   223
Empowering/Enabling Statements for Younger Children   225
Encouragement vs. Praise   226
The Language of Encouragement   227
Making Agreements and Following Through Handout   228
Mistaken Goal Chart   229
The Belief Behind the Behavior – A key for mistaken beliefs   230
Chart of Classroom Interventions by Mistaken Goal   231
Positive Discipline in the Classroom – Suggested Framework for Getting Started   233
Positive Discipline in the Classroom Leadership Tools   235
The Results of Rewards Handout   236
Solutions: Focus on Solutions   238
Substitute Strategies: Respect and the "Guest Teacher"   239
Substitutes: Sample Guest Teacher Checklist   242
Top Card Handout   243
Top Cards: Teaching Ups and Downs and Possibilities   244
Trauma: Working with Students Exposed to Trauma   245
Understanding Attachment and the Development of Beliefs   247
Trauma: Rebuilding the Foundation for Students with Insecure Attachments or Trauma   248

Teachers Helping Teachers Problem-Solving Steps 249

Teachers Helping Teachers Problem-Solving Steps   251
Teachers Helping Teachers Problem-Solving Steps – Detail   252

Moving it Forward 257

Asking vs. Telling   259
Do as I Say   261
Do vs. Don't   262
Encouragement Circles   263
Listening: Effective and Ineffective   264
Taking Care of Yourself   265

The Two Lists: Where Are We and Where Do We Want to Go? 267

"What" and "How" Questions   269

The Wright Family   270

About the Authors 272

Resources 274

Acknowledgments

We are grateful for the work of Alfred Adler and Rudolf Dreikurs whose passionate commitment to respect and dignity for all human beings continues to be radical work and provides a solid foundation for a better world.

We are deeply indebted to our master teachers, Jane Nelsen and Lynn Lott, for their vision for Positive Discipline in schools. They published the first *Positive Discipline in the Classroom Teacher's Guide* in 1992 followed by *Positive Discipline in the Classroom* with Stephen Glenn in 1993. The 1997 revision of *Positive Discipline in the Classroom Teacher's Guide* provided the basic ideas for most of the activities in this manual.

This manual would not be what it is without the incredible community of colleagues who keep this work alive and growing in so many different corners of the world. You inspire us. The non-profit Positive Discipline Association is a vibrant group of people who share their ideas and generate activities at an astounding rate. Your experience and recommendations enhanced this revision. We have made a sincere effort to give credit to those who have provided the framework for specific activities included in this manual. Many teachers over the years have made nameless contributions to Positive Discipline in the Classroom and their ideas have also been passed down among us. We appreciate the contributions and support of all who have made this manual possible.

Special thanks also to Carol Dores, Catherine Bronnert DeSchepper, Cheryl Erwin, and Kelly Gfroerer for careful reading and editing.

We extend deep gratitude to our families who are our best teachers and continuously hold space for us to work toward becoming our best selves.

Foreword

When we wrote the book, *Positive Discipline in the Classroom* and *Positive Discipline in the Classroom Teacher's Guide* for the two-day workshop, we had no idea it would have the impact it has had on so many people. We are especially humbled that the PDC work has attracted people like Teresa LaSala, Jody McVittie, and Suzanne Smitha who have become passionate about this work. We appreciate their experience and expertise in working with teachers and administrators in countless schools and workshops, and that they now bring their experience, expertise, and passion to the revision of this manual.

Jane Nelsen

Lynn Lott

Introduction

Positive Discipline weaves the teaching of social-emotional skills and character development into the fabric of each and every school day. In addition to specific lessons, adults model the skills they are teaching and integrate them into the discipline system used by the school. Adults also use these skills as they work together as colleagues (at Professional Learning Communities, staff meetings, and working collaboratively). The result is a campus-wide approach for effective discipline and a school that systematically and intentionally cultivates a positive school culture and climate.

The practices implemented through Positive Discipline are the foundation for *social justice and equity* in our learning communities and school buildings. Positive Discipline is also a *restorative practice* focused on building skills for repairing mistakes and healing relationships. When put into practice as designed, Positive Discipline is preventive: as individuals in the community develop more skills to self-regulate and problem solve, disciplinary incidents are reduced.

> *"We are preparing students for the tests of life, not just a life of tests."*
> - Maurice Elias

Positive Discipline in the School and Classroom Manual has grown out of the collective experience of the authors and their colleagues, using and teaching Positive Discipline in public, private, and parochial schools in diverse communities and student populations of schools over the last 30 years.

This manual combines *Positive Discipline in the School and Classroom: Teachers' Guide Activities for Students* and *Positive Discipline in the School and Classroom: Leaders' Guide Resources and Activities.*

Positive Discipline in the School and Classroom Manual, and the book, *Positive Discipline in the Classroom, 4th Ed.* by Jane Nelsen and Lynn Lott were designed to complement each other. Together they provide materials to empower schools to develop and implement a comprehensive school process that teaches mutual respect, fosters academic excellence and teaches students (in a structured, experiential manner) the basic skills they need to develop a strong sense of belonging and significance.

Positive Discipline in the School and Classroom Manual is organized to serve three primary purposes:

1. To provide the resources to teach the social-emotional skills necessary as the foundation for class meetings and the tools to lead your classroom into the process of Positive Discipline class meetings.
2. To provide the materials used in the Positive Discipline in the Classroom professional development training workshops.
3. To provide resources and ideas to inspire co-workers in your own school.

As interest is generated in your school community, we recommend inviting a Certified Positive Discipline Trainer (CPDT) to provide a full training for your school. If you or colleagues from your school are interested in training your own staff, it is highly recommended that you become a certified trainer (CPDT) through the Positive Discipline Association.[1]

---

1   Positive Discipline in the Classroom workshops are offered around the world as open workshops and also as custom workshops requested by individual schools or districts. Current schedules are posted at www.PositiveDisicpline.org.

The Theory Behind Positive Discipline

Positive Discipline is based on the work of Alfred Adler (1870-1937) and Rudolf Dreikurs (1897-1972), both Viennese psychiatrists. Central to the philosophy is the belief that every human being is equally worthy of dignity and respect. Dr. Adler was a keen observer of human action and understood behavior to be movement toward an internal sense of becoming a whole human being. He noticed the pattern of that direction was toward a sense of connection and contribution to the human community, something he called *gemeinshaftsgefuehl*. After World War I, Adler initiated a series of child guidance clinics in Vienna to teach parents and teachers more effective methods for working with young people, using the democratic principles of dignity and respect. He believed that children needed both order (structure and responsibility) and freedom in order to grow into responsible, contributing citizens of their community. Though he developed his philosophy almost a century ago without the aid of modern technology, current brain science supports his theories, which were based on his careful observation of human behavior. For more detail about the history of Dr. Adler and Positive Discipline, please see Positive Discipline Principles.

Trauma-Informed Practices

Based on brain science and development, Positive Discipline is a trauma-informed practice. Part of the training for educators includes:

- Developing a deeper understanding of how the brain adapts to toxic stress and how to respond to students who are triggered.
- Developing a deeper understanding of how the teacher's leadership is critical in modulating the stress level of their classroom (how they connect, integrate self-regulation practices, manage transitions, avoid contingent responses, etc.).
- Learning how to help students gain ability to be aware of their internal state, self-regulate and build positive relationships with peers and adults.
- Tools for building resilience, which comes from the deep belief that you matter to another human being and from the practice of repairing mistakes.

An initial concern has been that Positive Discipline will not be as effective for the 10% of the students that create 90% of the challenges. It is our experience that Positive Discipline tools are one of the most effective approaches for supporting these students. They benefit from deep practice in self-regulation. They benefit from the experience of being able to repair mistakes, but most importantly, they benefit from being in a community of peers that embraces differences and builds strong connections.

It is important to remember that Positive Discipline is not therapy and does not replace or eliminate the need for therapy. Working with students who have had significant neglect or exposure to toxic stress requires time, intentional focus and many consistent small steps.

Character Development

Character is sometimes defined as doing what is right because it is the right thing to do, what one does when no one is watching. Positive Discipline builds character by supporting intrinsic motivation: the development of an internal locus of control. Students work collaboratively to develop communities which align with the school's core values without the use of incentives or rewards. They develop a sense of social interest and awareness of actions that benefit the common good. In this model, adults do less managing and more leading.

Social Emotional Learning (SEL)

The Collaborative for Academic Social and Emotional Learning (CASEL) has identified five core social emotional competencies. They are:[2]

- Self-Awareness
- Social Awareness
- Responsible Decision-Making
- Self-Management
- Relationship Skills

The Positive Discipline curriculum teaches the 5 core competencies in every lesson.

---

[2] Competency chart (next page) is shared with permission from CASEL and also available at https://casel.org/wp-content/uploads/2017/01/Competencies.pdf.

Introduction

SOCIAL AND EMOTIONAL LEARNING (SEL) COMPETENCIES

SELF-AWARENESS
The ability to accurately recognize one's own emotions, thoughts, and values and how they influence behavior. The ability to accurately assess one's strengths and limitations, with a well-grounded sense of confidence, optimism, and a "growth mindset."
- IDENTIFYING EMOTIONS
- ACCURATE SELF-PERCEPTION
- RECOGNIZING STRENGTHS
- SELF-CONFIDENCE
- SELF-EFFICACY

SOCIAL AWARENESS
The ability to take the perspective of and empathize with others, including those from diverse backgrounds and cultures. The ability to understand social and ethical norms for behavior and to recognize family, school, and community resources and supports.
- PERSPECTIVE-TAKING
- EMPATHY
- APPRECIATING DIVERSITY
- RESPECT FOR OTHERS

RESPONSIBLE DECISION-MAKING
The ability to make constructive choices about personal behavior and social interactions based on ethical standards, safety concerns, and social norms. The realistic evaluation of consequences of various actions, and a consideration of the well-being of oneself and others.
- IDENTIFYING PROBLEMS
- ANALYZING SITUATIONS
- SOLVING PROBLEMS
- EVALUATING
- REFLECTING
- ETHICAL RESPONSIBILITY

SELF-MANAGEMENT
The ability to successfully regulate one's emotions, thoughts, and behaviors in different situations — effectively managing stress, controlling impulses, and motivating oneself. The ability to set and work toward personal and academic goals.
- IMPULSE CONTROL
- STRESS MANAGEMENT
- SELF-DISCIPLINE
- SELF-MOTIVATION
- GOAL SETTING
- ORGANIZATIONAL SKILLS

RELATIONSHIP SKILLS
The ability to establish and maintain healthy and rewarding relationships with diverse individuals and groups. The ability to communicate clearly, listen well, cooperate with others, resist inappropriate social pressure, negotiate conflict constructively, and seek and offer help when needed.
- COMMUNICATION
- SOCIAL ENGAGEMENT
- RELATIONSHIP BUILDING
- TEAMWORK

JANUARY 2017 — COLLABORATIVE FOR ACADEMIC, SOCIAL, AND EMOTIONAL LEARNING — www.casel.org

In addition, unlike many other programs, Positive Discipline teaches the competencies implicitly. The process of learning experientially builds self-awareness, self-management, social awareness, responsible decision making and relationship skills. Class meetings are the laboratory process in which all these competencies are practiced on a regular basis, supporting learning and the growth of new neural connections.

Social Emotional Learning (SEL): Social Skills Make a Difference

Numerous studies have demonstrated that a systematic approach to the implementation of social-emotional learning (SEL) programs offers significant benefits. A review of programs by Durlak, et. al., (2011)[3] showed that SEL programs:
- Improve students' achievement test scores across the spectrum by up to 11 percentile points.

---

[3] Durlak, J. A., Weissberg, R. P., Dymnicki, A. B, Taylor, R. D.,& Schellinger, K. B. (2011) The Impact of Enhancing Students' Social and Emotional Learning: A Meta-Analysis of School-Based Universal Interventions. Child Development, 82 (1), 405–432.

- Are effective in both school and after-school settings and for students with and without behavioral and emotional problems.
- Are effective for racially and ethnically diverse students from urban, rural, and suburban settings across the K-12 grade range.
- Improve students' social-emotional skills, attitudes about self and others, connection to school, and positive social behavior; and reduce conduct problems and emotional distress.

> "Social-emotional and life skills must be taught explicitly at the elementary and secondary levels. Like reading or math, if social-emotional skills are not taught systematically, they will not be internalized and become part of a child's lifelong repertoire of valued skills. Children also benefit from coordinated, explicit, developmentally sensitive instruction in the prevention of specific problems, such as smoking, drug use, alcohol, pregnancy, violence, and bullying."
> — Elias, 2001, 2006

The paper also noted that school-based programs are most effective when they are conducted by school staff (e.g., teachers and student support staff) and can be incorporated into routine educational practice. In addition, effective programs and approaches are sequenced, active, focused, and explicit (S.A.F.E.), meaning they:

- S: Use a **S**equenced set of activities to achieve skill objectives,
- A: Use **A**ctive forms of learning,
- F: Include at least one program component **F**ocused on developing personal or social skills, and
- E: **E**xplicitly target particular personal or social skills for development.

> Among the major reasons cited for dropping out of school, several involve social and emotional factors: not getting along with teachers or peers (35.0% and 20.1%, respectively), feeling left out (23.2%), and not feeling safe (12.1%).
> — National Center for Education Statistics 2002
> Dropout Rates in the United States, 2000

Like other effective programs, the Positive Discipline curriculum outlined in this manual is S.A.F.E.: Sequenced, Active, Focused, and Explicit.

Implementing the Positive Discipline Social-Emotional Curriculum

Changing the culture of a school does not happen overnight; in fact, it requires intentional commitment, patience, education, and practice. The way adults respond to inappropriate student behavior is an important model for student conduct. In a Positive Discipline School, every adult:

- Understands that the quality of relationships and school climate are absolutely critical to successful student learning,
- Seeks to establish strong connections between staff, students, and families in social and academic contexts,
- Implements principles of mutual respect, collaboration, and encouragement,
- Focuses on long-term solutions to misbehavior at individual, class, and school-wide levels,
- Views mistakes as opportunities to learn and misbehavior as opportunities to practice critical life skills, and
- Questions the tradition of adult control, rewards, and punishments.

Introduction

The long-term strategies for successful implementation of the Positive Discipline social-emotional curriculum include:

- Training all school staff,[4]
- The presence of an oversight team,
- A commitment to school-wide teaching of the full curriculum,
- Making a respectful climate and culture a school priority,
- Regular practice including regular class meetings,
- The use of behavior and climate data as feedback,
- Incorporating the model into school-wide practices (student council, students solving school-wide problems, staff meetings), and
- Engaging the broader community, including parents and caregivers.

School-wide Positive Discipline

Although incorporating social skills and character development training into a school has significant long-term positive impacts, they are only part of a comprehensive Positive Discipline implementation. Developing a school-wide discipline system that is consistent *and* leaves enough flexibility to allow for consideration of the individual student requires thought and commitment on the part of the school's staff and administration. It is the foundation of a culture of respect and equity within the school.

Leading all staff, students and families to build a learning community that models mutual respect and fosters academic excellence for all students is a huge task to accomplish the following:

- A general consensus among the school staff that **discipline is about teaching and learning—not punishment**. This does not mean eliminating consequences for serious or dangerous misbehavior. Such consequences are critical to civil society. Rather, it means rethinking everything that occurs up to that point. It also means rethinking how we implement consequences for serious or dangerous misbehavior and the downstream results of those consequences, so that students develop a *stronger connection* to their school community, rather than being pushed away. Repairing relationships after a student has spent time away from the community is an essential element of this practice,
- A principal and leadership team who believe that **rethinking discipline assumptions and practices to create more responsible, resilient and successful students is a high priority**,
- A principal, leadership team and staff who are **committed to increasing cultural competence** and who foster engagement and curiosity around issues of race, culture, class and gender,
- A school staff that understands improving discipline practices and school climate is far more demanding than merely adopting a new program. Rather, it is a **core school improvement strategy owned and managed well by the principal and staff**,
- A school staff that knows **improving discipline practices and school climate takes time** and who are willing to stay the course for three years or longer,
- A **willingness to collect and use discipline data** (including disaggregating by race or ethnicity),
- A school staff that understands **fostering a community of mutual respect to enhance student learning is a process** that will gradually include a larger and larger segment of the broader school community.

---

4   The Positive Discipline Association maintains a network of certified trainers. (For more information see www.positivediscipline.org)

Putting it Together: The Analogy of the Jumbled School House[5]

The jumbled schoolhouse analogy is a powerful tool to help visualize the importance of taking a whole-school mission driven approach to improving services and outcomes for students. Initially developed by Dr. Maurice Elias and the Developing Safe and Civil Schools (DSACS) team[6], the metaphor helps everyone understand that without a guiding framework, even the best intended practices can lead to fragmentation. Dr. Elias and his team of researchers assert that an effective social-emotional/character development framework is the essential piece that links the academic program, parent and community involvement, and all systems and programs within the school building. The resulting synergy helps ensure students receive the skills they need for success in life.

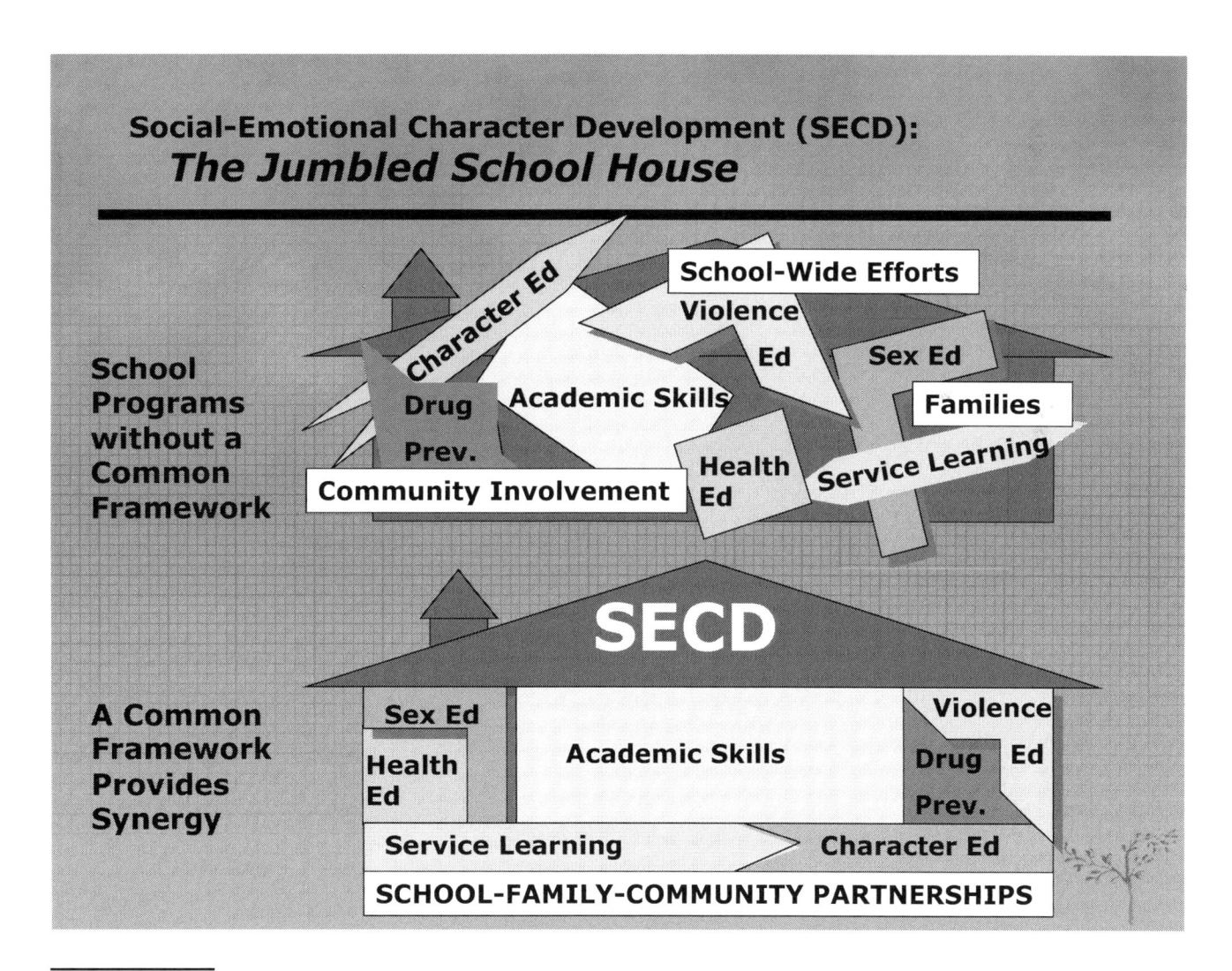

Social-Emotional Character Development (SECD): The Jumbled School House

School Programs without a Common Framework: Character Ed, School-Wide Efforts, Violence Ed, Sex Ed, Drug Prev., Academic Skills, Families, Community Involvement, Health Ed, Service Learning

A Common Framework Provides Synergy: SECD — Sex Ed, Health Ed, Academic Skills, Violence Ed, Drug Prev., Service Learning, Character Ed — SCHOOL-FAMILY-COMMUNITY PARTNERSHIPS

---

5 Permission to share the Jumbled School House granted by Dr. Maurice Elias.
6 Elias, Maurice J. and the DSACS_SECD Team (www.teachSECD.com). Guidelines for putting the pieces together: How to go from the jumbled schoolhouse to the synergized schoolhouse. Retrieved from https://www.positivedisciplinenj.com/resources

Notes

How to Use This Manual

This manual has three primary purposes:

- It is the Positive Discipline curriculum for teaching social-emotional learning.
- It is the resource for the training to become a certified Positive Discipline Classroom educator.[1]
- It provides resources and ideas to inspire co-workers in your own school.

It has been intentionally organized to move through the concepts of Positive Discipline in a scaffolded manner. Each big idea or concept is outlined on a blue face sheet: it serves as your guide or compass. The activities are tools designed to help students understand, learn and to use the concepts. You may have other activities or literature that supplement the activities in this manual.

- *The Introduction* sets the stage, connecting Positive Discipline to current educational practices, research and challenges. It clarifies the vision of building respectful relationships in schools, families and communities.
- The curriculum is presented graphically as the "House of Positive Discipline in the Classroom"
    - The *Preparing the Ground* section focuses on building basic social skills.
    - The *Essential Skills for Class Meetings* section focuses on the skills for effective class meetings.
- Positive Discipline Principles and the sections that follow comprise the resources for the Positive Discipline in the Classroom Educator Certification training.

Where do you start with the curriculum?

- Study a few Face Sheets (blue pages) and review the format for activities.
- Face Sheets explain the importance of each concept and suggest the order for teaching the activities that follow in that section.
- The format for activities gives objectives, materials and comments in the left margin, and directions in the right column.
- Many activities require some form of note-taking visible to all. Teachers can use document cameras, flip charts, or classroom boards. Under "materials," we have simply listed "board."
- Some activities have modifications, tips and/or graphics at the end of the activity.
- Once you have read an activity carefully, you may be able to teach it by only glancing at the bold headers as your cue for each step.

If this material is new to you and your students, we suggest you plan to teach most of the lessons in this manual in order.

- *Read each Face Sheet carefully.*
- Move through the concepts of *Preparing the Ground* at a pace that fits for you and your students.
- Then move through the *Essential Skills for Class Meetings*, again at a pace that fits for you and your students.

For a sample 10-week implementation, you can review "Positive Discipline in the Classroom, A Suggested Framework for Getting Started" in the Handout section of this manual.

---

[1] The schedule of training workshops is at www.positivediscipline.org

How to Use This Manual

If you and your students have some familiarity with Positive Discipline in the Classroom, you will find in this manual:

- Face Sheets that summarize the concepts and suggested approaches for teaching
- The list of *Preparing the Ground* and *Essential Skills* steps (see: The House of Positive Discipline in the Classroom), which can serve as a skills checklist
- A *new emphasis on skill building* before starting class meetings
- New activities for building and deepening your students' skills

You will want to cover all the concepts to ensure a solid foundation before you begin class meetings. However, because of your and your students' prior knowledge, you may discover creative ways to combine some lessons and may be able to shorten the time required to bring students' skill levels up to what is needed for successful class meetings. You may find the "Positive Discipline in the Classroom, A Suggested Framework for Getting Started" or the "Class Meeting Checklist" helpful, from the Handout section of this manual.

Our experience is that when class meetings are not running smoothly, it is usually because the students have not yet incorporated the basic (Preparing the Ground) skills. Although on the surface, class meetings may appear to be about problem solving, the real function of class meetings is to help students embody and practice the social skills they need to be responsible, respectful, resourceful citizens.

If you and your students are part of a school that has used Positive Discipline in the Classroom for many years, you will notice:

- The *increased emphasis on basic skill building* (Preparing the Ground)
- A concise summary and guide for teaching in each Face Sheet
- A movement toward focusing on the whole school. Evidence is now clear that school-wide culture and climate impacts students' ability to learn.[2]

Because of prior experience, you may:

- Decide to change the order for teaching the concepts (e.g., begin to meet in a circle from the first day of school to create your classroom guidelines),
- Combine some lessons or choose a favorite piece of literature that helps you to teach others, or
- Begin problem solving much sooner, reviewing only concepts needed to update your students.

Moving it forward

We challenge you to move Positive Discipline forward in your school. Here are some suggestions:

- Run Student Council using a class meeting format.
- Have the Student Council create the school-wide guidelines.
- Run staff meetings using a class meeting format.
- Create school-wide jobs.
- Include student representatives on appropriate school committees.

---

[2] The Impact of School Climate and School Identification on Academic Achievement: Multilevel Modeling with Student and Teacher Data Frontiers in Psychology, 2017: 8 2069 Published online 2017 Dec 5. doi: 10.3389/fpsyg.2017.02069

- Use data and data teams to continuously monitor and improve the school climate.
- Link discipline data with academic data.
- Update your student manual to be consistent with Positive Discipline.
- Ensure that your anti-bullying policy is consistent with Positive Discipline.
- Offer Positive Discipline parenting classes.
- Include all staff in Positive Discipline training (bus drivers, cafeteria staff, office personnel, playground staff, and after-care staff).

How long will it take to implement Positive Discipline?

There is no single answer to this question. What is important to remember is that *this is not a program that you put "on top" of what you are doing.* It asks for a fundamental shift in how we relate to each other, to students, and to their families. It is a movement from a traditional model of compliance and rewards/punishments to building a learning community based on democratic principles of equity, dignity, mutual respect, and focusing on solutions.

Small changes can happen quite quickly in a classroom, and it takes much longer to shift the culture and climate of an entire school.

- **In a classroom**, when there is consistent implementation, shifts will happen within a few weeks and student skills will continue to grow as they practice problem solving in regular class meetings.
- **In a whole school**, with intentional implementation, changes will be noticeable within the first year. Our experience is that it takes 2-3 years to develop the benefits in positive school climate and to create a sustainable infrastructure.

Keeping Parents in the Loop

Most schools have a parent-teacher organization or some structure that enables parents to be aware and involved to support the total school environment. Classroom teachers typically communicate through periodic newsletters to parents, keeping them informed about academic pursuits and events in the school and classroom. Whether you are implementing Positive Discipline in only your classroom or throughout the school, sharing information through your existing avenues helps parents understand the importance of what you do.

Many teachers include a few sentences in each newsletter about the lessons students have covered from this manual. Others have students complete a writing prompt about a book or lesson and then take it home to share. Most schools have an open-door policy allowing parents to visit. Parents are often amazed at what they see in class meetings, having never participated in anything like that as a student themselves.

As Positive Discipline becomes part of a school, integrating Positive Discipline language and concepts into school documents is important. Below is a sample document that can be included in the school handbook for an elementary school.

How to Use This Manual

What is Positive Discipline at [School]?

[School] has a long history incorporating Positive Discipline into our school culture. It is a program that encourages the development of healthy social and other life skills in a manner that is mutually respectful to adults and children. Positive Discipline uses both kindness and firmness at the same time and is neither punitive nor permissive. Interpersonal and intrapersonal skills, judgment, and the ability to respond to the limits and consequences of everyday life with responsibility and integrity are emphasized by our staff and administration in their daily student interactions. Highly compatible with [insert here the name of other character development programs that your school might have], Positive Discipline has as one of its fundamental components "Class Meetings".

Drawn by Yusho Ogata, a 5th grade student at Sharon, 1995-96

Held several times weekly for 15- 20 minutes, these meetings serve as the forum for students and teachers to give and receive compliments, learn effective ways to support each other through sincere compliments and communication skills, develop problem-solving strategies, and plan events as a team. Compliments help create a positive atmosphere that is conducive to a healthy classroom environment and effective problem solving. Students have opportunities to practice strategies like ignoring, using effective listening and speaking skills, role playing, developing win-win solutions, collaborating, and brainstorming for solutions. In the community that is their classroom, they can share and learn from each other under the guidance of their teachers. Essentially, the Class Meeting process is a microcosm for participatory democracy, and thus reflects a long-term goal of educating children to be effective citizens.

Parents are welcome to observe Class Meetings. Contact your child's teacher with questions, comments, or to find out when their class meets. Also, please feel free to call [your school's] counselors to discuss Positive Discipline or to borrow a Positive Discipline book. It can be helpful for parenting too.

In closing

Moving through this material in a step-wise fashion will grow cooperative and respectful relationships in your school and classroom, which will make your school the amazing place you want it to be. *We hope you enjoy the journey as much as we have.*

Positive Discipline Stories

A kindergarten class meeting

Ms. Brown's kindergarten class has learned how to use the agenda to solve problems. At the scheduled time, Ms. Brown uses her chime to cue students that their class meeting is about to begin. Because they are well practiced, everyone moves to form a circle, sitting on the floor. Ms. Brown starts their stuffed duck around the circle and students offer compliments. Ms. Brown looks at the agenda and sees that Trevor has drawn a picture sharing his problem.

She asks, "Trevor, is this still a problem for you?"

"Yes," he answers.

"Can you explain the problem to the class?"

"I get pushed playing Ninjas," he said. "I don't want to be pushed."

"Would you like to share your feelings while others listen, discuss without fixing or ask for help with this problem?"

"I want help. I don't want to be pushed."

Ms. Brown then passed the stuffed animal around the circle again. As the duck came around, each student offered a solution or passed. Some students offered that they didn't like Ninja play either: others suggested ways to play more carefully. One suggested that Trevor find another game. Ms. Brown wrote the ideas down as they were offered. After everyone had a chance to offer a solution (including Ms. Brown who passed this time) Ms. Brown read the suggestions aloud. Because Trevor put the problem on the agenda, Ms. Brown asked him which solution sounded best to him. He thought the whole class should stop playing Ninjas. Ms. Brown reminded Trevor that the class would have to agree to that since they were involved too. She suggested that the class vote. Trevor agreed. Ms. Brown had the class close their eyes and vote. The class voted to stop playing Ninjas. Ms. Brown was a bit surprised but also relieved. She suggested that at their next meeting they could discuss other things to do at recess instead of playing Ninjas. The meeting was adjourned, and the students quickly went back to their seats.

A middle school story

Ms. S. teaches pre-algebra to 8th graders. One of her three classes seemed especially challenging to her. She often told colleagues that she felt like she was "herding cats." These students seemed to take delight in making mischief. None of the behavior was malevolent and sometimes it was entertaining, but no matter how she planned, this class took longer to get work done and was always two or more days behind her other classes.

Three weeks into taking the Positive Discipline in the Classroom workshop sponsored by her school district, she decided to change her focus for the one class that was always behind. She decided to dedicate time, "however long it took," to get a set of agreements the whole class could agree to so they could move forward and get to work. She later admitted that even though she promised herself she would dedicate any amount of time, she thought they could pull it together and complete it in one class period. It took three.

The first day they didn't take her seriously. The second day they realized she was serious, but not being good at working together for a common goal, they were not able to come to full agreement. The third day they got it done. Now of course, they were a full week behind the other classes and Ms. S. was having serious second thoughts. By the time she shared this with her peers in the workshop however – only eight days after the agreements were completed - the "late" class had caught up with the others. Having a set of consistent agreements that they developed (and helped each other follow) dramatically changed the academic environment.

Positive Discipline solving recess problems

At an urban elementary school in Seattle, a group of third- and fourth-graders consistently created problems at recess. The staff's response was to deny these students recess privileges for a period of time, and then allow them to return to recess. Their behavior did not improve. After some thought, the administrative team decided to change their approach. Because the students were indoors anyway during recess, they decided to use that time to improve the students' skills at playing cooperatively. They began with simple games like "Chutes and Ladders." Despite the fact that the staff already believed these students lacked critical skills, they were surprised by the students' inability to take turns, to remember any game "rules" or to play together, even in a small group.

The teacher who supervised the students during recess began to teach the students how to play games, and helped them teach each other about how rules helped people play together. They started the group with very small steps and stopped frequently to invite the students to notice what was happening. As the students began to gain skills, they enjoyed their success with each other and seemed to learn more rapidly. Over a two-week period, the students progressed to less structured, more difficult indoor games, like checkers. The teacher then began to teach these students the rules of the games played outdoors at recess. After two weeks of working together indoors, the students took a recess "field trip" and found that they could play well with others. They were allowed to join their class at recess and were quite successful from then on.

Positive Discipline around the world! Currently Positive Discipline is being taught in 61 countries.

Positive Discipline in Iceland

The Grænuvellir School in Húsavík, Iceland has been a Positive Discipline Whole School since 2016. What a difference and joy this has made. Following the guidelines of Positive Discipline has made the atmosphere within the school significantly better. The students are happier, the teachers do and feel better and the parents are happier than ever before!

In October 2017 the Icelandic President, Mr. Guðni Th. Jóhannesson and his wife, first lady Eliza Reid came to Húsavík on an official visit and we had the pleasure to welcome them to Grænuvellir. Our oldest children, 5 years old, were eager to invite them to take part in a class meeting. They accepted. Everyone, including the guests, sat in a circle on the floor and the meeting started with compliments and appreciations, from both the children and the president. The children invited our guests to put something on the agenda, which they did. As one of the children said: "Presidents might need help solving problems like we do!" The president asked for help with a parenting challenges. His children, ages 4, 6, 8 and 10, were not eating their vegetables or going to bed promptly. The students did some problem solving with them and came up with wonderful solutions. None of their solutions included punishments or rewards. Suggested solutions included:

- *Let the children choose vegetables themselves in the store*
- *Let them prepare and cut up the vegetables*
- *Make sure they know that eating vegetables makes you healthy and strong*
- *Let the children choose if they want to eat their vegetables before dinner, after dinner or as a snack after dinner.*

It was amazing to witness! In the end both Guðni and Eliza thanked the children for a wonderful meeting and finished off as we always do, with giving hugs and high fives for a great meeting.

A few days after the meeting we received a thank you letter from the president which said that he and his wife would never forget this meeting. He believes that the Positive Discipline way of sitting in a circle with the children and problem solving is a great way to train the children to work together on finding solutions that are respectful to everyone. This type of work would create excellent skills for the future. We could not agree with them more. We are deeply satisfied with our decision to embrace Positive Discipline in our school, Grænuvellir!

How to Use This Manual

House of Positive Discipline in the Classroom

Growing
responsible, respectful, and resourceful members of the community

CLASS MEETING FORMAT
1. Compliments and appreciations
2. Follow up on prior solutions
3. Agenda items
   - Share feelings while others listen
   - Discuss without fixing
   - Ask for problem solving help
4. Closing activity or class planning
   (field trips/parties/projects)

Essential Skills for Class Meetings

Essential Skill # 1 Forming a Circle	Essential Skill # 2 Practicing Compliments and Appreciations	Essential Skill # 3 Respecting Differences	Essential Skill # 4 Using Respectful Communication Skills
Essential Skill # 5 Focusing on Solutions	Essential Skill # 6 Brainstorming and Role-playing	Essential Skill # 7 Using the Agenda and Class Meeting Format	Essential Skill # 8 Using and Understanding the Mistaken Goals

Essential Skills for a Positive Discipline Classroom

- Agreements and Guidelines
- Routines
- Meaningful Work
- Self-regulation
- Communication Skills
- Mutual Respect
- Building Cooperation
- Mistakes and How to Fix Them
- Encouragement
- Respecting Differences
- Buy-In for Class Meetings

Developing respectful relationships in schools, families, and communities.

Side labels: BUILDING THE HOUSE | LAYING THE FOUNDATION | PREPARING THE GROUND | VISION

Adapted from design by Deborah Owen-Sohocki

Essential Skills for a Positive Discipline Classroom: Preparing the Ground
Face Sheet

The big idea: Preparing the Ground
- This section provides a series of activities that teach basic social skills, self-regulation and self-management skills.

  - Agreements and Guidelines
  - Routines
  - Meaningful Work
  - Self-regulation
  - Communication Skills
  - Mutual Respect
  - Building Cooperation
  - Mistakes and How to Fix Them
  - Encouragement
  - Respecting Differences
  - Buy-In for Class meetings

  The following practices, skills and procedures are essential for a healthy classroom and school community:

The circle
Some classroom communities regularly teach with students in a circle. It is a wonderful format for teaching these lessons. However, it is important to distinguish *teaching in a circle* from a *class meeting*, which has its own unique format and is also in a circle. When teaching in a circle, the teacher is directing the process. In a class meeting, there is shared responsibility based on a clear structure and set of agreements.

Why preparing the ground is important
- Taking the time to methodically teach the foundational skills in this section will help your class learn how to work together more effectively and respectfully. The skills learned here will help students manage stress, develop self-regulation and learn to identify and express their thoughts, needs and emotions.
- **The ability to self-regulate and delay gratification are better predictors of academic success than intelligence.**
- When a classroom doesn't function smoothly, we often find that the students creating the disruption are those lacking these basic skills. Though it is common to think or wish that students would come to school with an ability to manage stress and self-regulate, many don't. (Many adults don't either.)
- *Preparing the Ground skills will need to be revisited many times as students (or the classroom) encounter challenges. It is* **the practice** *of repeating these tools and skills that empowers children to be "fluent."*

What else are students learning?

When students work together effectively they develop the following "Significant Seven"* perceptions and skills:

- I am capable.
- I can contribute in meaningful ways and I am genuinely needed.
- I can influence what happens to me in life.
- I have the ability to understand my personal emotions, to use that understanding to develop self-discipline and self-control, and to learn from my experiences.
- I have the ability to work with others and to develop friendships through communicating, cooperating, negotiating, sharing, empathizing, and listening.
- I have the ability to respond to the limits and consequences of everyday life with responsibility, adaptability, flexibility, and integrity.
- I have the ability to use wisdom and to evaluate situations according to appropriate values.

Recommended order for teaching *Preparing the ground*

- It is important to teach lessons from each section and that *you* determine the appropriate order for your students. This is the order we recommend:
    1. Agreements and Guidelines
    2. Routines
    3. Meaningful Work
    4. Self-regulation
    5. Communication Skills
    6. Mutual Respect
    7. Building Cooperation
    8. Mistakes and How to Fix Them
    9. Encouragement
    10. Respecting Differences
    11. Buy-In for Class Meetings
- If students are lacking the most basic ability to work together you may need to change the order recommended above. For example, student-generated classroom agreements and guidelines are an important first step, but your students may not be able to complete that task. To adapt for your class:
    - You may need to post temporary guidelines for behavior before your students begin school.
    - Teach routines and the lessons below, at an appropriate point.
    - When ready, teach "Agreements and Guidelines" to create *student-generated guidelines* to replace your temporary ones.
- These activities will also help you assess your students' skill levels and which basic skills or competencies need more work.

LITERATURE CONNECTIONS

Many Face Sheets include a few children's books chosen because they:

- Are easy to read
- Support and develop one or more concepts
- Are enjoyable for all ages
- Are generally consistent with Positive Discipline throughout. (An exception is that a few may mention rewards or punishment as an aside to the overall theme.)

Teachers in higher grades are adept at drawing multiple concepts emphasized in Positive Discipline from more complex literature. Such skill is beyond the scope of this manual. For this reason, no attempt is made to recommend books that would appeal only to middle or high school students.

* Glenn, H. Stephen, & Nelsen, Jane. (2000). *Raising self-reliant children in a self-indulgent world.* New York, NY: Harmony Books.

Notes

Agreements and Guidelines for the Classroom
Preparing the Ground: Face Sheet

Concept: Creating agreed-upon guidelines
- Guidelines are statements created by the group to determine their course of action.
- Having agreed-upon guidelines is a powerful way to lead a classroom.
- *Establishing guidelines* **with your students** *is one of the first things to do at the beginning of the school year or semester.*
- In many traditional classrooms, students walk into the classroom and the "rules" are already posted on the wall. There are three challenges from these kinds of rules:
  1. Students sense that they are imposed from above – and even if they make sense, they ask students to comply instead of cooperate.
  2. Students have heard the words in the rules many times and may have a general sense of what the words mean. However, they often have not linked the words to their own actions and remain disconnected from personal responsibility.
  3. The rules become background noise instead of an agreed-upon "living document" that teaches students awareness of their own behavior and that of those around them.

Important Note: Extending the process of establishing agreed-upon guidelines throughout the school changes the climate and culture of the entire school. School staff creates agreed-upon guidelines with each other and the student council takes agreed-upon guidelines from each classroom to create school-wide guidelines.

Why agreed-upon guidelines are important
- Guidelines create a "shared vision" for the classroom. As the teacher, *you are the steward of this shared vision*. It is what empowers you to lead your classroom instead of manage your classroom. (We lead people, we manage things.)
- It is the teacher's job to invite students to self-reflect and self-correct over and over again until, with practice, the students themselves will understand and "feel" what a smoothly functioning classroom is like.
- *Guidelines vs. Rules.* We use the word "guidelines" intentionally. This sets them apart from traditional rules that are inflexible and made by someone else without input from the group.

What else are students learning?
- The practice of pausing, reflecting, and then making small corrections increases students' awareness of the world around them.
- Students begin to transfer the skills of pausing and reflecting to academics.

Preparing the Ground: Agreements and Guidelines for the Classroom and Class Meetings

Recommended order for teaching *agreements and guidelines*

- ***Beginning the Almost Perfect School Year (BAPSY): Guidelines for our Classroom (extended version)*** is the most powerful way to engage students in creating guidelines that fit and have meaning. It challenges them to think more deeply about the meaning of words like "respect" and "considerate" and what they might sound like and look like in action. For example: Students have heard the word "respect" over and over again, but without having an opportunity to create an active definition, it has less meaning. For this reason, we suggest using BAPSY, especially with young children.
- ***We Decided: Guidelines for our Classroom (short version)*** This is a quick, simplified and effective process for generating classroom guidelines.
- ***We Decided: Guidelines for our Class Meeting*** (Using the Class Meeting Format and Agenda). Use later, before beginning class meetings. This is a quick and effective process for any additional guidelines needed for class meetings or other situations, e.g. time-out space, work with another teacher, etc.

Teaching is not enough

- Agreements and guidelines must be reviewed and practiced over and over again.
- Routines (refer to Routines Face Sheet) provide predictability and order that supports classroom guidelines.

■ Tips

- **Keeping the guidelines alive with "Check-ins."** Checking in with students regularly throughout the day (thumbs up/sideways/down) about specific guidelines helps students attune to the classroom environment and their own behaviors. It might sound like this, "How are we doing on our agreement about noise levels during reading? Show me with a thumb up/sideways/down." No comment is necessary. Follow with, "Take one breath and think of one thing that you can do (silently) to improve the environment. Then do it. Thank you." Regular check-ins like this help students learn to observe what is *outside* in their environment and then *inside* their own body and to be able to begin (with practice) to be aware that their behavior makes a difference.

  > Regular check-ins on created guidelines are necessary for students to make a connection between their actions and the classroom environment.

- The teaching doesn't stop. Guidelines are not written in stone for the whole year. It is common for classrooms to modify their guidelines when unexpected or unaddressed situations arise.
- Holidays and breaks. Students lose track of their agreements in the time leading up to and immediately after holidays and breaks. It is helpful to re-focus on routines and the 5 R's at those times (see Teaching Routines).
- New students. Have a plan about how you will introduce new students to the class guidelines. This can be a student job or an opportunity for whole class review.

Preparing the Ground: Agreements and Guidelines for the Classroom and Class Meetings

Beginning the Almost Perfect School Year (BAPSY)

Based upon a video clip done by Lisa Roy.

OBJECTIVE:
- For all stakeholders to work together on creating the needed guidelines for a safe and successful classroom and school.
- To create a shared vision of responsibility in the classroom.
- To teach self-reflection and self-regulation.

MATERIALS:
- Board
- 4-5 pre-prepared template sheets (model below)
- Large post-it notes or small sheets of paper (recycled is fine)
- Tape

COMMENTS FOR TEACHERS:
- This activity can be split over several days.
- Everything about this process helps establish a democratic classroom. Jointly creating guidelines is foundational for Positive Discipline in the classroom.
- Practice is important. Note step 11.
- Once developed, guidelines are not set in stone and should be revisited throughout the year as members of the class, including the teacher, notice the need for modification.
- Plan for how you will acclimate new students to the guidelines.

DIRECTIONS:

1. Prepare ahead.
- 4-5 blank chart papers like the template shown below.

2. Say to students.
- "What do we all want to do to make this the best school year ever? One where together we ALL learn, teach, feel safe, and get along?"

3. Write on board: To create the best school year ever, we will...

4. Voice, Write, View.
- Write each student's shared idea on a piece of paper (or large post-it)
- Post them on board.
- Have students help in any way they can (scribe/ courier/ tape etc.)
- **Tip:** If a student makes an inappropriate suggestion, *connect before correct.*

Example: Student: "We should have 5 recesses!" Teacher: "Wouldn't that be fun! However, we all have to operate within the school's guidelines." (And then move on.)

5. Sort and title.
- Working together, move the posted ideas into 4 or 5 groups of words/ideas that fit together.
- Give each group a title. For example: "Have fun," "Be respectful," "Make new friends," "Take care of our environment," "Help each other learn," etc.

6. Model use of template.
- Using one of the prepared blank templates enter one title in the top "We will" box as shown below (e.g., "Help each other learn.")
- Ask for and record ideas that go in the "We say this, we do this" boxes. What will we actually say or do?
- Complete the chart by inviting students to finish the "Our Guideline:" box. For example, "We will help each other learn because it is fun and more interesting."

7. Small group work.
- Divide the class into groups.
- Give each group a remaining category, all the papers from that category, markers and blank prepared template sheet.
- Give groups 10-15 minutes (depending on age) to fill in sheets.
- Monitor progress, offer support.

Preparing the Ground: Agreements and Guidelines for the Classroom and Class Meetings

TEMPLATE:
Have 5 of the following templates (large paper) made before you begin this activity.

We will:	
We say this:	We do this:

Our Guideline: We will _____ because _____.

EXAMPLE

We will: Help each other learn	
We say this:	**We do this:**
- I know how to do that - want some help? - Come join us - Would you like to work with me? - You did a great job on that! - Come sit by me. - Can I join you? - I'm interested in that, too. - What do you think about it? - You can borrow this book. - Thanks for sharing your information with me.	- Make sure everyone is involved in a group. - Work quietly during silent time. - Help each other. - Share things. - Notice each other's work. - Laugh together. - Listen to each other. - Practice together.

Our Guideline: We will help each other learn because it is fun and more interesting.

8. Post and Review.
- Post charts
- One at a time, read the chart aloud (older students can do this)
- Ask, "Does anyone have questions about these guidelines?"
- Ask for a "thumbs-up" from class members to show that they can live with that group's completed guideline.
- If someone has a concern about a guideline ask, "How would we want to change this so that you and the others could agree with it?" Note that you, the teacher, are a member of your classroom community. If there is a guideline that you can't agree with, respectfully offer one that you can agree with.
    > For example, if the students have included, "No homework" say, "I can't live with that guideline. You need practice. I can work with you to keep the homework interesting."
- When a change is offered, check with the class again to make sure all can live with it. Then rewrite it. For example, you might rewrite "No homework" as "Keep homework interesting."
- Repeat for each chart.

9. Signing on.
- When all sheets are completed have each student sign each sheet (in any white space) as acknowledgment of their agreement. (This can be done at the end of the activity, the next day, or another designated time.)

10. Follow through.
- Leave the guidelines up. Refer to them often.
- Comment when you *notice students following the guidelines*. For example: "Thank you, Abdul, for bringing in books on this topic today. You're helping us accomplish our goal of learning new things this year." Or "Thanks, Mary, for raising your hand before speaking. That is what we said we'd do to show respect to speakers in our class."
- Comment when you *notice students NOT following the guidelines*. Speak with that student privately, asking them to check their behavior against the class guidelines and let you know what needs to change.

11. Moving it forward: Reflection and self-regulation.
After the posters have been made, check in with the class **several times a day** to pause and reflect:
- "Show me with a thumb up, sideways or down how we are doing on [guideline]." ("Show me how you think we are doing on our 'listen while others talk' guideline.")

Preparing the Ground: Agreements and Guidelines for the Classroom and Class Meetings

- "Think of one small thing *you* can do to help us meet this guideline better. Please do it now."
- It is important to do this when things are going well so students can see their progress.
- When following through, it is important to remain non-judgmental. Continue it **several times a day throughout the year.**
- Your non-judgmental observations help students become more aware.

For example: "I can tell you are excited about the field trip tomorrow and it is harder to listen while others talk."
Or,
"I notice our classroom has the sound of students hard at work. I'm enjoying listening to you work, help each other and solve problems."

Tips

- This activity is worth repeating, even if students have done it in previous years.
- For parent involvement/support: Ask a couple of student volunteers to type up a sheet of the Class Guidelines (with only the guideline from the bottom of each template) with a place for the student to sign, the teacher to sign, and the parents to sign, if you would like to be sure parents understand what the class guidelines are. Explain the process in your class newsletter or ask students to explain it to their parents. Encourage students to keep the agreement in the front of their notebook.
- In some schools, students take their 4 or 5 guideline statements on an 8 x 11 piece of paper with them in the hallway and to specialists. This shows other teachers the class' own expectations.
- School guidelines. Each class can submit suggested guidelines for common areas to their student council. The student council can then discuss and choose the school guidelines, which in turn, can be shared with each classroom and posted throughout the building.

Modifications

- In higher grades, "Looks Like" and "Sounds Like" are more appropriate headings for the columns "We Say This" and "We do this" on each template.
- For kindergarten and 1st grade, spread this out over several days. Use role-play to demonstrate what people say and do to follow the guidelines. Add picture clues to the guidelines to help non-readers remember what they say.
- Some classes leave the original templates up all year. When students seem to have a good grasp of what each of the guidelines means, it is certainly possible to take the templates down and have a few volunteers make one poster with only the guidelines on it. Signatures in white space indicating support is still a good idea.

Preparing the Ground: Agreements and Guidelines for the Classroom and Class Meetings

We Decided: Guidelines for our Classroom

OBJECTIVE:
- For all stakeholders to work together on creating the needed guidelines for a safe and successful classroom and school.

MATERIALS:
- Board
- Materials for a poster

COMMENTS FOR TEACHERS:
- This is a quick, simplified and effective process for generating classroom guidelines; however, it is not as powerful as BAPSY. Use guidelines in BAPSY for additional tips or fine-tuning.
- The power of this activity comes from making the list, engaging the students in following the guidelines and follow through. *The follow-through in step 4 is as important as the guidelines themselves.*
- Often students don't make the connection between individual behavior (theirs) and the climate of the whole group. The internal reflection process teaches students to notice themselves in their environment.
- The climate of the classroom is extremely important. If there is a pattern of problem behavior not being addressed by the guidelines, share your concerns and ask the class to review and revise.

DIRECTIONS:
1. **Brainstorm and record.**
   - Ask students to brainstorm what we want to do to have a safe, effective, and fun classroom for learning.

   For example: listen while others talk, be polite, be respectful, take care of our things, put things away, only one person talks at a time, etc.

2. **Vote.**
   - Ask students to vote for the three they think are the most important.
   - Tally the votes and choose the top 3 – 5 ideas to be "class guidelines."

3. **Making poster and sign on.**
   Have student volunteers make a poster to display chosen guidelines. Use their words, for example:

   OUR CLASSROOM - WE DECIDED:
   Listen while others talk
   Respect each other
   Help each other learn

   - Have each student sign the poster as acknowledgment of his/her agreement.

4. **Moving it forward (the follow through).**
   After the poster has been made, ask the class **several times a day** to pause and reflect:
   - "Show me with a thumb up, sideways or down how we are doing on [guideline]. ("Show me how you think we are doing on our 'listen while others talk' guideline.")
   - "Think of one small thing YOU can do to help us meet this guideline better. Please do it now."
   - It is important to do this when things are going well so students can see their progress.
   - When following through, it is important to remain non-judgmental. Continue this process **several times a day throughout the year.**
   - Your non-judgmental observations help students become more aware.

   For example: "I can tell you are excited about the field trip tomorrow and it is harder to listen while others talk."
   Or,
   "I notice our classroom has the sound of students hard at work. I'm enjoying listening to you work, help each other, and solve problems."

Creating Routines for the Classroom
Preparing the Ground: Face Sheet

Concept: Routines
- Routines are commonplace tasks with clearly defined steps students follow. For example, lining up, turning in assignments, sharpening pencils, and accomplishing any number of daily expectations.
- Routines are typically planned by teachers in advance.
- Routines must be taught and practiced over and over.
- After routines are taught, mistakes are best corrected when teachers ask questions instead of telling students what to do.

Why routines are important
- Routines set a rhythm and pattern for the classroom.
- Routines are essential to create an environment of safety. This is particularly important for students who have been exposed to trauma.
- Routines typically allow daily tasks to be more efficiently accomplished.
- Performing some tasks by routine can free our minds to be more creative in other endeavors.
- When the "routine is the boss" there is less conflict.

What else are students learning?
- Repetition gives students a sense of confidence.
- Students gain a sense of safety and predictability in the classroom.
- Students learn sequences of behavior that are regular and established.
- Practicing routines in the classroom transfers an understanding of systems and process in the community such as checking out at the grocery store and returning library books.

Recommended process for teachers to teach routines
- Design the layout of the classroom with designated spaces to meet the needs of the class (quiet vs. noisy work areas, locations for materials, locations for equipment, etc.)
- Create steps for transitions, use of materials, turning in work, etc. (See list of routines to consider for the classroom, located at the end of the activity, "Teaching Routines")
- Teach and role-play routines.
- Prepare students for interruptions in routines through role-plays. The **Cooperative Juggling** activity can be used as a starting place for teaching this concept. After the class has mastered juggling add an unusual object (rubber chicken) as a surprise. Students usually struggle to maintain the "routine" they established and it can lead to productive discussions.
- Follow "The 5 R's of Routines."

Preparing the Ground: Creating Routines

The 5 R's of Routines

Review Expectations. "What is our routine for ____ (walking in the hall, getting homework in, bathroom passes etc.)?" Ask instead of tell.

Reflection. Ask students to reflect on how it is going, "How are we doing?"

Responsibility. "Think about how you could help make it better."

Results. "What can we achieve? How will we know that we have met our mark?"

Rehearse. Again, and more than once.

Teaching Routines

OBJECTIVE:
- To teach your classroom routines

MATERIALS:
- Varies depending on routine

COMMENTS FOR TEACHERS:
- Routines are a critical part of the social infrastructure of the classroom.
- It takes some students, especially those exposed to trauma, a long time to learn routines.
- Teaching a routine involves active practice.

The 5 R's of Routines:
1. **Review expectations**
2. **Reflection**
3. **Responsibility**
4. **Results**
5. **Rehearse**

DIRECTIONS:

1. **Select a routine you plan to teach.**
2. **Share with students the problem that the routine will solve.**
   For example,
   - "As a class, we often move from one room to another. We have to do that in a way everyone is safe and we don't bother others."
   - "When you hand in your homework, it has to go in one place so I can find it easily and quickly."
3. **Share your outline of the solution, your *routine* way of solving the problem.**
   Students like to be engaged in solutions. If you ask for their input, they will engage their thinking brains. For example,
   - "Before we move as a class we will line up against this wall. I'll know we are safe and ready to move when everyone is there and can easily hear my whispered voice.
     - What kind of voice is appropriate in the hall?
     - How will you and I know your voice is quiet enough?"
   - "This box is where your homework belongs.
     - How will I know the homework is yours? (It will have my name.)
     - If homework is due in the morning, what time does that mean?"
4. **Practice and/or role-play.** Have your students practice the routine in various scenarios. Adding scenarios helps students think about the routine and become more flexible with challenging situations. For example,
   - "Let's practice lining up when everyone is calm. How did we do? What would make it better? Should we try it again or add another challenge?"
   - "Let's practice lining up – but pretend I lost track of time and we have to do it in a hurry. This is harder, but what do we need to remember to do about voices? How did we do?"
   - "Let's pretend we are walking in the hall and it is too noisy. How am I going to get your attention in a way that is respectful? What could I do?" Practice their solution.

5. **Moving it forward.** After you do the initial teaching and practice you will need to revisit your routines regularly. Think of the "5 R's of Routines" as a continuous practice.
   - **Review Expectations.** "What is our routine for ____ (walking in the hall, getting homework in, bathroom passes)?" Asking the students is more powerful than telling. It feels like a challenge that they can take on and less like a lecture.

Preparing the Ground: Creating Routines

- **Reflection.** Ask students to reflect on how it is going, "How are we doing?" Many teachers increase engagement by asking students to use the thumbs up/sideways/down for this process.
- **Responsibility.** Invite each student to see what they could do to make an improvement in the group's work. "Think about how you could help make it better." Some classes do this silently; others pair share or share to the whole group.
- **Results.** "What can we achieve? How will we know that we have met our mark?" Setting a specific goal about what it will look like/ sound like and by when, helps students be able to reflect later. Your class may want to set up a rating scale or a time frame to challenge itself toward improvement.
- **Rehearse.** "Would it be helpful to role-play this or practice it again so that we each know what we can do?" "What part is our biggest challenge?" Rehearse again, and more than once.

Common routines to be taught to students include:

Attendance	New students
Cleaning up	Noise levels in the classroom
Coming and going from lunch or recess	Other students' property
Distributing materials	Paper headings
Exchanging papers	Phone answering in the classroom
Fire drills	Putting backpacks away
Food, drink, or gum in the classroom	Signals for getting attention.
Going home	Student supplies
Going to the bathroom	The teacher's desk/property
Hall passes	Transitions in the classroom
Hats and coats in the classroom	Turning in work
How to calm down when the room is excited.	Using cell phones, electronics
How to use the positive time out area	Using the computers
Late students	Using the pencil sharpener
Lining up	Valuables in the classroom
Make-up work after absence (where to find it, where & when to turn it in)	What to do when work is finished early
	When teacher is absent and substitute is present
Morning work or warm up activity	When teacher steps out of the room briefly
Moving to other spaces	

Teaching Routines: How Do We Line Up?

OBJECTIVE:
- To help students get an embodied sense of what lining up feels like.
- To have fun while learning and practicing a skill.

MATERIALS:
- Flip chart & marker

COMMENTS:
- Once a class has practiced lining up this way and knows how it feels, it serves as a reference point. You can ask, "Remember when we all practiced lining up last week? Let's do that again right now."
- Notice in this activity that the students are using the 5 R's of routines. They are creating and *reviewing expectations*. They are *reflecting*, taking *responsibility*, and noticing the *results* of their actions. They have started *rehearsing*. For long term success, they will need to practice and remember what they have set up.

DIRECTIONS:

1. **Set Up.**
   - Tell your students, "We are going to work together as a group to create our routine for lining up."
   - Divide the room into two groups.

2. **Role-play.**
   - Tell group 1, "When I say 'go', I want you to line up. Your job will be to make mistakes in how you line up while still staying safe. You can think of things that you have seen other students do that make it hard to get into line quickly or quietly."
   - Tell group 2, "When I say 'go', you will be the observers. Your job will be to watch carefully and notice as many mistakes as you can."
   - Start the process by saying, "Go," and then at an appropriate moment in the role-play, instruct group 1 to stop and stay where they are.

3. **Pause and reflect with group 2.**
   - Ask group 2, "What improvements could this group make?" (Be prepared to coach them to articulate their suggestions in terms of what *to do* instead of what not to do.)
   - Scribe their ideas on a flip chart. E.g.: walk quietly, give personal space, face forward, stand behind the person in front of you, single file, etc.

4. **Repeat role-play with improvements.**
   - Instruct group 1, "Go back to your seats. We are going to try it again. When I say 'go' this time, your job will be line up again using *all* these improvements. You can still make other mistakes that your observers might not notice."
   - Tell group 2, "When I say 'go', you will be the observers. Your job will be harder now. You will need to watch carefully and notice as many mistakes as you can."
   - Restart the process by saying, "Go," and then at an appropriate moment in the role-play, instruct group 1 to stop and stay where they are.
   - Ask group 2, "What other improvements could they try to make the line even better?" Examples might include, hands at side, push in their chairs.
   - Add those ideas to the flip chart.

5. Groups 1 & 2 switch roles. Role-play with Group 2.
- Ask group 1 to sit down.
- Tell both groups, "Now we are going to switch roles."
- Tell group 2, "This time when I say, 'go' you will be lining up. This will be harder. You will have an opportunity to make mistakes, but you need to follow all of the guidelines on our chart. You'll have to make small mistakes.
- Tell group 1, "This time when I say, 'go' you will be the observers. It won't be easy. Some of their mistakes might be hard to see!"
- Restart the process by saying, "Go," and then at an appropriate moment in the role-play, instruct group 2 to stop and stay where they are.
- Ask group 1, "What other improvements could they try to make the line even better?"
- Have group 2 sit down.

6. Final role-play with the whole group.
- Notice out loud, "This is a long list!" Read the list aloud without judgment or comment.
- Challenge your class, "I bet we could do all of this all together. We can put all of this into action. Pause and think about what you need to do. This time when I say go, we'll all line up together." Ask the group to get in line as well as they possibly can, putting into action everything that they learned.

7. Pause and reflect with the whole group.
- What did you notice? What will it take to do this well? How can we help each other?

Variations for teaching and practicing lining up: It can be helpful to practice this routine pretending that the class is in an unexpected situation. It will build their skill. "Let's pretend we're going to be late for music class," or, "Let's pretend we're having a fire drill."

This activity can be done with teachers in preparation for having them teach it to their students. When this activity is done in a workshop for teachers, it invites teachers to:
- Notice how routines provide safety, predictability and engagement.
- Experience how routines can be taught and what else kids are learning when they are actively involved in establishing and practicing routines.
- Experience the effectiveness of 'do's' vs 'don'ts' when setting guidelines for behavior.

Meaningful Work
Preparing the Ground: Face Sheet

Concept: Meaningful work

- Meaningful work is defined by Michael Steger as work that:
    - Makes sense (we know what is expected and have the resources to accomplish the task),
    - Has a point (we have to be able to understand the "why" of it), and
    - Contributes to the greater good in some way.
- Although the idea of meaningful work applies to academics, it also refers to work aimed toward the good of the classroom community.

Why meaningful work is important

Meaningful work is important because students:

- Learn about the different types of work needed for a classroom and school community to function.
- Understand that their contributions (and by inference, *they*) are needed and valued.
- Are provided the opportunity to learn and practice a variety of new skills.

What else are students learning?

- Students learn responsibility, empathy, that they are capable, and able to contribute.
- They learn how to learn from others.

Activities

In this section, there are no activities to teach. However, a creative list of classroom and school-wide jobs and support materials are provided.

- Remember to involve students as you develop and enhance your jobs.
- Remember to "take time for training."
- Make sure students understand what each job is and how to successfully accomplish the task.
- Have the students fill out a "job training sheet" listing the important and necessary aspects of each job. They can teach each other and add to the list as they learn from doing the task.

LITERATURE CONNECTIONS

Piper, Watty. *The Little Engine That Could.* New York: Platt & Munk, 1983.

Preparing the Ground: Meaningful Work

"First, the work we do must make sense; we must know what's being asked of us and be able to identify the personal or organizational resources we need to do our job. Second, the work we do must have a point; we must be able to see how the little tasks we engage in build, brick-by-brick if you will, into an important part of the purpose of our company. Finally, the work that we do must benefit some greater good; we must be able to see how our toil helps others, whether that's saving the planet, saving a life, or making our co-workers' jobs easier so that they can go home and really be available for their families and friends."

Michael Steger
http://www.psychologytoday.com/blog/the-meaning-in-life/200906/meaningful-work

"Meaningful work is one of the most important things we can impart to children. Meaningful work is work that is autonomous. Work that is complex, that occupies your mind. And work where there is a relationship between effort and reward — for everything you put in, you get something out..."

Malcom Gladwell in an interview with Charlie Rose
http://37signals.com/svn/posts/1483-malcolm-gladwell-on-meaningful-work-and-curiosity

The best motivation for doing a job well is the satisfaction of doing it.

Rudolf Dreikurs, *Social Equality: The Challenge of Today*
Contemporary Books, Ontario 1971 p.12

Preparing the Ground: Meaningful Work

Classroom Jobs

This list includes many job options, some of which are not so traditional. Some jobs will need more than one student. You may start with one set of jobs at the beginning of the year and modify them as your students become more skilled. Students need time to learn how to do a job well, and jobs need to be rotated regularly to give each student a chance to learn a variety of classroom responsibilities. In elementary school, there should be enough jobs for every student to have at least one at all times. In secondary school, classroom jobs still provide an important function. Jobs continue to help students by giving them a sense of significance and providing support for teachers. Jobs that secondary teachers have used are indicated by an asterisk. Students always have ideas for more ways to be helpful. Ask them!

Attendance taker*

Board cleaner

Calendar updater*

Door holder

Electrician (lights/computers)*

Emergency bag carrier

Energy/water czar (helps the class keep a small environmental foot print)

First responder/nurse helper (Band-Aids)

Greeter (for guests, new students)*

Guideline carrier (carries an 8 x 11 copy of the class guidelines to specialty classrooms like PE, art)

Hand sanitizer/washing monitor

Helping hand*

Jobs monitor/assistant

Letter carrier

Library book carrier

Line leader

Lunchbox carrier

Messenger*

Mindful moment leader* (or self-regulation monitor)

Mystery job (does something to help the class feel good once that week)

New student buddy/helper*

Noise level monitor*

Paper passer-outer*

Patrol

Pencil sharpener

Pet caretaker

Plant caretaker

Problem Solving "guides" (one boy and one girl who can help students through the steps of problem solving)*

Recycler*

Representative to Student Council*

Snack distributor*

Substitute welcomer and assistant*

Substitute/floater (does the job for the students who are absent)*

Table cleaner

Teacher assistant*

Thank-you card maker*

Timekeeper*

Uncrumpler (helps students who feel like "Charlie")*

Vacuumer/sweeper

Weather checker

Later when you are doing class meetings, these can also be included:
    Class meeting leader*
    Class meeting note taker*
    Helpful not hurtful monitor*

*Indicates jobs also useful in a secondary classroom.

School-wide Jobs

In addition to classroom jobs, many schools have school-wide jobs. This can happen at the level of a whole classroom or by individual students. It is important to engage students in deciding how these jobs are assigned and rotated.

School-wide jobs: Whole classroom

In some schools, classrooms (or advisory rooms) take on school-wide jobs to develop ownership beyond the classroom. It is helpful to rotate these jobs with the school terms (quarter or semester).

Examples of whole classroom jobs include:

- Managing lost and found (check in once per week),
- Outdoor game box organization (including ball retrieval),
- Front entrance area cleaning,
- Bulletin board management,
- Checking in on bathrooms (class assigned to each one),
- Acknowledgement bulletin board (some schools do this electronically),
- School plant watering, and
- Managing compost center in cafeteria.

School-wide jobs: Individual students

Individual school-wide jobs introduce the concept of job applications, fitness for a particular job, interest in different types of work, contributing to the wellbeing of the community, responsibility, and many relational skills.

- Jobs typically last a term (quarter or semester). Students re-apply for new jobs each term,
- There are enough jobs for the majority of interested students to participate at least one quarter or semester,
- Typically, jobs are done during part of the student's lunch break, arrival time, or shortly before dismissal, and
- Staff does need to be allocated to support some jobs.

Job descriptions and "hiring"

Sample job descriptions and interview protocols are on the pages that follow. Job descriptions can be created that fit each school and include the following:

- Purpose or need for the job,
- Responsibilities for the job (how, where and when to do),
- Skills needed for the job, and
- Critical standards to keep the job and what happens if standards are not met. Typically, this involves a warning and if the problem persists, loss of the job for the term.

Examples of individual student jobs

Job Title - Description

- Air Regulators - Pump and maintains school balls
- Beachcombers - Sweep and maintain sandbox area
- Book Elves - Library helper: shelves, straightens, dusts books
- Bus Coordinators - Encourage bus riders to be prompt to bus
- Chef Assistants - Assist cooks
- Conference Room Coordinators - Clean and organize
- Computer Movers - Transport computers
- Employee Photographers - Take picture of student employee of the week
- Equipment Coordinators - Hang tetherball and other recess equipment
- Hall Helpers - Monitor hall during arrival and dismissal (to answer questions and remind others of guidelines).
- Host/Hostess - Show new students around school
- High-Rise Engineers - Raise and lower flag
- Library Specialists - Assist librarian
- Literacy Boosters - Read to and with younger students
- Lunchroom Sanitizers - Assist janitor in lunchroom
- Malt Shop Engineers - Sets up ice cream sales
- Office Runners - Help office secretary
- Paper Technicians - Fills copy machines with paper
- Pledge and Announcement DJs - Lead pledge of allegiance
- Reader Board Organizers - File and organize letters for the reader board
- School Environmentalists - Collect litter on school ground. Older students can track data on electricity, water, garbage and share with school.
- Scuff Removers - Keep hallways scuff free. (Students often like this job. Make a small slit in a tennis ball and squeeze it onto an old broom handle. Students can walk the halls and wipe off the scuffmarks.)
- Supply Regulators - Retrieve lost balls and clothing
- Tutors - Assist students in academics

    Adapted from Totem Falls Elementary, Snohomish, WA

Story: The "Bags" job.

At Sharon Elementary School in Charlotte, North Carolina, the literacy teacher took responsibility to create a bag labeled for each K or 1st grade student who was struggling with reading and writing. Three days per week, she pulled out and reviewed the previous assignment, and then dropped a simple reader and a short writing task appropriate for each child into the bag. Fifth grade students ate lunch quickly, left to pick up their assigned buddy, went to the literacy room and pulled the bag for their student. They worked 15 minutes, returned materials and walked their buddy back to class. Teachers reported progress for their students and were eager to involve additional children in the program. In addition, friendships were formed that helped with playground and bus behavior, among other things. Older students were very responsible about moving around the building unsupervised and about completing tasks with their buddies.

Preparing the Ground: Meaningful Work

Sample Job Description

Job title:	
When is it done?	
Where is it done?	
When this job is done well you will see:	
To do this job well be careful to:	

The first person to learn this job this year: _____.

You can consult with _____ to improve the job description or to ask questions. (In a classroom, this might be another student who has had the job, for school-wide jobs this is typically the adult supervisor.)

© Positive Discipline Association ■ www.PositiveDiscipline.org

Sample School Job Application

Name:

Date:

Classroom (Homeroom):

Grade:

Job Desired:

I would be good at this job because…

Hobbies or special interest:

Chores or job history:

References:

Name   Phone number

1. _____   _____

2. _____   _____

3. _____   _____

Sample Job Interview Guide

1. Tell us a little about yourself.

2. Review application together.

3. We want to establish a team atmosphere. What makes you think you'll be a good team player?

4. Give us an example of a situation in your life where you demonstrated leadership qualities, problem solving tools or team player abilities.

5. Do you have any personal growth goals? What are they?

6. Why should we hire you for this job?

7. What is your strongest quality or one you are most proud of?

School-wide Jobs – Sample Letter to Parents

Adapted from Totem Falls Elementary, Snohomish School District, Washington

Dear parents of…

One of the goals we have for all students in our school is that they become caring, compassionate, responsible, and dependable citizens in our school, in our community, in our country, and in our world. We believe that if our students begin to understand their role as a citizen in our school, they will be able to transfer that knowledge to the larger community. We want our students to know that their contributions make a difference here. It takes all of us doing our part to make our school a place to be proud of and a great place to learn.

We are beginning a new program this fall called "Team [name of school]." Students will be able to perform different jobs around the school and become "employees" of Team [name of school]. The program will give students the opportunity to apply for, interview for, and learn the skills to be successful at the job. They will then perform the job to the best of their ability and participate in an assessment process to gain even more skills.

We have identified many jobs that will provide needed services at school. Most of the jobs take less than 15 minutes a day and can be performed during recess. There are a few jobs that will take students out of class for up to 10 minutes.

We will start the program on a small scale and expand it as we all learn together. Short job descriptions and an application are attached to this letter. If your child is interested in applying for a job on our team, they should complete the application and return it on or before [date].

We are excited about giving our students an opportunity to make a real contribution to our school community. Our schools, communities, and our world need involvement and participation from all citizens.

If you have questions please feel free to call our team coordinators [name and number].

Notes

Self-regulation
Preparing the Ground: Face Sheet

Concept: Self-regulation (Self-control)

Self-regulation is the ability to control or modulate one's emotions, wants, impulses, and actions. A student's ability to recognize and name emotions is an important step in learning self-regulation. Self-regulation depends on the prefrontal cortex and provides the basis for all social skills, success in joining groups, flexibility, and self-discipline.

The importance of spending time teaching, developing, and practicing self-regulation (theirs and yours) cannot be over emphasized. Lack of self-regulation skills in one or more students creates challenges for the entire classroom community. *All students* benefit from regular brain-breaks and self-regulation exercises. Although there is concern that taking time to do brain breaks will interfere with academic learning, research now shows that frequent, intentional breaks enhance student learning and social interactions. Initially these short breaks might need to be every 10 to 15 minutes. As students gain skills the spacing can increase.

Why self-regulation is important

- Self-regulation has been found to be a crucial component of school readiness, academic success and positive health outcomes.
- Students lacking in self-regulation skills have trouble learning, can be disruptive in classrooms and often interfere with the learning of others.
- Self-regulation is a critical skill for students to manage transitions in a school day.

Developing self-regulation and self-control

- Developing the skills of self-control takes practice. With practice, new brain pathways are built.
- The content of the activities in this section deliberately focuses on emotional awareness of self and others as this is an essential first step in developing self-regulation.
- The *process* of doing all the activities (in this and other sections) enhances self-awareness by requiring reflection, input, and planning skills.
- Students learn to identify and name feelings (emotional and physical), which gives them more control over their actions.
- Students learn to use basic brain science to understand themselves.
- Teachers must guide students into, through, and out of transition times with clearly thought out routines.
- **Teachers must hold students accountable with kindness and firmness**, until they demonstrate understanding and self-control.

> "Regulation... means available to interact, neither too low or too high... So, if a kid is not regulated, you can't work on answering why questions, or work on shared problem solving, or anything else... Kids can't work at higher developmental levels if they aren't regulated."
>
> From *Respecting Autism. The Rebecca School DIR Casebook for Parents and Professionals.* Stanley I. Greenspan, MD and Gil Tippy, Psy D. Vantage Press, NY, 2011 Page 12.

Preparing the Ground: Self-regulation

What else are students learning?
- To develop and use more language to express their own feelings,
- To manage anger, and
- To make the connection between sensations in their body and their emotions, so that they can recognize the body's "warning signal."

    For example, a second grader described that he felt his "tummy shake" just before he hit another student because he was angry. He learned to recognize the feeling in his stomach as a warning "stop" signal. He then developed a plan for those times, which was to walk away and use various self-regulation skills to calm down (breathe, quiet time out, squeeze Koosh ball).

Recommended order for teaching *self-regulation*
- *Brain in the Hand*
- *Positive Time Out*
- *More Activities for Self-Calming and Self-Awareness*
- *Glad, Mad, Sad, Scared: The Wheel of Feelings*
- *Feeling Faces Quilt*
- *Feeling Faces Chart*
- *More Activities for Emotional Awareness*

■ **Tip: The teaching doesn't stop.** There are opportunities to weave self-awareness and emotional intelligence into all sorts of school activities.

LITERATURE CONNECTIONS
Bang, Molly. *When Sophie Gets Angry, Really, Really Angry.* New York: Blue Sky Press, 1999.
Bang, Molly. *When Sophie Feels Really, Really, Hurt.* New York: Blue Sky Press, 2015.
Baskwill, Jane. *If Peace Is...* New York: MONDO Publishing, 2003. (Note: good for time-out space.)
Chryssicas, Mary Kaye. *I Love Yoga.* New York: DK Publishers, 2005.
Curtis, Jamie Lee and Laura Cornell. *Today I Feel Silly and Other Moods that Make My Day.* New York: Joanna Cotler Books, an Imprint of Harper Collins Publishers, 1998.
Everitt, Betsy. *Mean Soup.* San Diego, CA: Harcourt Brace Jovanovich, 1992.
Freymann, Saxton, and Joost Elffers. *How Are You Peeling?* New York: Arthur A. Levine Books, 1999.
Modesitt, Jeanne. *Sometimes I Feel Like a Mouse: A book about feelings.* New York: Scholastic, 1992.
Nelsen, Jane, Ashlee Wilkin and Bill Schorr. *Jared's Cool-Out Space.* Positive Discipline, 2013.
Parr, Todd. *It's OK to Be Different.* New York: Little Brown & Company, 2001.
Parr, Todd. *The Feelings Book.* New York: Little Brown & Company, 2005.
Parr, Todd. *The Peace Book.* New York: Little, Brown and Company, 2004. (good for a Time Out space)
Slobodkina, Esphyr. *Caps for Sale.* New York: Scholastic Inc., 2009. (Note: mirror neurons explain the behavior of the monkeys in this book.)
Sosin, Deborah. *Charlotte and the Quiet Place.* Berkley, CA: Plum Blossom Books, 2015.
Spelman, Cornelia Maude. *When I Feel Angry.* New York: Scholastic Inc., 2000.
Vail, Rachel. *Sometimes I'm Bombaloo.* Singapore: Scholastic Press, 2002.
Verde, Susan. *I Am Peace: A Book of Mindfulness.* New York: Abrams Books for Young Readers, 2017.
Witek, Jo. *In My Heart: A Book of Feelings.* New York: Abrams Appleseed, 2013. (for K-1)

ONLINE RESOURCES

https://www.naeyc.org/resources/pubs/yc/mar2017/teaching-emotional-intelligence

https://casel.org/what-is-sel

Preparing the Ground: Self-regulation

The Brain in the Hand
Based on work by Daniel J. Siegel, MD*

OBJECTIVE:
- To teach students and teachers about their brain
- To understand how the brain responds when stressed.
- To invite students to think about self-regulation proactively.

MATERIALS:
- Board

COMMENTS FOR TEACHERS:
- We function best when we have access to all parts of our brain. Under stress, the prefrontal cortex doesn't work well and we lose our problem-solving skills.
- When the part of our brain that allows us to think and respond respectfully is not functioning well, we can help ourselves and others by taking some time to "come back into ourselves."
- Dr. Siegel's language makes this easy to explain. To watch his video, do an internet search for Daniel Siegel and "Brain in the Hand."
- For further details on this model for the brain, study *Parenting from the Inside Out* by Daniel J. Siegel, MD & Mary Hartzell, New York: Jeremy P. Tarcher/Putnam, 2003, p. 171 - 183.

DIRECTIONS:

1. Setting the stage.

Invite students to think of a time they got really upset. List a few examples on the board of things that are upsetting to them (no names).

- Ask, "Can you remember if it felt like you had a choice about what you did?"
- "Did it matter to you what the other person was feeling or thinking?"

2. Introducing the "brain in the hand".

- Explain that you will use your hand to model a brain. (See drawings next page.)
- Point to the base of your palm. The part of your brain that is closest to your spine and near the base of your skull is called the **brain stem**. It is your survival brain. It keeps you safe and when things "look dangerous." It can tell you to fight, freeze or run away (flight).
- Fold your thumb across your palm. The middle part of your brain is where feelings arise and your memories are stored (limbic area). It is also where you have your "safety radar" (your *amygdala*).
- Fold your fingers over your thumb so you have a fist. The outer layer of your brain is called the **cortex**. It is where your thinking and planning happens.
- Point to your fingernails. The area of the cortex that is right up front is the **prefrontal cortex**. It is where the brain processes information about how we relate to others. It gives us the ability to:
  - Understand others' feelings
  - Calm ourselves
  - Make choices
  - Make moral decisions
  - Sense what is going on for others (read body language).

3. Flipping our lid.

Explain, "When we are really stressed or upset, the prefrontal cortex shuts down and no longer works with the rest of our brain. It goes offline."

- Lift the fingers up so they are straight and the thumb is still across the palm.
- "We say, 'We flip our lid.'"
- Explain that we "flip our lid" when the thinking part (prefrontal cortex) of our brain isn't working. It becomes hard to use our problem-solving skills.

© Positive Discipline Association ■ www.PositiveDiscipline.org

Preparing the Ground: Self-regulation

BRAINSTEM:

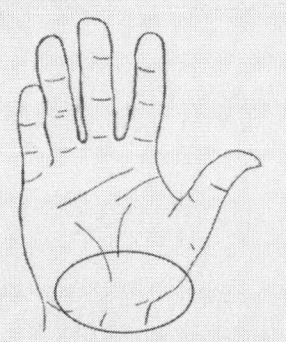

LIMBIC AREA:

PREFRONTAL CORTEX:

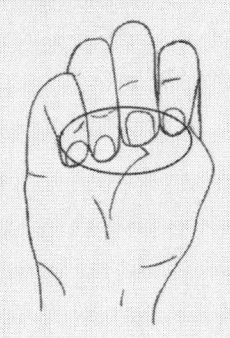

FLIPPED LID:

4. Reflection.
Ask students:
- "Do you sometimes flip your lid or have you ever been with someone who flipped their lid?" Invite students to share (no names). "What did that look like?" "Feel like?"
- "When you are really upset, have you ever done something and later thought, 'Why did I do that?' or 'I really wish I hadn't done that!' or 'What in the world was I thinking when I did that?'" (Allow some thought about why that might happen if the pre-frontal cortex is not working at that time.)
- Explain, "When you are "flipped" (hand with fingers straight), you can't learn very well either. It really helps to calm back down so that you can solve problems."

5. A little more brain science: *Mirror neurons.*
Explain to your students: "Our brains are built so that we learn by copying. When you see someone yawn do you notice that sometimes you feel like yawning? Even babies copy what they see. Our brains also mirror feelings. When we are with other people who are sad, we can feel their sadness. The nerves (neurons) that do this are called **mirror neurons**."
- Holding up one hand as a "flipped lid" ask students, "What might happen to someone near that person because of mirror neurons?" (They are likely to flip their lid too.)
- Holding both hands in the "flipped lid" positions, ask students, "What might happen if two people approach each other like this?" (They might get into a fight.)
- "What might students need to do to find their thinking brains and solve their problem?" (Move away, calm down, un-flip their lids).

6. Exploring self-regulation.
- It is helpful to have a list of useful strategies posted for when someone has a "flipped lid." For example:
  ◦ Invite the students to share what they have found helpful to calm or re-gather themselves. Make a list of some of the tools.
  ◦ When someone else has a flipped lid, I could: Not take it personally, invite them to breathe deeply, give them space, etc.
- Students may want to post these lists in their positive time out space once it is created.
- Invite the students to share what they have found helpful to calm or re-gather themselves.

Positive Discipline in the School and Classroom Manual
by Jane Nelsen, Lynn Lott, Teresa LaSala, Jody McVittie, and Suzanne Smitha

Preparing the Ground: Self-regulation

■ Tips

- Invite students to reflect on the Brain in the Hand while they are reading. "How is the character feeling? Has that person flipped their lid?"
- In his book, *The Whole Brain Child*, Dr. Siegel simplifies this by using the terms the "upstairs brain" (the prefrontal cortex) and the "downstairs brain" (the limbic area and brain stem). This is another way of talking about the brain, especially for younger students.

■ Extension

Students find this kind of brain science very useful. They can use this in addition to information on mirror neurons. There is a short (14 minute) video on mirror neurons on YouTube. Search "Mirror Neurons PBS".

For a story with a good example of mirror neurons at work see:
Slobodkina, Esphyr. *Caps for Sale*. New York: Scholastic Inc., 2009.

*"The Brain in the Hand" is the work of Daniel J. Siegel, M.D., first published in his book, *Parenting from the Inside Out* (2003) and more recently published in *The Whole-Brain Child* (2011). Dr. Siegel is not associated and/or affiliated with, and does not endorse and/or sponsor the Positive Discipline Association and/or its activities.

Preparing the Ground: Self-regulation

Positive Time Out & Creating the Space

OBJECTIVE:
- To teach that Positive Time Out can be encouraging and empowering (helpful) instead of punitive (hurtful).

MATERIALS:
- Chart paper
- Marking pens

COMMENTS FOR TEACHERS:
- "Where did we ever get the crazy idea that in order to help students do better, first we have to make them feel worse? Students (and adults) do better when they feel better."
  - Jane Nelsen
- Positive Time Out teaches students self-discipline and self-control through an understanding of the value of "cooling off" until rational thinking is available to them again.
- Overuse of the Positive Time Out area may indicate that the student doesn't feel belonging or doesn't feel significant. It can be a reminder to connect and learn what is going on for the student.
- Time limits are not recommended. Different people need different amounts of time to self-regulate.
- Another resource is *Positive Time Out and Over 50 Ways to Avoid Power Struggles in the Home and the Classroom* by Jane Nelsen, 1999

DIRECTIONS:

1. **Reframing "time out."**
   - Ask students, "What is the purpose of a 'time out' in sports?" (They will probably mention things like: catch your breath, re-group, or make a new plan.)
   - Explain, "Everyone needs a time out once in a while, because we all make mistakes and need to regather. It is even better to use a time out when you feel like you are about to 'lose it.'"
   - Say, "It helps to have a place to sort out feelings, calm down, and then make a decision about what to do."
   - "How might a space like this help our classroom?"

2. **A time out place for our classroom.**
   - Explain, "We are going to design a place in the room for the Positive Time Out space. The goal is to create a space where we can calm ourselves, so we can feel better and then do better. It is not a place used for punishment."

3. **Designing the space.**
As a group brainstorm and come to consensus on:
   - Where in the classroom will it be?
   - What items would be helpful there?
   - What will the theme/name be? (Common names include Hawaii, the chill spot, the alone zone, the calming quarter.)

4. **Guidelines for a time out space.**
   - Brainstorm guidelines for your time out space. Invite your students to think about what will be helpful. Examples might include: It is space for being quiet, we join the group again when we are ready, one person at a time.
   - Ask them to consider common objections of many teachers, such as, "What if students misbehave just so they can go listen to music?" or, "What if students want to stay in time out all the time because they would rather play with toys or sleep in the bean bag chair?" Proposed guidelines should include solutions to these concerns.
   - Vote to select those that are needed. Post them in the Positive Time Out space.

5. **Moving it forward.**
   - Establish a time frame for creating the time out area.
   - Check in with the students about once a week initially to make sure that the guidelines are working.
   - Challenges that arise from using the space are great class meeting agenda items.

Positive Discipline in the School and Classroom Manual
by Jane Nelsen, Lynn Lott, Teresa LaSala, Jody McVittie, and Suzanne Smitha

Preparing the Ground: Self-regulation

▪ Tips

- **It can take time for students to learn how to use Positive Time Out respectfully.** Some teachers are worried students will go to the cool-down spot just to play or to avoid doing their work. If this is one of your concerns, bring it up as students are setting the guidelines.
    - It is better to *ask* instead of *tell*. For example, "Do you think that this will be a space to use to play?" "What would happen if you use the space just to avoid work time? When would you get your work done?"
    - When a problem develops, it is an opportunity to review guidelines and focus on solutions. Let the class share how they feel about the space being used this way, as well as their ideas for correcting the problem. When only one student is consistently misusing the space, consider individual problem solving.
    - Some classrooms have a sand timer for students to use for themselves. It is not recommended that the space have a pre-set time limit. Some students self-regulate quickly. Others cannot.

- **Refusing to use Positive Time Out.** A frequent question from teachers is, "What happens when the student won't go to the cool down spot?" One reason students refuse to go is that they associate going to "time out" with being bad, or being punished. Another reason is that when someone has "flipped" they are not totally in their thinking brain. Some strategies that have worked for others are:
    - Offer a choice. "____, you seem upset. Do you think you can cool down at your desk, or would it be helpful to go to the cool-down spot?"
    - Offer an ear. "____, I can tell you are upset. I'd be glad to listen to what is going on for you after I _____. Do you want to wait at your desk or would it be more helpful to go to the cool down spot?"

- **Space in another classroom.** Some teams of teachers invite students to use the calming down space in the other classroom, so that they are not as near the incident or people that were the trigger. It is best to do this only in extreme situations. When students are able to stay in the same room they:
    - Miss less class; may be able to absorb some of the content being covered at the time.
    - Do not risk being embarrassed by having to leave class or show up in another class.
    - See how peers can transition from feeling upset to becoming self-regulated.

- **Problems.** Use any problems that come with time out space as opportunities to learn and practice problem solving.

- **Supplies.** Many time out areas include books, stuffed animals, stress balls. Some classrooms have a sand timer for students to use for themselves.

- **Listening friends.** After students have learned about listening skills, a listening friend can be part of the time-out plan. This means a student can choose a friend who will go to time out with them and just listen while the student talks about what is upsetting. Sharing while someone just listens is very healing.

- **Choosing a theme.** One ninth-grade class designed a Positive Time Out area that looked like Hawaii, complete with a palm tree, a mural of sand and the ocean, beach chairs, and headphones for listening to Hawaiian music. A 4th grade classroom brought in a tent and "went camping."

- **When space is a problem.** One classroom's solution for a lack of suitable time out space was to have every student create a stand-up card. Students displayed their card on their desk when they needed to let others to know that they were taking a time out.

- **Follow through is important.** The next time a student is struggling to self-regulate ask, "Would it help you to take some Positive Time Out or go to [name of your cool down area]?" It is helpful to do this as privately as possible to support the student in maintaining dignity. Positive Time Out is more effective when it is chosen rather than when it is ordered. If the student refuses (which is less likely if they have helped create the Positive Time Out area), you could ask if they would find it helpful to choose a listening friend to go with them.

More Activities for Self-calming and Self-awareness

OBJECTIVE:
- To integrate self-regulation and self-calming into daily activities.
- To practice self-regulation.

COMMENTS FOR TEACHERS:
- "Neurons that fire together wire together." - Donald Hebb Self-calming skills need to be practiced many times a day.
- Pausing to self-regulate resets the brain and gives students space to learn.
- Students who have more than one way to self-regulate will become more "fluent" in re-gathering themselves.
- Body awareness is a very useful tool to grow the body's ability to self-regulate. Body awareness increases left-right brain connections, which also improves the ability to recognize and handle emotions.
- These activities are meant to be used more than once. Teachers can use a variety of these tools each day to bring students back to self-awareness.
- Know and be aware of your students' developmental capabilities.
- Be aware of your students' needs for movement and interaction. Use pair shares and activities that involve some movement regularly.
- Consult with professional resources who can help you help children with special needs.

BREATHING ACTIVITIES
Practicing slow breathing will help students grow their self-control. The exhalation communicates a message to the brain. It is linked to the parasympathetic nervous system, so the slow exhalation is calming.

Belly Breathing. Sit comfortably, put one hand on your chest and one on your stomach. Slowly inhale through your nose, pushing your belly out and then expanding the rib cage. With your hands, feel your stomach and your lungs expand. Exhale through your nose, emptying your lungs and then collapsing your belly. Repeat several times. See resources for videos.

Finger Breathing. Hold one hand up in front of you. Using a finger from the other hand, begin with your thumb and trace up as you inhale slowly. Trace down the other side of the thumb and exhale. Breath in again as you move the tracing finger up the first finger etc.

Hot Chocolate. Invite students to cup their hands as if they are holding a cup of hot chocolate. Invite them to slowly breathe in and smell the imaginary chocolate. Then blow slowly to cool the chocolate. Repeat 3 or 4 times.

Square in the Air. Breathe in to a count of 4. Hold for a count of 4. Breathe out for a count of 4 and hold again for a count of 4. Repeat. As you show this technique, draw a square in the air with your finger. Begin in the lower left corner start by moving your finger up for the first breath in. Model drawing one side of the square for each count of 4.

The Hissing Breath: Inhale a long, deep breath through the nose, and then out the mouth with a hissing sound, slow and long. Extending the exhale will allow students to slow down their inner speed.

MOVEMENT ACTIVITIES
Freeze/Melt Teach the class to "freeze" when you say, "freeze." Have them notice their body. When you believe they have frozen (this will be far from perfect at the outset), quietly give the next instruction or question. For example, "When I say melt, quietly give me a thumb up if you can remember our guidelines for walking in the hall."

The Ten Countdown: Teacher stands facing class and raises both hands above their head, spreading fingers open. Students copy, facing teacher. Teacher begins counting slowly from ten, and everyone moves hands down, ending at "one" with hands at sides.

Stretch it Out: Everyone stands up, stretches high, stretches low, and side to side for a count to 20. Eyes can be closed if desired and comfortable.

Tension Stretch: Have students stretch and move their bodies in the following ways: reach for the sky, touch toes, arm circles, neck circles, knee to chest. Practice until students can hold/do each of these stretches up to 20 seconds.

Preparing the Ground: Self-regulation

Movement Spelling (or Math). Have your students stand up. Tell them to reach up for vowels, reach down to your toes for consonants and then pick some words to spell. (Do this with them). You can also do this with mental math choosing to go one direction for odd numbers and one for even. You can start with simple math problems and get more complex.

Wet Dog Shake: Have your students think about how a dog shakes when it is wet. Say, "Do a body check and notice where all of the tension is currently showing up in your body. Pretend to glue your feet to the floor. Now, imagine you are feeling soft raindrops all over your body. We're going to shake like a wet dog shakes and when we do, all the tension is going to leave our bodies. Keep your feet firmly in place while you shake and bounce out the tension. Move your legs first… then shake your arms…hands and then the whole body. Think about a dog shaking off water as you shake away imaginary droplets of stress. Repeat several times with a deep breath in between."

Yoga. Encourage greater body awareness by beginning the day with a few minutes of simple yoga, stretching or slow, rhythmic, synchronized body movement. Some schools lead the entire school in yoga on closed circuit "Morning Announcements." See resources.

Where are your elbows? Caroline Goodell at the Institute for Body Awareness has a simple process for teaching students to become more body aware. Focusing on their bodies helps them be able to calm down internally and brings them back to the present moment. She created a game called "Where are My Elbows?" You can use this in combination with the "Freeze/Melt" activity above.

1. While staying calm yourself, say, "Freeze."
2. Then say, "Don't look but see if you can guess – without looking – if your knees are bent (pause) or straight."
3. Melt and look. Thumbs up if you guessed right.
4. Ask the students to move again and repeat the process with a different body question.
5. Repeat one more time. Here are some other body part suggestions:
   - Are your shoulders up or down?
   - Are your elbows bent or straight?
   - Are your hands in fists or open?
   - Are your toes scrunched or flat?
   - Is your tummy pushing out or relaxed?
   - Is your forehead relaxed or tight?
   - Is your weight more on your left foot, right foot, or both feet the same?
   - Is your head tilted or straight?

MINDFUL MOMENTS

Have your class practice quiet moments. They may only be able to start with 10 seconds. Gradually help them learn how to breathe slowly and deeply for increasing amounts of time. (Can they feel their breath in their nose? Throat? Can they breathe slowly enough that they feel it differently? Can they hear their breath in the back of their throat if they breathe really quietly?) See resources.

Chime activity.: Ring a chime and invite students to listen carefully and raise their hand when they can no longer hear the sound of the chime. Gradually extend the silent time before you ring the chime until students are able to sit in silence for 20 seconds or more.

Food activities. Give each student a small piece of food (slice of apple, slice of orange, several raisins). Invite students to taste and eat slowly, being aware of taste, texture, smell and the feeling of their mouth.

Silence/Stillness Silence is not something you use to control or reduce chaos in a room, but is instead a state of mind you help children develop.

- Silence/stillness allows students to access internal awareness and resources. Silence/stillness is a skill that must be taught.

- Softly encourage students to become more still, more quiet, and to listen for minute sounds from the environment.
- Initially ask them to be silent for small amounts of time, gradually extending the time to increase their capacity.
- Make a poster that says simply, "Silence" or "Stillness" and quietly post it periodically.
- Silence can be contagious and it won't happen all at once.
- Montessori schools have used this practice for years. Montessori Association websites offer more teaching suggestions.

TEACH BRAIN SCIENCE
Being aware of what is happening in their brains helps students self-regulate.

Brain in the Hand. After teaching the Brain in the Hand (Daniel J. Siegel, MD), use it as a non-verbal signal. For example, "Class, I'm beginning to feel (show your hand "half-flipped") and I'm guessing you are too. Let's (take some deep breaths, use a mindful moment, listen to music for 30 seconds) to see if we can bring ourselves to here (show hand with fist closed)." After the activity say, "I'm feeling (show hand). Show me how your are doing now".

MUSIC
During work time. Play quiet nature sounds or soft music. (If you can't hear the music, the noise level in the room is too loud).

During transitions. If you use music to signal transitions, the music should be clearly different so students know which cue to follow.

During quiet time. Set aside a few moments each day to just listen to calming music. This can be particularly useful as students transition in as they arrive or after lunch or recess.
Music sources: Search Youtube for "Brain Music" or nature sounds.

Textured Objects to Hold, Squeeze, or Sit Upon
Some students benefit from squeezing dense, spongy items (if impulse control is an issue, make sure the item is on a string, tied to the leg of their desk) or holding stuffed animals while they work or are in a positive time out space.

- Educate students on the appropriate use of such objects.
- Occupational therapists serving schools often have materials for checkout like large balls, bumpy seats or wedges for sitting.
- Weighted vests can also be helpful for some students with special needs.

Tips
There are many ways to augment self-regulation skills.

- In some classrooms, a self-regulation monitor is a classroom job. The student with this job pauses the classroom on a regular basis, and leads a self-regulation activity.
- In some classrooms, any student can call for a "mindful moment" by following a routine to invite the class to notice that it is not regulated and leading a short self-regulation activity.

RESOURCES

Brain Gym activities also stimulate right-left brain connections; see www.BrainGym.org

Bowen-Irish, Tere. *Drive Thru Menus: Exercise Posters for Attention and Strength & Leader's Manual.* Framingham, MA: Therapro, Inc., 2004. www.Theraproducts.com *Drive Thru Menus* is a workbook with posters that offer 10 quick, easy exercises for improving attention and strength in elementary age students. They are fun for students and support body/mind awareness, self-control and focus.

Mindful Games Book and Activity Cards, Susan Kaiser Greenland https://www.susankaisergreenland.com

Mind Up Curriculum

Mindyeti.com

Sesame Street lesson with Elmo on belly breathing: https://www.youtube.com/watch?v=7zxBRBhxbNo

Yoga 4 Classrooms Activity Cards, Lisa Flynn http://www.yoga4classrooms.com/activity-card-deck

Preparing the Ground: Self-regulation

Glad, Mad, Sad, or Scared: The Wheel of Feelings

Saskia deRaat Riley and Teresa LaSala
Adapted from Dr. Gloria Willcox's Feeling Wheel*

OBJECTIVE:
- Increase students' vocabulary for describing feelings.
- Develop a classroom tool to help identify feelings.

MATERIALS:
- Board
- Chart prepared in advance as shown below
- Markers

COMMENTS FOR TEACHERS:
- Four basic feelings are a starting point for many students who are not used to naming feelings.
- Once students have a verbal (cognitive) connection to what they are feeling on the inside they can rapidly increase their internal awareness *and* matching vocabulary.
- When students can identify and have words for their feelings it is much easier for them to self-regulate and express themselves effectively.
- A sample list of feeling words is included so that you have a reference. In this activity, however, it is hoped that a growing list develops *from* the students.

DIRECTIONS:

1. **Introduction: feelings are important.** Invite a discussion about why feelings are important. For example, they help us recognize/understand:
   - The people we love
   - Danger
   - What makes us human
   - How to solve problems
   - How people see the world differently

2. **Words and Feelings.** Explain that most feelings can be described using just one word. This can be surprisingly difficult for both children and adults.

3. **Identify basic feelings.** Explain that human emotions can more or less be grouped into these four "basic emotion" categories (Glad, Mad, Sad, Scared). Refer to and post prepared chart.

4. **Brainstorming: expanding awareness.** Together we are going to brainstorm more words to describe the four basic emotions.
   - Taking one basic emotion at a time, brainstorm other words that are more specific but are still related to the feeling. Write words on the chart in the appropriate quadrant. (Repeat for each basic emotion.)
     For example, "If we imagine feeling glad, what other words might describe that feeling?" Students may respond with happy, excited, and hopeful.
   - It is important that the words come from the students. You may need to allow some thinking time to help them stretch. (This list will grow throughout the year.)
   - Students will notice that some words fit in more than one quadrant.

5. **Using the chart.**
   - Ask the students how having the chart in the classroom might be helpful to them. As they practice noticing whether they are glad, mad, sad or scared they will get more specific in naming their emotions.
   - Explain that we often experience more than one feeling at a time, and it can be confusing. Focusing on the basic emotions helps to sort it out.
   - Our body's sensations can help us tell the difference between mad, sad, glad and scared. (A discussion about what different students notice in their bodies can be helpful.)

Positive Discipline in the School and Classroom Manual
by Jane Nelsen, Lynn Lott, Teresa LaSala, Jody McVittie, and Suzanne Smitha

Preparing the Ground: Self-regulation

6. **Moving it forward.**
    - Post the chart where it can be seen from the positive time out area.
    - Add to the chart whenever new words come up in discussion or reading.
    - Encourage students to use the chart to identify their own feelings when they complain to you or have concerns.
    - Incorporate the chart into academic lessons where possible. (Reading: What do you think the character in the story was feeling? Writing: What is your character feeling? What kinds of descriptive words would help your readers know what your character is feeling?)

*Gloria Wilcox's feeling wheel can be found at:
https://med.emory.edu/excel/documents/Feeling%20Wheel.pdf

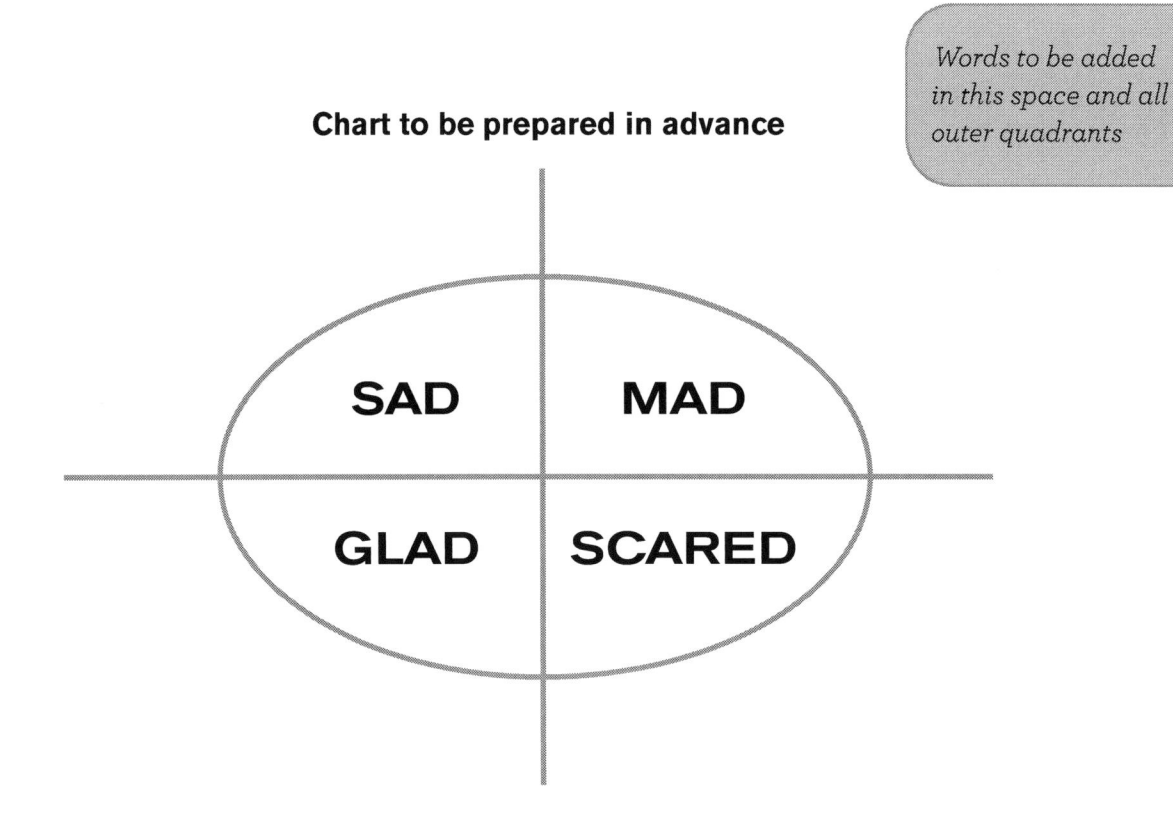

Chart to be prepared in advance

| SAD | MAD |
| GLAD | SCARED |

Words to be added in this space and all outer quadrants

Examples of Feeling Words

GLAD	SAD	MAD	SCARED
Amused	Alone	Acrimonious	Afraid
Appreciated	Apathetic	Angry	Anxious
Brave	Ashamed	Annoyed	Ashamed
Cheerful	Betrayed	Betrayed	Confused
Comfortable	Bored	Critical	Cornered
Confident	Confused	Disappointed	Discouraged
Content	Depressed	Disgusted	Distrustful
Creative	Disappointed	Distressed	Embarrassed
Curious	Discouraged	Distant	Fearful
Daring	Distant	Enraged	Frightened
Energetic	Embarrassed	Frustrated	Helpless
Enthusiastic	Grieving	Furious	Horrified
Excited	Guilty	Grumpy	Humiliated
Fascinated	Helpless	Hateful	Inadequate
Gleeful	Hopeless	Hostile	Insecure
Gratitude	Humiliated	Humiliated	Insignificant
Happy	Hurt	Hurt	Intimidated
Hopeful	Inferior	Impatient	Mortified
Intimate	Insignificant	Infuriated	Overwhelmed
Joyful	Isolated	Irritated	Shocked
Loved/Loving	Lonely	Jealous	Skeptical
Nurturing	Lost	Perturbed	Submissive
Optimistic	Miserable	Provoked	Surprised
Peaceful	Overwhelmed	Rejected	Tense
Playful	Rejected	Resentful	Threatened
Powerful	Remorseful	Sarcastic	Uncertain
Proud	Resigned	Selfish	Unsafe
Relaxed	Sleepy	Shocked	Violent
Relieved	Solemn	Skeptical	Vulnerable
Respected	Stunned	Tense	Worried
Safe	Stupid	Violent	
Satisfied	Tired		
Secure	Tortured		
Successful	Weary		
Surprised	Wounded		
Thankful			
Tickled			
Trusting			
Valuable			

Preparing the Ground: Self-regulation

Feeling Faces Quilt

OBJECTIVE:
- To expand student awareness of feelings and the words to describe them.

MATERIALS:
- 3" x 8" sheets of white paper
- Camera and ability to print pictures
- Board

COMMENTS FOR TEACHERS:
- Many children are thrilled and they want to do more than one feeling.
- That is an opportunity to explain that people sometimes have different facial expressions for the same feeling. However, noticing a person's face is a good place to start to try to understand how they feel.
- You may have duplicate feelings. That is an opportunity to explain that not everyone looks the same with their feelings.

DIRECTIONS:

1. **Introduce body language/facial expressions.**
   - Ask students, "What are some clues that help us guess how people are feeling?" (They tell us. We can see it in their face. We can tell by how they act or move.)

2. **Linking facial expressions with feelings.**
   - Put on an exaggerated feeling face and ask students to guess what you might be "showing." For example, open your eyes wide and make your mouth "O" shaped for "surprised."
   - Try another feeling and see if they can guess the feeling.

3. **Generate a list of feeling words.**
   - Brainstorm and record with students a long list of feeling words.
   - Invite them to include feeling words that aren't used so often for example: reluctant, offended, perplexed.

4. **Create a feeling faces quilt.**
   - Explain that together you will be making a feeling faces chart for the classroom.
   - Ask each student to pick a word (from the list) that they think they could demonstrate in their face.
   - Pass out pieces of paper about 3 x 8 inches and have them write the feeling in big letters.
   - Then with a camera have each child hold the title (paper with the feeling name) under their chin as you take a picture of the feeling face.
   - Print up the pictures and make a wall chart.

5. **Moving it forward.**

Use the chart in your classroom to help identify feelings and continue to expand student vocabulary for emotions. Ideas include:

- Encourage students to name their feelings. If they get stuck, have them walk to the chart.
- Use the chart to talk about feelings in the stories being read.
- Use the chart to guess how someone might feel.

© Positive Discipline Association ■ www.PositiveDiscipline.org

Preparing the Ground: Self-regulation

Feeling Faces
Illustrations by Maia Goodman

appreciative	excited	delighted	glad	pleased
happy	cheerful	joyful	loving	playful
calm	surprised	thrilled	sad	angry
tired	bored	scared	hurt	annoyed
confused	disappointed	guilty	worried	jealous
irritated	challenged	provoked	defeated	confident

Positive Discipline in the School and Classroom Manual by Jane Nelsen, Lynn Lott, Teresa LaSala, Jody McVittie, and Suzanne Smitha

Preparing the Ground: Self-regulation

More Activities for Emotional Awareness

OBJECTIVE:
- To integrate emotional awareness into daily activities.

COMMENTS FOR TEACHERS:
- Students who have a large vocabulary of "feeling words" can better express their emotions using language instead of problem behavior.

FEELINGS CHECK-IN
Have cards with feeling words. When students come into the room, they can pick a card that matches what they are feeling and put it on their desk or in their "name pocket." Some classrooms have a clothespin with each student's name. The student moves their clothespin to the picture/word that matches their feeling. For another example of a check-in board see http://www.naeyc.org/files/yc/file/200611/BTJFoxSupplementalActivities.pdf

BE A SCIENTIST AND DISCOVER
Have students pay close attention to what is happening in their bodies when they have strong feelings. Ask, "What happened right before you lost control?" Students can share their observations at class meetings.

FEELING WORD OF THE DAY
Pick 30 or 40 feeling words (some familiar, some less familiar). Begin discussing a feeling word a day as part of your morning activities.

WORD CHART
Start a feelings word chart or use your chart from Glad, Mad, Sad, or Scared. Invite students to add to the word chart when they find new feeling words in their reading or hear them in the halls.

ROLE-PLAY
Role-play situations using puppets. Have the puppets say what they are feeling.

DRAWING FEELINGS
This is a good follow up lesson to **Brain in the Hand**. Provide each student with a simple outline drawing of a person. With markers, pencils or crayons invite them to color in the "body" to show what their body feels like when they are flipped. Encourage the students to use color.

On another day, you can ask students to color another "body" to show what it looks like when they are not flipped. It can be the basis for an interesting discussion. Children as young as kindergarten have learned from this.

Communication Skills
Preparing the Ground: Face Sheet

Concept: Communication skills

Communication is the process of sharing information with at least one other person.

- There is a sender, a message and a receiver. The skills of communicating involve learning to be an effective "sender" as well as an effective "receiver."
- Listening, expressing desires or feelings effectively and respectfully are skills that need to be taught. It takes practice.

Why communication skills are important

- They give students a sense of both connection and autonomy.
- They help students express thoughts, feelings and ideas in a respectful manner and empower them to influence the world around them.

What else are students learning?

- Patience,
- Projecting voice,
- Public speaking skills,
- A connection between feelings and thoughts,
- Powerful words and communication can influence and make changes in the world, and
- Communication takes practice.

Recommended order for teaching communication skills

This section has activities to practice "sending" and "receiving" communication.

- **Sending:** *Bugs and Wishes, I-Messages.* All children can learn "I-messages" but for younger children (10 and under) who are not fluent in speaking about emotions, Bugs and Wishes is an easier first step.
- **Receiving:** *Listening 1, Listening 2* depending on the skill set of your class.

■ Tips

- Up to this point in the manual, lessons have been presented in a linear order. It may be appropriate for your class to augment these communication lessons by developing problem solving skills. You could use **Four Problem-Solving Suggestions**, **Wheel of Choice** and/or **Solution Table** from Essential Skill #5: Focusing on Solutions. Most of the skills in these lessons can be used independently of class meetings.
- Sometimes students will look at the adult instead of the student to whom they are talking. It is important to remind students to look at the person to whom they are talking.
- Communication skills need continual practice and review.

LITERATURE CONNECTIONS

Binko, Howard. *Howard B. Wigglebottom Learns to Listen*. Marina Del Ray, CA: Thunderbolt Publishers, 2005.
Lester, Helen and Lynn Munsinger. *Listen Buddy*. Boston, MA: Houghton Mifflin, Harcourt, 1995.
Moss, Pegg. *Say Something*. Gardiner Maine: Tillbury House, 2004.
Scheuer, Karen. *A Bug and a Wish*. Houston, TX: Strategic Book Publishing and Rights Co, 2014.
Williams, Barbara. *Albert's Impossible Toothache*. Cambridge, MA: Candlewick Press, 2003.

Preparing the Ground: Communication Skills

Bugs and Wishes

OBJECTIVE:
- To provide students with a format for problem solving.

MATERIALS:
- Magic wand
- "Bug" about the size of your hand. (Ladybugs are recommended rather than scorpions or spiders.)
- Board

COMMENTS FOR TEACHERS:
- Bugs and Wishes is a simplified form of "I- Messages."
- Bugs and Wishes are meant to be used one-on-one in private for problem solving. *This is not a class meeting process. It is taught in the circle for practice but used for one-on-one problem solving.*
- Once students learn how to use "bugs and wishes," you will start hearing the expression in their own conversations.
- Teaching students how to respond is an important part of the activity.
- Young students are prone to say, "It bugs me…and I *wish* you would *stop*." While this is an acceptable beginning, students should to learn to say what they wish the other person would actually *do* to correct the problem.
- The bug and the wand can be kept on the Solution Table in the classroom. See "Solution Table" activity.

DIRECTIONS:

1. **Getting ready.**

   On a piece of flip chart paper make two columns. Title one column "Bugs" and the other "Wishes."

2. **Brainstorming.**
   - With students seated in a circle, brainstorm and record typical classroom problems that "bug" them, such as:

     Breaking in line

     Borrowing without asking

     Pushing

     Talking during work time

     Telling secrets

     Interfering with other work
   - Let students do the brainstorming. If they don't mention something you think is a typical problem, say, "What about _____?"
   - Then brainstorm and record some "wishes" to match the "bug list." For example, across from the column for "cutting in line," they might put "go to the end of the line."

3. **Adding a new tool.**
   - Tell students that you will share a new tool for using words to help express what is bothering them. It's a good way to let others know how they feel about a problem without being bossy.
   - Say, "We will be practicing some examples in our circle, to learn. But this is something you use with each other, one-on-one."
   - Bring out your "Bug" and your "Magic Wand" as props to help them remember the words.
   - Give them an example using one of the above problems, saying: **"It bugs me when** people break in line, **and I wish people would** go to the end of the line," holding the bug up when you say "bugs" and the wand up when you say "wish."
   - It takes practice for students to be able to say what they want (suggest a solution) instead just "I wish you would stop."

4. **Prepare to Practice.**

   Tell students to think of a similar example, and use the word "people" instead of using names (as in the example above).

Preparing the Ground: Communication Skills

5. Practice.
Pass the bug and wand around the circle. Give each student a chance to practice (or pass) making their own bugs and wishes statement, or one from the brainstormed list.

6. Learning how to respond.
(This might happen on a separate day)
- On another piece of chart paper write: "Respectful Responses."
- Tell students, "Before we start using Bugs and Wishes, it is important to learn how to respond to one of these statements."
- Brainstorm with the students ideas for responses, being sure to include things like: "I'm sorry," "I didn't know it bothered you," "Thank you for telling me," "I'll think about that," "I'll do ___ instead," or, "It bugs me when you ___ and I wish ___."
- Suggestion: Write (or have students write) the most useful examples on sentence strips to be posted in the classroom. (Note that you will use these again later.)

7. Practicing responses.
- Give students an opportunity to practice responses.
- Read from your initial list of brainstormed "Bugs and Wishes" problems (steps 2 and 3 above), and ask volunteers to practice responding by using suggestions from the Respectful Responses list.
- For example, while holding the bug and the wand say, "If someone said to you, 'It bugs me when you cut in line and I wish you would move to the back' how could you respond using one of the respectful responses?"
- Have students role-play several examples while holding the bug and the wand. Practice the role-plays until you sense that students "get it."

8. Moving it forward.
- After you are confident everyone understands, explain that "Bugs and Wishes" are used in the classroom for one-on-one communication.
- Use the bug and magic wand to tell someone how you feel and what you would like to have happen. Then the other person can respond respectfully.
- Some teachers have students make bugs and wands to use at home. They send home an explanatory note.

9. Modeling and following through.
- Use the phrases yourself.
- Follow through by quietly noticing/acknowledging students who use the phrases during the day.
- During a Class Meeting ask students to share a time when they used a Bugs and Wishes statement and how it may have helped solve a problem.

I-Messages[1]

OBJECTIVE:
- To teach the communication skill of "I-messages," or "I-statements."

MATERIALS:
- Board

COMMENT FOR TEACHERS:
- Many students find it hard to express their feelings and may blame others first. This activity encourages students to name their feelings and to make a request to solve the problem.
- This activity is similar to "Bugs and Wishes," adapted for older students.
- It is expected that you have done activities in the self-regulation section to introduce feeling words.
- Some students will struggle to put feelings into one word. It may be helpful to review the Sad, Mad, Glad, Scared activity.
- Thoughts and feelings are often confused. It is common for people to start a sentence with "I feel" and then share a thought. This happens frequently with "I feel that ___" and "I feel like ___" statements.

DIRECTIONS:

1. Feelings and words to describe them.
- Post the Feeling Faces or Sad, Mad, Glad, Scared chart so that the class has their list of words for feelings.
- Remind students that feelings happen inside us and are not what we do.
- Remind students that there aren't good or bad feelings. Feelings are always okay. It is what we do that matters.

2. I-messages (part one).

Invite the students to practice "I-messages" by filling in the following blanks using these feelings: discouraged, angry, disappointed, and excited. I feel _____ when _____. The statements might look like:
- I feel discouraged when I can't figure out a problem.
- I feel angry when someone breaks a promise.
- I feel disappointed when I have too much homework.
- I feel excited when I get to play with my friends.

3. Using I-messages.
- Explain that I-messages can be useful to tell people what you are feeling and to ask for what you want.
- There is a difference between just complaining to someone and actually asking for what you want.
- Invite the students to think about what they would like *instead*.

4. Completing I-messages.

Have students finish a few of the sentences they brainstormed using "wish" or "would like" as in the samples below. Ask them not to use anyone's name in the statement and to use "people" instead. For example:
- I feel discouraged when I can't figure out a problem and I wish people would help me.
- I feel angry when people break a promise and I would like them to not make promises they can't keep.
- I feel disappointed when I have too much homework and I wish I could have a day off.
- I feel excited when I get to play with my friends and I wish I had more time with them.

Ask for a volunteer to choose a different example and create a complete statement.

---

[1] Thomas Gordon coined term "I" Messages in the 1960's.

Positive Discipline in the School and Classroom Manual
by Jane Nelsen, Lynn Lott, Teresa LaSala, Jody McVittie, and Suzanne Smitha

5. Learning to respond.
- Ask students what kinds of responses are appropriate when someone shares feelings and a wish.
- Write down samples. They might include: "I'm sorry." "I didn't know it bothered you." "Thank you for telling me." "I'll think about that," "I'll do ____ instead."
- *Note: you will use this again later when you create a classroom solution table.*

6. Moving it forward.
- Quietly acknowledge students who use the phrases at other times during the day.
- Use the phrases yourself.
- In a class meeting or classroom discussion ask students to share a time when they used an "I-message" at school or somewhere else and how it may have helped solve a problem.
- Make a template that says: "I feel_____ when _____ and I wish_____." Post it in the room. You might also make templates of the responses.

Listening 1: Effective and Ineffective Listening

OBJECTIVE:
- To teach effective listening skills

MATERIALS:
- None

COMMENTS FOR TEACHERS:
- It is often easier to talk than to be an effective and respectful listener.
- Developing listening skills requires practice. Practice, practice, practice!
- If time allows, do the second and third role-plays again, with the other person taking the lead.

DIRECTIONS:

1. Overview.
You will have students work in pairs for three short role-plays, and you will process after each.

2. First role-play.
- Have both students talk at once about their favorite TV show, their pet, or what they did over the weekend. Insist that both are to talk continuously until you tell them to stop.
- Ask students, "What did you learn from the other person?"

3. Second role-play.
- In the same pairs, have one student share (it can be the same sharing) and have the other student act bored (but not say anything.) The second student can look around, focus on their fingernails or something else.
- After about 20 seconds, stop the sharing and ask the partners who were talking what they noticed.
    - "How did it feel to share like that?"
    - "Did you get the impression that the other person was listening? Why or why not?"
    - "What were you thinking or deciding about the other person?"
- Ask, "How *do* you know when someone is listening? Invite the class to share a few ideas.

4. Third role-play.
- Using the same partners, have the same person share, but this time have the partner listen carefully. (Use some of their ideas about listening carefully). The listener remains quiet.
- Ask the "sharers" how it felt this time.
    - What were they feeling, thinking or deciding about the other person?
    - How did they know the other person was listening?
- Some classes make a list of the kinds of body language that indicate listening. What kind of body language gives you the sense that the other person is not listening?

5. Moving it forward.
- Keep this skill fresh by asking (both when things are going well, and not so well), "How are we doing with our listening skills? Let me know with thumbs up, thumbs down or thumbs sideways. Think about what *you* can do to make it a little bit better."

Positive Discipline in the School and Classroom Manual
by Jane Nelsen, Lynn Lott, Teresa LaSala, Jody McVittie, and Suzanne Smitha

Preparing the Ground: Communication Skills

Listening 2: Effective and Ineffective Group Listening

OBJECTIVE:
- To teach effective listening skills

MATERIALS:
- Markers, flip chart paper

COMMENTS FOR TEACHERS:
- It is often easier to talk than to be an effective and respectful listener.
- Developing listening skills requires practice. Your role is to respectfully require practice (over and over again).

SAMPLE POSTER:

Effective Listening Skills

1. Look at the speaker
2. Be quiet while they talk
3. Think about what they are saying
4. Try to hold still

DIRECTIONS:

1. **Setting the stage.**

   Tell students that you are going to ask them to observe communication skills. Have each student spend a moment thinking of something that happened or a movie they saw this week and get ready to talk about it for about 30 seconds.

2. **Role-play: Talking.**
   - Have all students talk at the same time.
   - After a signal for them to stop, ask how many of them felt that they were heard.

3. **What was learned?**
   - "What did you learn from the experience?"
   - "Was good communication occurring?"
   - "What is needed for good communication to occur?" (Speaking *and* listening)
   - "What do we need to do to be effective listeners?"
   - Record all of their ideas on poster paper labeled "Effective Listening Skills."

4. **Moving it forward.**
   - Hang the poster of the list of effective listening skills in the room.
   - Use the poster as a tool for reflection at other times. If students are not using effective listening skills, quietly refer them to the poster to find something they could do that would be useful.
   - Keep this skill fresh by asking (both when things are going well and not so well), "How are we doing? Let me know with a thumb up, thumb down, or thumb sideways to indicate response. What can each of you do to make this better?"

Extension

After doing the above, ask a volunteer to share an interesting experience, such as a favorite vacation.

- Have the other students wave their hands in the air as if they want to speak.
- Tell everyone to stop. Process with the class and the volunteer about their feelings. Ask how many would find the waving of hands distracting.
- Next have the volunteer share again, but this time everyone should use effective listening skills. (Refer to the "Effective Listening Skills" poster as a reminder of what they decided.)

Mutual Respect
Preparing the Ground: Face Sheet

Concept: Mutual respect

- We define mutual respect as *respect for yourself (regarding yourself in a way that honors your dignity) and respect for the situation (honoring the needs of the situation and the dignity of others)*. This is quite different from the usual operating definition which sounds more like "I respect you, you respect (obey) me."
- Respect is a *feeling*. Obedience and compliance are *actions* and often a result of fear instead of respect.
- Mutual respect invites cooperation, which is different from compliance or obedience and more powerful in a classroom setting.
- Disrespect from students is often the result of being put in a "dignity double bind." When a student has the perception (true or not) of being disrespected, that student is in a double bind. They can comply – and lose dignity *or* somehow not comply (with body language, hurtful behavior or outright defiance). While this maintains dignity, it also often gets the student in trouble. Maintaining a sense of dignity (self-worth), however, is so important that many students don't have access to other options in the moment.

Why mutual respect is important

- Mutual respect is necessary to establish a classroom and school community.
- It is important for students to understand both components of mutual respect: respect for themselves (and their own morals) and respect for others.
- Without mutual respect, it is extremely difficult to establish a classroom environment that students experience as safe and trustworthy. Naming self-respect as an important component of mutual respect supports students in standing up for their own values.
- A community built on mutual respect shows respect for the uniqueness of each individual and that individual's perceptions.
- Our uniqueness as individuals is one of our greatest values, both to ourselves and to our society.

> *The essentials for living in a democratic society can be simply stated...The principle implies mutual respect, respect for the dignity of others and respect for oneself. The principle is expressed in a combination of firmness and kindness. Firmness implies self-respect; kindness, respect for the others.*
>
> - Rudolf Dreikurs
> *Social Equality: The Challenge of Today*
> Contemporary Books, Ontario 1971 p.115
> Emphasis in original

What else are students learning?

- An increased sense of empathy and compassion by seeing the world from someone else's perspective.

Recommended order for teaching mutual respect

- **Charlie** invites reflection on the impact of our actions and words as well as exploring ways for helping both others and ourselves gain a sense of belonging.
- **Mutual Respect** focuses on self-respect as an important piece of mutual respect.

Preparing the Ground: Mutual Respect

LITERATURE CONNECTIONS
Byers, Grace. *I Am Enough.* New York: Harper Collins Children's Books, 2018.
Estes, Eleanor. *The Hundred Dresses.* New York: Harcourt Children's Books, 2004.
Henkes, Kevin. *Chrysanthemum.* New York: Greenwillow Books, 1991.
Jeffers, Oliver. *Here We Are: Notes for Living on Planet Earth.* New York: Philomel Books, 2017.
Jeffers, Susan and Chief Seattle. *Brother Eagle, Sister Sky: A Message from Chief Seattle.* New York: Scholastic Inc., 1992.
Steptoe, John. *Mufaro's Beautiful Daughters: An African Folk Tale.* New York: Scholastic Inc., 1987.

A teacher's story

I went through the "Charlie" exercise with my grade three class on Wednesday and they loved it. I suggested hanging Charlie up to remind us that words have long lasting effects. My students were very enthusiastic about this, but they were sad Charlie would hang by himself and feel lonely. What did they do? They each drew a stick figure friend to keep him company. This was a giant step for my kiddos anyway, but when they suggested that a corner of each of their drawings should be wrinkled (because we've all had hurtful words affect us), I knew they were on the right track. We had a wonderful and respectful discussion on that topic.

Jenn – third grade teacher

Preparing the Ground: Mutual Respect

Charlie

Similar to the crumpled man or crumpled heart activity, origin unknown.

OBJECTIVE:
- To provide students with a visual image of the long-lasting effects of disrespectful comments.

MATERIALS:
- One sheet of chart paper with a simple face or stick figure of "Charlie" drawn on it.
- Paper for posters if doing modifications.

COMMENTS FOR TEACHERS:
- Use a name for "Charlie" that is not the name of a student or staff member.
- In step #4 it is important to use language that refers to *belonging* instead of *feeling better*.
- It is important to think before we speak about how our comments might be received by another person.
- While the activity seems simple, secondary students have really appreciated this activity. They use it with each other. For example, overheard in a middle school hallway, "Ouch, Dude, that was a Charlie."

DIRECTIONS:

1. **Preparation.**
   - Hold up the chart paper drawing of Charlie.
   - Introduce him as "Charlie," a regular kind of guy who switches schools and for some reason isn't very well liked.

2. **Brainstorm.**
   - Ask students to share comments they might hear that could hurt Charlie's feelings.
   - As they volunteer examples, with each comment, crumple the chart paper until it forms a ball.

3. **Reflection about Charlie - ask students:**
   - "How is Charlie different now?" (He is, of course, quite wrinkled.)
   - "How do you think Charlie is feeling at the end of his first day of school?"
   - "Do you think he wanted to come back to school for a second day?"
   - "Do you think he felt students wanted him to be a part of their class?"

4. **Reflection about what to do next – ask students:**
   - "What could you say or do with Charlie to help him feel that he belonged at this school or that he was welcome?" Smooth out the paper a little as you hear each helpful comment.
   - "Now what do you notice?"
   - "What do you suppose is going on for Charlie?"
   - "Is it possible to completely remove the wrinkles?"
   - "Do we all have some "wrinkles?""

5. **Moving it forward.**
   - "What did you learn from this that might change how we work as a group or how you interact with others?"

- **Extension**
   - "Sometimes people have "Charlie" days. How would you know? What might we notice?" (It is helpful to write these ideas down and post the list.)
   - "If you saw someone who looked like they were having a "Charlie" day how might you help them "uncrumple" and feel that they belong?" (Scribe and post this list.)
   - "If you were having one of these bad days, how might you ask for help from one of your friends or classmates?" (Scribe and post this list.)
   - This activity can also be used in discussions around bullying. Students clearly understand that once someone has been hurt (wrinkled) they are never completely the same afterwards.

Positive Discipline in the School and Classroom Manual
by Jane Nelsen, Lynn Lott, Teresa LaSala, Jody McVittie, and Suzanne Smitha

Preparing the Ground: Mutual Respect

Respect for Self and Others

OBJECTIVE:
- To teach the meaning and importance of mutual respect.

MATERIALS:
- Board

COMMENTS FOR TEACHERS:
- Mutual respect allows a person to respect others and to practice self-respect.
- The concept of self-respect can be a challenge for some students. Naming it as part of mutual respect is very helpful.
- Self-respect gives students the capacity to honor their own morals and values; their sense of right and wrong.

DIRECTIONS:

1. Introduce the idea of disrespect.
- Ask class members to think of a time when they felt hurt or criticized.
- What were they thinking or deciding about themselves? About the other person?
- As appropriate, share a couple of your own experiences. (Some teachers start with this.)
- Ask class members if they can think of a time they criticized or hurt someone else.
- What were they thinking or deciding about themselves or the other person?

2. Self-respect.
- Have students think of a situation when they said "Yes" when they meant "No." (Or "No" when they meant "Yes.")
- What kinds of things make it hard to say what you really want?
- How might this affect one's sense of self-respect?

3. Maintaining self-respect.
Have the students brainstorm some ideas for things they can do or say so they are able to maintain their sense of self-respect. Examples:
- "I don't care for that idea."
- "I want to be your friend, but I have other plans tonight."
- "I'd like to play with you, but I don't want to play that game."
- "I'd like to do something with you this afternoon, but that doesn't sound like fun to me."

4. Moving it forward. Options:
- Ask students to notice when others are showing self-respect and invite sharing.
- Do a thumb up/sideways/down for "respect checks" during the day.
- Ask for compliments about self-respect during a class meeting.

Extension

At the end of the discussion, ask for volunteers to make two posters for the classroom. Options include:
- We're here to help each other, not hurt each other.
- Mutual respect means respecting others and myself.

Building Cooperation
Preparing the Ground: Face Sheet

Concept: Building cooperation
- Cooperation is the process of working and being able to overcome obstacles together.
- Learning requires action on the part of the learner and happens more effectively in a community of peers who work together to learn.
- Cooperation helps students gain a sense of connection and belonging in the classroom.
- Cooperation is not just a "feel good" concept. It changes how the brain learns and more directly meets the needs of many students in our culturally diverse classrooms.

Why cooperation is important
- As teachers we can *invite, encourage*, and support learning but we cannot "make" students learn. Cooperation is necessary for learning to occur. (The learner has to agree to learn.)
- Many students live in cultures that are highly collectivist. These students learn better in groups, so skill building for group work is essential.
- Support and engagement from peers is an important source of motivation for almost all students.
- When students are provided the needed skills for learning together and are in an environment where peers cooperate, learning becomes engaging and attractive enough to create movement without incentives or competition.
- Students cannot solve problems if they are always looking to be the winner or expecting to be a loser.
- Competition creates stress, which sometimes can be fun or helpful. However, for students who already have high stress levels, competition (the threat of either winning or losing) can put them over their "lose it" line and decrease their ability to engage or learn.
- In many classrooms "incentives" and "competition" are used to move students in the direction of learning. There is now excellent evidence that incentives and competition are counter-productive in both the short and long term. (See *Drive* by Daniel Pink or YouTube video.)[1]

> *A common cultural archetype connected with deep culture is a group's orientation toward either collectivism or individualism. Collectivism and individualism reflect fundamentally different ways the brain organizes itself. Turns out our brains are wired to favor a communal view of the world. Humans have always sought to be in community with each other because it enhanced our chances of survival....*
> *In [North]America, the dominant culture is individualistic, while other cultures of many African American, Latino, Pacific Islander and Native American communities lean more toward collectivism.*
>
> Zaretta Hammond
> Culturally Responsive Teaching and the Brain, p. 25
>
> See below for information on the research about collectivism and individualism.

---

[1] Pink, Daniel H. (2009). ***Drive: The suprising truth about what motivates Us.*** New York, NY: Penguin Group.

Preparing the Ground: Building Cooperation

What else are students learning?
When students work together effectively they discover the power of groups, the value of differences and how differences enhance learning.

Recommended order for teaching *building cooperation*

Creating a Win/Win: Exploring Power. This discussion invites students to think about and discuss how power is used in their world, including the classroom.

The following additional activities give students a "felt" sense of working together to create cooperation and a win/win environment. Any of these activities can be used to invite students to grasp how working together creates better results for everyone. Each has a slightly different focus. We recommend that you do at least one in addition to "Exploring Power."

Cooperative Juggling
Rope Activity
Moving the Ball
Crossing the Line
Arm Wrestling

LITERATURE CONNECTIONS
Brown, Marcia. *Stone Soup.* New York: Aladdin Paperbacks, 1997.
Jeffers, Oliver. *Here We Are: Notes for Living on Planet Earth.* New York: Philomel Books, 2017.
Moss, Lloyd. *Zin, Zin, Zin!* New York: Simon & Schuster Books for Young Readers, 1995
Muth, Jon J. *Stone Soup.* New York: Scholastic/Weston Woods, 2003. (Story set in China)
Muth, Jon J. *Three Questions.* New York: Scholastic Inc., 2002.

RESOURCES
Drive: The suprising truth about what motivates Us. http://www.youtube.com/watch?v=u6XAPnuFjJc

Hammond, Zaretta *Culturally Responsive Teaching and the Brain.* Thousand Oaks, California: Corwin, 2015.

For more information on deep cultural differences, you can explore the work of Geert Hofstede, Gert Jan Hofstede, Michael Minkov and their research teams: www.hofstede-insights.com

Exploring Power: Building Cooperation

OBJECTIVE:
- To explore how we use and/or respond to power in relationships.
- To help students discover that problem solving is most effective when power is shared.

MATERIALS:
- Prepared chart as shown on following page for scribing

COMMENTS FOR TEACHERS:
- Cooperation is more powerful than compliance.
- When students have bought in to a process, they are less likely to resist or sabotage it.
- This activity is especially important for secondary students. It is similar to the activity **Exploring Power: Finding Win/Win Solutions.**
- It is sometimes frustrating for students to work cooperatively at school because they have not yet learned the necessary skills. Most students do have the skills to cooperate with friends.

DIRECTIONS:

1. Prepare for scribing: a four-column flip chart as below.

2. Ask and record. (Someone tries to control you)
Ask, "What do you experience (or what happens) when you sense that someone is trying to control you?"
- "What do you feel?"
- "What do you do?"
- "What do you learn, decide or realize from that?"

(Some students prefer having adults boss them around so they can rebel or avoid responsibility)

3. Ask and record. (You try to control others)
Ask, "How do you try to control or manipulate others, including teachers?"
- "What do you feel?"
- "What do you do?"
- "What do you learn, decide or realize from that?"

4. Ask and record. (You work cooperatively with others)
Ask, "What happens when you work cooperatively with others to complete a task?"
- "What do you feel?"
- "What do you do?"
- "What do you learn, decide or realize from that?"

5. Reflection.
Using language appropriate for your grade level:
- Invite the students to notice that you have been talking about control. How does control relate to power?
- Go back to the chart. Based on what you learned, what will be the most effective way for us to solve problems together?
- What skills might we need to work together effectively?

6. Moving it forward.
- Ask students to observe and think about power as you move forward in learning about class meetings.

Preparing the Ground: Building Cooperation

CHART

	Feeling	Doing	Learning/Deciding
They control you			
You control them			
You work together			

■ Extension

Have students do the "Cooperative Juggling" activity so they can experience working together.

Preparing the Ground: Building Cooperation

Cooperative Juggling

OBJECTIVE:
- To experience cooperation instead of competition.
- To understand the need for *practice* as part of learning.
- To build a sense of community.

MATERIALS:
5-7 Koosh balls or soft bean bags.

COMMENTS FOR TEACHERS:
- This is a wonderful activity to invite older students to help with younger students.
- Notice how the group can work with each other so all students are engaged and can be successful. For example, if you have a child with a cast on, how might the group work together to create a solution?
- Occasionally a student will recommend just passing the balls to the person next to them. That takes away from the fun of this activity. We recommend responding by noting that though it would be easy, it wouldn't be as much of a challenge – so it wouldn't be as much fun.

DIRECTIONS:

1. Setting up the juggling.
- Ask for 6 - 12 volunteers to stand up and form a circle with you. (You can do it with more students, but it becomes more complicated.)
- Ask others in the room to be observers.
- Share with the group that they are going to learn cooperative juggling.

2. Juggling Round 1.
- Tell your students that their goal in juggling is to keep the balls in the air and not to let them hit the ground.
- Quickly start tossing the balls in the air in the general direction of the students in the circle.
- After a few moments of chaos, tell everyone to freeze.

3. Pause, reflect and make a plan.
- Ask, "What is going on?" (Chaos!)
- "What could we do to make this work better?"
- Invite the group to offer suggestions. These will include things like: make a pattern, making eye contact, and calling someone's name before a ball is thrown, throwing gently. If they don't suggest creating a pattern it is important to suggest it.
- Review the group's ideas (including yours if it is needed), e.g., "What I heard was that you want to try to make a pattern, make eye contact, and throw gently."
- Ask the students to return the balls to you.

4. Juggling Round 2 (Practice with one ball).
- Ask the group if they would be willing try incorporating the suggestions by starting with just one ball to establish a pattern and get practice.
- Ask them to make sure that each student only gets the ball once. (One easy way to do this is to direct them to hold their hands out if they have *not* had the ball, and to put them down once they have received it.)
- Start by throwing the ball to one student.
- Finish the pattern by having the last student throw the ball back to you.
- Ask the students if everyone can remember who they got the ball from and to whom they threw the ball.
- Ask the students if they want to practice one more time with just one ball. (Follow their decision.)

Positive Discipline in the School and Classroom Manual
by Jane Nelsen, Lynn Lott, Teresa LaSala, Jody McVittie, and Suzanne Smitha

Preparing the Ground: Building Cooperation

5. **Juggling Round 3.**
   - Ask the group to follow the same pattern they just used. Let them know you will now add more balls.
   - Begin "juggling" again using the pattern and the other guidelines, adding balls so that the whole circle is active again.

6. **Pause and reflect.**
   - How did we do?
   - Observers (the other students in the class), what did you notice?
   - What did we learn from this process?
   - How many of us did it take to be successful?
   - What happened after we took time to practice?
   - Can you think of some things even now that could make our juggling better?

7. **Moving it forward.**
   - What did it take for us to get better at working together?
   - How could we apply this to our classroom?

Extension

- Many of the students may want to be part of this experience. You can repeat the process with other students. Each time start with the "messy" juggling, followed by soliciting their ideas. You (and they) will find that each successive group will have ideas that are a slight improvement on those of the previous group. They will discover that they get better at the process just by watching.
- As an extra challenge, you can do a fourth round of juggling by slipping in a "surprise object" to juggle (a plastic wrench, rubber chicken, or awkward object). This surprise upsets the routine and invites a discussion about what happens when routines get interrupted by unexpected events. Afterwards, process by asking questions like, "What can our classroom do to prepare for the unexpected?" "How do routines help us deal with the unexpected?"

Preparing the Ground: Building Cooperation

Rope Activity

Adapted by Sahara Pirie from activity presented by David Colestock at 2007 NASAP

OBJECTIVE:
- To explore cooperation and build community.
- To notice the cultural pervasiveness of the pressure to win (while others lose).

MATERIALS:
- Two or more ropes (one per 8-10 participants) 15-20 feet long, with a knot tied in the center (Long jump ropes work well)
- More than a simple overhand knot is recommended
- You can make it more complicated by putting 2 or 3 knots on top of each other or tying a bowline knot

COMMENTS FOR TEACHERS:
- Because this is a challenging activity, it may be best for students 8 years and older.
- Many qualities can be lifted from this activity, such as cooperation, leadership, communication and motivation.
- When using multiple ropes and different kinds of knots, interesting things come out about competitiveness, fairness, etc.

DIRECTIONS:

1. **Setting up the activity.**
   - Lay knotted ropes out on the floor - fully extended. One for each team.
   - Create one team of 6-8 participants for each rope. (Remaining students can be observers.)
   - Ask the participants to find a spot on either side of the knot such that roughly half the participants are to the left of the knot and half are to the right.
   - Tell the team members to choose to pick the rope up with either one hand or two, *and let them know that once they have picked up the rope, they should not let go of it until the activity is complete.* They may slide their hand(s) along the rope, but they are not to let go.

2. **Untying the rope.**
   - Ask the participants to untie the knot without letting go of the rope - that is, if they picked the rope up with one hand, that hand must stay in contact with the rope until the activity is complete.
   - If they picked the rope up with both hands, both hands must stay in contact with the rope until the activity is complete.
   - Optional: Give them a 5-minute time limit. (Not always recommended).

3. **Pause and reflect. Ask students:**
   - What did you notice?
   - What were you thinking or deciding?
   - How did you decide what to do?
   - How did the group work together?
   - Did I tell you this was a contest? Why did you assume it was (if they did make that assumption)?
   - What happened when one team finished first?
   - What else did you notice?

4. **Moving it forward.**
   - What did we learn from this activity that we could use to make our classroom a better place for learning?

Extension

Some additional questions to explore: How did the time limit affect your behavior? What might have happened if I'd stopped you before you had a chance to be successful? How are you feeling about yourself and your 'teammates' now, compared to before the activity?

Positive Discipline in the School and Classroom Manual
by Jane Nelsen, Lynn Lott, Teresa LaSala, Jody McVittie, and Suzanne Smitha

Preparing the Ground: Building Cooperation

Moving the Ball

OBJECTIVE:
- To explore differences between "win/lose," "lose/lose," and "win/win" experiences.

MATERIALS:
- Several soccer-size balls, one per group

COMMENTS FOR TEACHERS:
- This is a quick interactive activity that generates discussion about competition and win/win solutions.
- Not all classes have the self-regulation skills to be able to do this activity.
- You can change the rules in step 3, depending upon the age of your students and room space.

SAMPLE POSTER:

For Win/Win Solutions we will:

1. Talk *and* listen for mutual understanding.
2. Treat all with respect.
3. Find solutions that work for all involved.

DIRECTIONS:

1. **Divide** the classroom into different-sized groups of 5 to 8 students per group, saying we're going to play a new game.
2. **Instruct** the groups to form circles around the classroom.
3. **The "rules" of the game.** Announce that each group will receive a ball and must pass the ball around their circle to each member in the group, who in turn must perform each of the following tasks before passing the ball:
   - Bounce the ball once in front of them and catch it,
   - Hold the ball as high as they can above their head while standing on one foot,
   - Pass the ball around their own body from the right hand to the left, and then
   - Pass the ball to the person on their left, and
   - Do this sequence as quickly as possible!
   - The group that finishes first will be the winner.
4. **Start the game.**
   - Pass the balls, tell them to go and stop everyone when one group "wins," giving them a cheer.
   - Try it again.
   - Dismiss or minimize any complaints that may be emerging about this being unfair because of unevenly sized teams.
5. **Reflect and learn.** After a couple of rounds, stop everyone and process thoughts, feelings and decisions by discussing:
   - "What did you notice about the game?"
   - "How did the winners and losers feel?"
   - Discuss the meaning of win/lose, lose/lose, or win/win situations.
   - "Did this game create win/lose, lose/lose or win/win situations?" (Some might say lose/lose, because the game wasn't set up to be "fair" so the winners had nothing to be proud of).
6. **Win / Win solutions.** Share that if we want to achieve a "Win/Win" Solution, three things are necessary:
   - People must communicate to understand each other's ideas and needs.
   - They must treat each other respectfully.
   - They must look for a solution that works for all involved.

© Positive Discipline Association ■ www.PositiveDiscipline.org

7. **Turning the game into a win/win.** Brainstorm ideas that might lead to a win/win solution. Some possibilities include:
   - Have the same number of people on each team.
   - Just have fun; it is a game, so it doesn't matter who finishes first.
   - Do the whole thing in one big circle with several balls starting at different points in the circle and set a timer to see if we could improve our speed as a whole class.
   - If time permits, try one of these ideas.

8. **Moving it forward.**
   - When we begin to have class meetings, what kind of solutions do we want for our class: lose/lose, win/lose, or win/win?
   - What are some things we need to remember in order to achieve win/win solutions?
   - The class may want to write guidelines for win/win solutions in their own words to post in the room. (See sample poster.)

Extension

Discuss the similarities and differences between games and class meetings. You might want to create a chart to compare similarities and differences. A sample is below.

GAMES AND CLASS MEETINGS

Similarities	Differences
Everyone usually participates.	Games are often win/lose.
People work as a team.	Games are more for fun.
We should use each person's strengths.	Class meetings are more serious.
People have strong feelings sometimes.	We're solving problems in class meetings.
Both help us have a good school year.	In a class meeting, we wait to talk until we get the object.
Both help us learn how to get along together.	There is usually more discussion in a class meeting.
	We are sharing important stuff in class meetings.

Crossing the Line
Glenda Montgomery

OBJECTIVE:
- To explore the idea that "winning" does not have to mean someone loses.
- To allow students to see that when they understand the concept of "win-win," they can work together for the benefit of everyone.

MATERIALS:
- One 2-foot piece of string or ribbon for each pair

COMMENTS FOR TEACHERS:
- Bringing up the difference between win/lose and win/win invites us to challenge our unexamined cultural understanding that in order for someone to win, someone must lose.

DIRECTIONS:

1. **Setting up the activity.**
   - Divide into pairs and give each pair a 2-foot length of string or ribbon.
   - Ask each pair to:
     - Find a space
     - Face each other standing 3 feet apart
     - Lay the ribbon on the ground between them (acting as a border between each person's space)
   - Read the following aloud:

   "There are three rules.
   1. The goal is to win.
   2. You win when the other person crosses the line into your territory.
   3. You may not talk to or touch the other person."

2. **Crossing the line.** Let the groups go for a couple of minutes before asking them to stop.

3. **Pause and reflect.** Suggested questions:
   - "What were you feeling as you tried to win?"
   - "What thoughts were running through your head?"
   - "Did anyone WIN?" "How did you do that?" (Often someone will have given up and let another person "win.")
   - "Who gave up?" "How did that feel?" "What thoughts were you thinking?" "Were you making any decisions about yourself or your partner?"
   - "Were there any pairs in which both people won?"
   - "How could you have had two people win?"
   - "Did I say that only one of you could win?"
   - "Why do you think you assumed only one of you could win?"
   - "If you thought from the beginning that both of you could win, how would that have changed things?"

4. **Moving it forward.**
   - Ask, "If our goal as a class is to have everyone succeed, how can we do that without having anyone lose?"

Preparing the Ground: Building Cooperation

Arm Wrestling

OBJECTIVE:
- To explore the idea that "winning" does not have to mean that someone loses.
- To allow students to see that when they understand win-win, they can work together for the benefit of everyone.

MATERIALS:
- Poster shown below

COMMENTS FOR TEACHERS:
- Students can turn potentially competitive situations into cooperative interactions where everyone "wins."
- A win/win solution is not always achievable, but it is possible with this activity.

SAMPLE POSTER:

To achieve win/win solutions we will:
1. Talk and listen for mutual understanding.
2. Treat all with respect.
3. Find solutions that work for all involved.

DIRECTIONS:

1. **Play the "game."**
   - Have students get a partner and sit facing each other with elbows propped on a desk between them (or have them lie on the floor facing each other, elbows propped) to arm wrestle.
   - Tell them they will have 15 seconds to see if anyone in the room can get their partner's arm down as many as 5 times.
   - Shout, "Go!"
   - After 15 seconds, stop them, check for winners.

2. **Discuss "winning" and "losing."**
   - Identify the winners, and ask, "What does that make the others?" (losers)
   - Discuss how that feels to everyone.
   - Ask, "How do you like the fact that I made the rules just because I'm the teacher, or I'm bigger?"
   - Ask, "How does it feel to be in a situation where someone has power over you?"

3. **Explain that it takes cooperation to create "win/win" solutions.** Use your poster to share with the class.

   To achieve win/win solutions we will:
   - Talk and listen for mutual understanding.
   - Treat all with respect.
   - Find solutions that work for all involved.

4. **Pause and reflect.** Provide think/talk time. Tell the class they have a few minutes to talk with their partner to see if they can come up with a win/win solution for this game.

5. **Repeat the initial "game,"** again allowing about 15 seconds. (What you hope will happen is that two students will cooperatively allow their arms to flip back and forth, tallying equal "downs" for each of them.)
   - If no one has thought of the solution, give a hint, asking if anyone can think of a way they could cooperate and help each other.

6. **Moving it forward.** What are the implications for the classroom regarding:
   - Cooperation?
   - Win/win solutions?
   - Helping each other?

Positive Discipline in the School and Classroom Manual
by Jane Nelsen, Lynn Lott, Teresa LaSala, Jody McVittie, and Suzanne Smitha

Notes

Mistakes and How to Repair Them
Preparing the Ground: Face Sheet

Concept: Mistakes and how to repair them

- A mistake is an error in action or a misunderstanding.
- Students often struggle with the difference between "I made a mistake" and "I am a mistake (I am stupid, lazy etc.)." This perception makes it difficult for students to take the necessary risk to learn from their mistake.
- Being able to recognize and repair mistakes is the foundation of all restorative practices.
- As human beings, we struggle with mistakes. We may think that the mistake we made shows we are stupid, inept, or unworthy, etc. When we think these negative thoughts, we are speaking in code for the hidden message "I am a mistake."
- Seeing adults make and repair their own mistakes regularly is a powerful learning tool.
- Asking for and accepting apologies takes practice and courage.
- "I'm sorry," is only an appropriate response when the feelings are sincere. (Students are often told/taught to say, "I'm sorry," even when they are not.)
- When students make a mistake and need to leave the classroom, their return is an ideal opportunity to connect and repair the relationship.

Why learning about mistakes and repair is important

- When *mistakes are seen as an opportunity to learn,* students do better socially and academically.
- When students trust that mistakes are opportunities to learn, they are less likely to lie or blame others for things that they did.
- Making amends and using sincere apologies (actions or words) invites students to take responsibility for their mistakes.
- Repairing and learning from mistakes is empowering.
- Respectful relationships are sustainable only if we know how to reconnect after making mistakes.
- When a repair is made, reconnection is possible.

> *Repair: v.*
> - *To fix or mend a thing suffering from damage or a fault.*
> - *To put right a damaged relationship or unwelcome situation.*
> - *Make good such damage by fixing or repairing it*
>
> *Repair: n. The action of fixing or mending something.*
>
> Google Dictionary

What else are students learning?

- Students who recognize mistakes as part of learning can accept other people's mistakes as well.
- Students become more helpful and more compassionate to others.
- Students gradually build their courage to be imperfect.

Recommended order for teaching Mistakes and How to Repair Them

- *Mistakes: Making vs. Being* (for younger or older students)
- *Mistakes Messages*

Preparing the Ground: Mistakes and How to Repair Them

And then one or more activities on repairing mistakes/making amends:

- **The R's of Recovery from a Mistake**
- **Apologizing: How to Do It**
- **Apology of Action: Repairing Relationships**
- **Apologizing: How to Accept an Apology or Repair**
- **Apologizing: How to Ask for a Repair**

LITERATURE CONNECTIONS

Berenstain, Stan and Jan. *The Bike Lesson.* New York: Beginner Books, 1964.
Fox, Mem. *Harriet, You'll Drive Me Wild.* New York: Voyager Books, Harcourt Inc. 2000.
Henkes, Kevin. *Lilly's Purple Plastic Purse.* New York: Greenwillow Books, 1996.
Jones, Charlotte Foltz. *Mistakes That Worked.* New York: Random House Children's Books, 1991.
Pett, Mark and Gary Rubinstein. *The Girl Who Never Made Mistakes.* Naperville, IL: Jabberwocky, 2011.
Saltzberg, Barney. *Beautiful Oops.* New York: Workman Publishing Co., 2010.

Mistakes: Making vs. Being for Younger Students

Adapted from an exercise by Bob Bradbury

OBJECTIVE:
To help students:

- See mistakes as opportunities to learn instead of deciding they are bad or inadequate.
- Recognize "I made a mistake" is different than "I am a mistake" or "I am stupid."

MATERIALS:

- A small cup or glass
- A tray or other container to hold the spill

COMMENT FOR TEACHERS:

- When someone is able to think, "I made a mistake," they feel guilty. When someone believes there is something wrong with them, "I am stupid or am defective in some way," they feel shame.
- This is easily adapted for older students. See Mistakes: Making vs. Being for Older Students.

DIRECTIONS:

1. **Making a mistake (demonstration).**
    - Set a small glass of water on a tray beside you as you read a story.
    - "Inadvertently" reach to get a sip of water and knock it over.
    - Act surprised or a little upset before pausing and reflecting.
2. **Reflection.**
    - Ask, "Did I *make* a mistake or *am* I a mistake or *am* I stupid?"
3. **Discussion.**
    - Ask students, "What makes something a mistake?" (Lots of things may be suggested.)
    - Ask students, "Is a person ever a mistake?" (No.)
    - If the discussion appears to imply that people "are" mistakes, gently guide the discussion away, even if it means saying, "I don't believe a person ever IS a mistake; we all make mistakes."
4. **Moving it forward.**

Follow up questions include:

- "What could I do about my mistake?"
- "What can we do when we make mistakes?"
- "Can I repair this mistake?"
- "What could I learn from my mistake?"
- "What might you do for someone who thought they were the mistake instead of just making a mistake?"

Modifications/Additions

- Another option is to ask the students to watch as you do a demonstration. Show the students that the glass is empty and that there is water in the pitcher. As you continue to talk, look at them and begin to pour the water, missing the glass. It is fun to then look at what you were doing and notice what has happened with surprise.
- Consider adding stories to bolster this. The Amelia Bedelia books are useful to some groups but they require some language sophistication and are confusing (not funny) to kids who still think concretely.
- Make a "reminder poster" that the students decorate. Older students can make their own poster.

> Mistakes are wonderful opportunities to learn.

Mistakes: Making vs. Being for Older Students
Adapted from an exercise by Bob Bradbury

OBJECTIVE:
To help students:
- See mistakes as opportunities to learn instead of deciding they are bad or inadequate.
- Recognize "I made a mistake" is different than "I am a mistake" or "I am stupid."

MATERIALS:
- Varies based on the "mistake" chosen for demonstration

COMMENTS FOR TEACHERS:
- When someone is able to think, "I made a mistake," they feel guilty. When someone believes there is something wrong with them, "I am stupid or am defective in some way," they feel shame.
- This activity is a variation of the version for younger students.

DIRECTIONS:

1. **Making a mistake (demonstration).**
   - Plan and make an obvious mistake. (For example: reviewing homework from the wrong day, asking students to open the wrong book, or confusing one group's work with another etc.)
   - Ideally the students will notice. You respond with surprise.
   - If the students don't notice, acknowledge your own mistake with a bit of drama.

2. **Reflection.**
   - Ask, "Did I *make* a mistake or *am* I a mistake or *am* I stupid?"

3. **Discussion.**
   - Ask students, "What makes something a mistake?" (Lots of things may be suggested.)
   - Ask students, "Is a person ever a mistake?" (No.)
   - If the discussion implies that people "are" mistakes, gently guide the discussion away, even if it means saying, "I don't believe a person IS ever a mistake; we all *make* mistakes."

4. **Moving it forward.**
Important follow-up questions include:
   - "What could I do about my mistake?"
   - "What else can we do when we make mistakes?"
   - "Can I repair this mistake?"
   - "What could I learn from my mistake?"
   - "What might you do for someone who thought he was a mistake instead of just making a mistake?"

Extension

Invite students to make and display a poster that says, "Mistakes are opportunities to learn."

Mistakes Messages

OBJECTIVE:
- To help students be aware of beliefs about mistakes.
- To teach students healthy concepts about mistakes.

MATERIALS:
- Board

COMMENTS FOR TEACHERS:
- With practice, students can learn to value and celebrate mistakes.
- It is important for you to model making and repairing mistakes.
- When students aren't nervous about making mistakes, they are more composed. They can think more clearly and are less likely to err.
- Teaching students that mistakes are opportunities to learn is not an invitation for them to make mistakes on purpose.
- When the whole class really understands that we learn from mistakes, they will not mind having their names on the class meeting agenda. Instead they will see it as an opportunity to get help and learn from their classmates. They will be able to be more responsible for their actions.

DIRECTIONS:

1. Reflect on messages from mistakes.
- Invite students to remember and think about messages they get, both stated and implied, about mistakes.
- Write these messages on the flip chart, board or doc cam as newspaper headlines. Some typical messages might be:
   o Mistakes are bad.
   o You shouldn't make mistakes.
   o You are stupid, bad, inadequate or a failure if you make mistakes.
   o If you make a mistake, don't let people find out. If they do, make up an excuse even if it isn't true.

2. Reflect on decisions about mistakes.
Ask, "Based on these messages, what decisions did you make about yourself or about what to do regarding mistakes?" Some typical decisions:
- I'm bad when I make mistakes.
- People will think less of me if I make a mistake.
- If I make a mistake, I should try not to get caught.
- It is better to make excuses and blame others than to accept responsibility.
- If I get caught or accept responsibility I will experience blame, shame or pain.
- I had better not take risks if I know I can't do something perfectly.

3. Reflect on the impact of messages from mistakes.
Wonder aloud with your students about how helpful these "mistakes messages" are.
- "Are they (the messages) helpful to us?"
- "When you heard these messages, what did you decide about yourself?"
- "What do you do to avoid making mistakes or to hide them?"
- "Can you learn without making some mistakes?" (No.)

4. Moving it forward.
Ask students:
- "What did you learn from our brainstorming?"
- "How many of you would be willing to take responsibility for your mistakes if you knew that others would be helpful, not hurtful?"

Preparing the Ground: Mistakes and How to Repair Them

The R's of Recovery from Mistakes

OBJECTIVE:
- To teach students the steps of recovery so they have tools to help take the guilt, shame, and blame out of mistakes.
- To understand that making mistakes is not as important as what we do about them.

MATERIALS:
- "R's of Recovery" Chart (below)

COMMENTS FOR TEACHERS:
- Recovering from mistakes requires that we make amends or apologize when possible.
- Using the "Three R's of Recovery" can make a relationship stronger than it was before the mistake.
- Some teachers prefer to start with a more comprehensive discussion. See the modification below.
- While we focus on the actual mistake, when a repair is made, it mends the relationship, the real casualty of most mistakes.

"R's" of Recovery

1. **Recognize.** "Oops, I made a mistake."
2. **Reconcile.** "I'm sorry."
3. **Repair.** "How can I fix this?"

DIRECTIONS:

1. **Recovering from mistakes.**
   - Tell students that we are going to learn how to recover from mistakes.
   - Show the poster and tell students that you will review and then practice each step.

2. **Recognize** (Step 1).
   - Ask your students, "If you realize you made a mistake and want to apologize or repair it, what kinds of things are important before you apologize or make amends?"
   - Brainstorm a list. For example:
     ○ We have to take responsibility for making a mistake.
     ○ All involved need to calm down.
     ○ All involved need to be honest.
     ○ We cannot make excuses.

3. **Reconcile** (Step 2).
   "What are some simple words we can say to the person we hurt?"
   - "I'm sorry."
   - "I apologize for what I did."
   - "I'm sorry and I'll try not to do that again."

4. **Repair** (Step 3).
   - "To repair something, we try to make it better for the person we hurt, which depends upon what we did."
   - Brainstorm a short list of common mistakes where an apology would be appropriate (taking something without asking, cutting in line, interrupting a conversation, etc.).
   - Have volunteers think about ways to repair a few of these mistakes.

5. **Moving it forward.**
   - Ask the students if they can think of a time when they made a mistake and could use the "Three R's." Invite them to share their example with another student.
   - Have the students take turns role-playing their situation. One partner will play the part of the person who was offended or hurt while the other partner practices using the "R's of Recovery."

© Positive Discipline Association ■ www.PositiveDiscipline.org

■ **Modifications** (Discussion to precede the activity):

PUTTING MISTAKES IN PERSPECTIVE

1. Explain
"Mistakes are not as important as what we do about them. It takes a big person to be able to repair mistakes."
- "Can you think of a time when someone hurt you by making a mistake and never apologized or tried to repair the mistake?"
- "Did it change how you felt about that person?" "What might happen when we make a mistake and do nothing about it?"

2. Recognizing mistakes
- "How do you know when you've made a mistake?"

3. Reconcile
Share how reflection, attempting repair and offering a genuine apology are key steps toward reconciliation.

Explore feelings about apologies and repair.
- "Have you ever received an apology that helped you feel better afterwards?"
- "Do you think more or less of someone who apologizes or repairs their mistake?"
- "What did you think about the person who apologized?" (What often comes out is that students respect and appreciate others who offer genuine apologies or repairs. They do not see them as weak.)
- Ask students if they remember hearing someone say, "I'm sorry," because an adult told them, "Say you are sorry," and they didn't seem to be sorry.
- "How did it feel to hear that?"
- "Have you ever offered an apology that was not sincere?" "For what reason?"
- "Have you ever had someone apologize to you (sincerely) before you were ready to accept the apology?"

Preparing the Ground: Mistakes and How to Repair Them

Apologizing: How to Do It

Appreciation for the main ideas in this activity is expressed to an anonymous 5th grade teacher from Snohomish, Washington.

OBJECTIVE:
- To learn how to apologize.
- To understand how apologies can reduce chances of additional hurt feelings.
- To understand how a repair can help prevent the same mistake from happening again.

MATERIALS:
- Poster – see below
- Optional: Puppets for steps 1 and 3

COMMENTS FOR TEACHERS:
- Instead of apologizing and admitting our mistakes, we often try to justify ourselves.
- When justifying our actions, the person we hurt:
    - May not feel heard.
    - Is often unable to "hear" our apology, accept it or forgive us.
- When an apology is accepted, both parties may feel better. The person apologizing feels they've righted a wrong and the other person feels understood and validated.

The 3 Step Apology
1. I'm sorry for _____.
2. I will try not to do it again.
3. Will you accept my apology?

- Use activity **Apologizing: How to Accept an Apology or Repair** to teach how to accept an apology.

DIRECTIONS:

1. Apologies that don't work.
Share the following interaction (or one appropriate for the age of your students). Puppets work very well to model this conversation for younger students.

Jean: "It really upset me that you were talking when I was talking."
Sheree: "Well, I needed to tell Jack to meet me after school."
Jean: "I'd like an apology."
Sheree: (With a tone of voice that is defensive) "Well, I'm sorry, but I had to tell Jack or else he would have taken the bus instead of walking with me!"

2. Why are some apologies ineffective?
- "How well do you think Sheree's apology addressed Jean's problem?"
- "What was missing from her apology?"
- "What was in the apology that wasn't helpful?"

Note: Sheree may have had a good reason for saying what she did, but it probably sounded like an excuse to Jean who was upset at the time. When someone is confronting you about what you did, they don't want to hear your reasons at that point. "Reasons" only come across as excuses in the moment.

3. Share the Three-Step Apology.
1. I'm sorry for _____.
2. I will try not to do it again.
3. Will you accept my apology? (If the answer is no, the students may either need more time to calm down, or help to solve the problem.)

4. Model the Three-Step Apology.
Replay the scene with Jean and Sheree using the three-step apology. Ask students what they noticed.

5. Moving it Forward.
While this is a very structured way to respond to a mistake, apologies tend to become more elaborate and personal with practice.

- Have the students brainstorm common mistakes that they would like an apology for, or apologies they would like to give.
- Use this list to practice (in pairs or with volunteer role-players).
- Hang the poster in the room for future reference.

Apology of Action: Repairing Relationships

Concept of Apology of Action is from Responsive Classroom Newsletter, Winter 1998

OBJECTIVE:
- To teach students how to repair their mistakes and their relationships.

MATERIALS:
- Board

COMMENTS FOR TEACHERS:
- Apology of action can help students think about repairing mistakes differently.
- As human beings, we feel awkward, uncomfortable or hurt when we've made a mistake or someone has hurt us. Often, we don't know what to do with those uncomfortable feelings. They are really internal information like radar, that lets us know that some repair is necessary.
- Because we don't know what to do with our feelings, sometimes we do nothing and try to ignore them. Sometimes we avoid the person we hurt or who hurt us.
- Learning how to repair relationships is an important skill when building a learning community.
- To be successful, students will need practice and follow-up.
- Occasionally there is disagreement about whether someone's feelings are "really" hurt. *If someone claims their feelings have been hurt, it is important to accept that.*
- Apologies of action are related to the mistake or problem.

DIRECTIONS:

1. Exploring hurt feelings. What creates hurt?
- "How many of you have had something happen to you that hurt your feelings?"
- "How many of you have ever done anything by mistake or on purpose that hurt someone else's feelings?"
- "What kinds of things might be hurtful to others; what have you seen or heard?" (Brainstorm and scribe list)

2. Responding to our feelings.
- "When we hurt someone, how does that change our relationship with that person?" ("Is it harder to talk to them?" Do we pretend nothing has happened, or avoid them?")
- "What do you feel when you see someone else being hurt?"
- "What uncomfortable feelings do we get from being hurt or from making a mistake?" (A knot in my stomach, my thoughts keep racing, I feel like I don't like the person or myself anymore.)
- "What might those feelings be telling us?" (Something isn't right, I need to do something, I wish I hadn't done that.)

3. Repairing the mistake and the relationship.
- Explain that when we make a mistake we often try to repair it. "If you spell something wrong, you correct it." "If you spill something, you wipe it up."
- "We've all been taught to say, 'I'm sorry.' Does, 'I'm sorry' help you or the other person feel better?" "Sometimes saying, 'I'm sorry' doesn't repair the relationship."
- "What else helps people feel better when feelings have been hurt? The things we do to help repair our mistake are called an *apology of action*. An apology of action is related to what caused the hurt."
- Use the brainstormed list of things that have hurt people's feelings (above) and think of actions that might repair the mistake. Ask, "What actions might help you reconnect?"
- Help the class generate a list of apologies of action related to the list brainstormed in #1 above. This might include writing a note, drawing a picture, helping the other person with something, or asking what would be helpful.
- "What happens to the relationship with the other person after you have made a repair?"

4. Moving it forward.
You can help students keep practicing by:
- Noticing when they are using apologies of action,
- Keeping a list of ideas that have worked, and
- Pointing out apologies of action in the literature you are reading.

Preparing the Ground: Mistakes and How to Repair Them

Apologizing: How to Accept an Apology or Repair

OBJECTIVE:
- To learn how to accept apologies and repairs.

MATERIALS:
- Poster – see below
- Optional: Puppets for steps 3 & 6

COMMENTS FOR TEACHERS:
- Repairing relationships can be challenging and messy. It is hard.
- Many of us find accepting apologies awkward and don't do it very well. This approach may seem overly structured but gives a foundation and a common language for an important skill.
- Sometimes the person who has been hurt is not ready to repair the relationship or deal with the hurt feelings as soon as the person who made the mistake or caused the hurt feelings.
- Each person is entitled to their own feelings. We need to respect the space and pace each person needs to finish the repair.

Accepting an Apology
[Name], thank you, I accept your apology.

Receive an Apology
[Name], thank you, I need to cool down, think about it, and I'll get back to you later.

- The person making the apology wants everything to be repaired and it sometimes is not that satisfying.
- When an apology is accepted, both parties are able to feel better. The person apologizing feels they've righted a wrong, and the other person feels understood and validated.

DIRECTIONS:

1. **Are we ready to make a repair?**
   - Invite students to, "Raise your hand if…"
     - "You've felt hurt because of something someone said or did."
     - "When that person apologized you felt better."
     - "You have ever responded to an apology with, 'It's okay' when it really wasn't okay."
     - "When that person apologized, you were still so mad or hurt that you weren't ready to hear what they had to say."
   - Reflect, "Would you agree, sometimes we are ready to accept the apology and sometimes we are not?"

2. **How do we respond when we are ready to accept an apology?**
   - Teach the language for responding to an apology that you are ready to accept.
     "[Name], thank you, I accept your apology."

3. **Practice accepting an apology.** This step is important: if students are going to gain the skill, they must see it in action.
   - Role-play this in some age appropriate situations. Examples are given below. Follow each with the response to an apology.

     Apology: "I am sorry I bumped into you. I will try not to do it again. Will you accept my apology?"

     Response: "[Name], thank you, I accept your apology."

     Apology: "I am sorry, I didn't mean to hit you when I threw the ball. I will try not to do it again. Will you accept my apology?"

     Response: "[Name], thank you, I accept your apology."

     Apology: "I am sorry, I had no idea that was important to you. I will try not to do it again. Will you accept my apology?"

     Response: "[Name], thank you, I accept your apology."

     Apology: "I am sorry, I didn't realize that you didn't want me to share that information. I will try not to do it again. Will you accept my apology?"

     Response: "[Name], thank you, I accept your apology."

4. **What makes accepting an apology hard?** Brainstorm and scribe a list of the things that make it hard to accept an apology. This may include: my lid was flipped, I was still too angry, I didn't feel heard, it didn't seem like the apology was real, I didn't trust the person, they say that all the time and don't do anything differently.

Positive Discipline in the School and Classroom Manual
by Jane Nelsen, Lynn Lott, Teresa LaSala, Jody McVittie, and Suzanne Smitha

Preparing the Ground: Mistakes and How to Repair Them

5. **How do we respond when we are not ready to accept an apology?**
   - Teach the language for an apology that you are not yet ready to accept or repair.
   - Say, "It is important to acknowledge the other person's effort:"
     "[Name], thank you."
   - Say, "Then it is important to express your position."
     "I need to cool down."
     "I need to think about it."
     "I need to get back to you later."
   - Put it together: "[Name], thank you, I need to cool down, think about it and I'll get back to you later."

6. **Practice receiving an apology when you are not quite ready to accept it.** This step is important: if students are going to gain the skill, they must see it in action.
   - Role-play this in some age appropriate situations. Examples are given below. Follow each with the response to an apology.

     Apology: "I am sorry I bumped into you. I will try not to do it again. Will you accept my apology?"

     Response: "[Name], thank you, I need to cool down, think about it and I'll get back to you later."

     Apology: "I am sorry, I didn't mean to hit you when I threw the ball. I will try not to do it again. Will you accept my apology?"

     Response: "[Name], thank you, I need to cool down, think about it and I'll get back to you later."

7. **Moving it forward.** Notice opportunities to model this with your students.

Apologizing: How to Ask for a Repair

OBJECTIVE:
- To learn and practice how to ask for a repair.

MATERIALS:
- Poster – see below
- Optional: Puppets for step 3

COMMENTS FOR TEACHERS:
- This activity expects that students have already practiced responding to an apology or repair (Apologizing: **How to Accept an Apology or Repair**).
- A review of "I-messages" or bugs and wishes including the responses would be helpful.
- We all are responsible for our own feelings, and when harm has been done (intended or not), it hurts relationships. Both parties are responsible for making the repair.
- Repairing relationships can be challenging and messy.
- Each person is entitled to their own feelings. We need to respect the space and pace each person needs to finish the repair.

Asking to Make a Repair

"[Name], I felt ____ when you ____ and I wish we could make a repair."

DIRECTIONS:

1. **What do we do if we feel like a repair is needed?** Invite students to, "Raise your hand if…"
   - "Someone hurt you and you didn't know how to ask for a repair."
   - "You hoped for an apology and didn't get one."
   - "Anyone has ever asked you to fix a mistake."
   - "Anyone has ever asked you for an apology."

2. **How do we ask someone to help repair a mistake?** Your students may know how to do this. Invite them to offer ideas. You can help them with more specific language.
   > "[Name], I felt ____ when you ____ and I wish we could make a repair."

3. **Practice asking for a repair.** This step is important: if students are going to gain the skill, they must see it in action.
   - Role-play this in some age appropriate situations. Examples are given below.

     State: "[Name], I felt hurt when you bumped in to me and I would like a repair."

     Apology: "I am sorry. I will try not to do it again. Will you accept my apology?"

     Response: "[Name], thank you, I accept your apology."

     State: "[Name], I felt hurt when you threw the ball and I would like a repair.

     Apology: "I am sorry, I will try not to do it again. Will you accept my apology?"

     Response: "[Name], thank you, I accept your apology."

4. **Moving it forward.** Notice opportunities to model this with your students.

Notes

Encouragement
Preparing the Ground: Face Sheet

Concept: Encouragement

- Encouragement is defined as:
    1. To inspire with courage (Courage < Old French corage, < Latin cor heart)
    2. To spur on: to stimulate, to give heart to
- Another way of understanding courage is the movement we make in the direction of being our best selves. Encouragement, then, is the space we make for others to have courage, to move toward becoming their best selves.
- In Positive Discipline, which is designed to help children feel encouraged, **encouragement**:
    - Is different from praise because it is non-judgmental (does not include words like good, best, perfect).
    - Is descriptive and personal. "I notice_____", "I appreciate_____", "I have faith____."
    - Is non-comparative; does not compare one student with another.
    - Invites internal motivation instead of doing things for someone else's approval.
    - Can be non-verbal (spending time, listening carefully, eyes showing that the adult is delighted to see the student) or verbal (I notice… I appreciate… I have faith…).
    - Is most effective when offered privately; it's not important that others hear it. (It does not highlight one student as an example to teach others.)
    - Can be offered even when things are not going well.
    - Provides opportunities for students to develop the perceptions: "I am capable," "I can contribute," and "I can influence what happens to me and how I respond."
    - Teaches the life skills and social responsibility students need to be successful in life and relationships.
    - Enhances self-esteem by inviting an internal locus of control.

> *Examples of encouraging statements.*
> - *It took courage to stand up for yourself like that.*
> - *Thank you for helping me.*
> - *I noticed you seemed upset this morning.*
> - *You listened carefully in your group this morning.*
> - *Have you noticed how much you have learned?*
> - *I trust your judgment.*
> - *This is hard, isn't it?*
> - *I'm curious about how you will solve this.*
> - *How did your game go last night?*
> - *What is your suggestion?*
> - *Can you teach me about ____?*

Preparing the Ground: Encouragement

Why learning about encouragement is important for students
Encouragement:
- Invites students to feel worthwhile without needing the approval of others.
- Builds community.
- Enhances self-confidence, self-reliance and self-esteem.
- Invites self-reflection and self-evaluation.
- Gives students tools to connect with each other.
- Contributes to a student's sense that someone knows them: that they matter. This understanding builds resilience.

> "People do better when they feel better. A misbehaving child is a discouraged child and the most powerful motivation for change is encouragement. When we strive to encourage others and ourselves, we are actually helping develop courage to face life's challenges."
>
> Nelsen, Jane, et al., *Positive Discipline: Teachers A-Z*. Three Rivers Press, New York

What else are students learning?
- Students learn to recognize strengths: theirs and others
- Students become more facile in seeing positive aspects of challenges as they become more confident in their own strengths.

Recommended order for teaching *encouragement*
We recommend that encouragement activities be used regularly throughout the year. They create an important underpinning for a positive classroom environment.

LITERATURE CONNECTIONS
Bang, Molly. *When Sophie Thinks She Can't*. New York, New York: Blue Sky Press, 2018.
Brown, Don. *Teedie: The Story of Young Teddy Roosevelt*. Boston, MA: Houghton Mifflin Books for Children, 2009.
Dillon, Diane. *I Can Be Anything! Don't Tell Me I Can't*. China: Scholastic, Blue Sky Press, 2018.
McCloud, Carol. *Have You Filled a Bucket Today?* Northville, MI: Ferne Press, 2006.
Rappaport, Doreen. *Eleanor, Quiet No More*. New York: Disney/Hyperion Books, 2009.
Rath, Tom, and Mary Reckmeyer. *How Full Is Your Bucket?* New York: Gallup Press, 2009.
Tillman, Nancy. *You're Here for a Reason*. New York: Feiwel and Friends, 2015.
Yamada, Kobi. *What Do You Do With a Chance?* Seattle, WA: Compendium, 2017.
Yousafzai, Malala. *Malala's Magic Pencil*. New York: Little Brown & Co, 2017.

Encouragement Activities

OBJECTIVE:
- To give students practice in the art of giving and receiving encouragement.

MATERIALS:
- For activities 4 & 5: The "Charlie" poster from the Mutual Respect activity, "Charlie"

COMMENTS FOR TEACHERS:
- Encouragement in Positive Discipline is different from praise. See face sheet.
- Using encouragement creates a positive school, classroom and class meeting climate.
- Modeling this will help students catch the spirit!
- Teachers need encouragement too. Consider using these ideas with some of your colleagues.

DIRECTIONS:
Use these activities regularly throughout the year as needed.

1. **Activity: Encouragement Circle**
   - Ask if there are any students who feel they need encouragement. If so, have them sit in the center of a class circle.
   - Go around, giving each of the other students an opportunity to offer an encouraging statement.
   - (If doing class meetings, take this activity to circle time.)

2. **Activity: Encouragement Notes**
   - Have students practice by writing notes of encouragement to each other.
   - They could pick one student per day, so that each in turn gets notes of encouragement.

3. **Activity: Encouragement Partners**
   - Assign student partners for the week.
   - Each pair watches for encouraging things to say and do for each other.
   - (If doing class meetings, they might be asked to compliment their partner).

4. **Activity: Moving the "Charlie" Activity Forward**
Connect it to the concept of encouragement.
   - Remind the students how after "Charlie" was crumpled up, they shared ideas to **give Charlie a sense that he belongs and is important.**
   - Make a list of those ideas.
   - Let the students know that those are all "words of encouragement." Encouragement doesn't make judgments. It helps people see that they are worthy just as they are.

5. **Activity: Expanding the Charlie Activity**
   - Ask students, "If you have had a bad day, like Charlie, what could you do or say to others that would help you feel more a part of our classroom or school community?"
   - Brainstorm, write down and post ideas. Ideas may include:
     - "Can I help you with that?"
     - "Would you please play with me?"
     - "I'm having a bad day. Could you help me?"
     - Offer to help the teacher or ask for a job.
     - Check with the "Uncrumpler" (if that is one of your classroom jobs).

Preparing the Ground: Encouragement

6. **Activity: Encouragement Place Mats.**
    - Get one place mat sized piece of construction paper for each student.
    - Write one compliment for each student (one per sheet).
    - Pass out the placemats.
    - Set aside time for students to get up and write compliments on each other's placemats.

Respecting Differences
Preparing the Ground: Face Sheet

Concept: Respecting differences

- Respecting differences highlights the fact that each person sees and interprets the world in their own way, and no one's perception is necessarily the "right" one.
- We are often drawn to spend time with people who are similar. This can appear to be exclusive and limits our ability to learn from each other's differences. This is not right or wrong, but in problem solving it is helpful to be inclusive, work together and learn from each other's perspectives.
- We each make meaning of the events around us in the context of our own experiences.
- Differences can be a challenge for students, but they are a powerful and rich asset to any community.

Why respecting differences is important

- Students often see differences as bad or as "I am right, you are wrong." Some students who perceive themselves as different begin to believe that they are bad or that something is "wrong" with them. These perceptions can be compounded by systemic structures that may intensify inequity.
- Embracing differences contributes to respect and compassion for self and others.
- Different points of view are extremely useful in problem solving.
- The ability to see the world from another person's (different) point of view is one of the key skills needed for the development of empathy.
- Understanding differences is essential to continuously build cultural responsiveness (the ability to effectively interact with people across cultures).
- New data on community resiliency also demonstrates that diverse communities are much more resilient. http://www.stockholmresilience.org/

What else are students learning?

- The skills to be equitable, inclusive and respectful in relationships with others they perceive as different (culture, race, physical, gender, learning styles, socio-economic class, religion, emotional differences),
- How to celebrate and share their own identities while holding space for classmates to do the same,
- How to safely share their own life experiences. For example, in one classroom, after discussions about differences, one student felt comfortable enough to teach her classmates about her physical tics and Tourette Syndrome. This helped her classmates understand her behavior, addressed their fear of the unknown, and gave her the opportunity to speak for herself. She gained a sense of belonging in the classroom and the other students gained empathy, knowledge, and understanding.

Preparing the Ground: Respecting Differences

Recommended order for teaching *respecting differences*

- **Animal Kingdom** is the most powerful activity to teach this concept. Though the activity is long, teachers feel that it is worth the time invested and students enjoy it. When whole schools use Positive Discipline, students may have already done this activity in previous years. It is worth repeating because discussions vary as students mature.
- *Experiencing Differences*
- *You Decided*
- **Note:** There are additional activities in the Essential Skills for Class Meetings, Respecting Differences section of this manual.

LITERATURE CONNECTIONS

Adler, David A. *A Picture Book of Jackie Robinson.* New York: Holiday House, 1994.
Byers, Grace. *I Am Enough.* New York: Harper Collins Children's Books, 2018.
Cannon, Janell. *Stellaluna.* New York: Scholastic Inc., 1993.
Choi, Yangsook. *The Name Jar.* New York: Knopf, Borzoi Books, 2001.
DeRolf, Shane. *The Crayon Box That Talked.* New York: Random House, 1966.
Dismondy, Maria and Kim Shaw. *Spaghetti in a Hot Dog Bun.* Wixom, MI: Making Spirits Bright, 2008.
Giles, Andreae and Guy Parker-Rees. *Giraffes Can't Dance.* New York: Orchard Books, 2001.
Jeffers, Oliver. *Here We Are: Notes for Living on Planet Earth.* New York: Philomel Books, 2017.
Lionni, Leo. *Little Blue and Little Yellow.* New York: Alfred A. Knopf, 2009.
Lobel, Arnold. *Frog and Toad Together.* New York: Harper Festival, 1999 - 1972. (Note: Many of the Frog and Toad books teach about different perspectives.)
MacLachlan, Patricia. *Through Grandpa's Eyes.* New York: Harper & Row, 1980.
Munch, Robert. *The Paper Bag Princess.* Toronto, Canada: Annick Press Ltd., 1995.
Parr, Todd. *It's Okay to Be Different.* Boston: Little, Brown & Company, 2001.
Rappaport, Doreen. *Eleanor, Quiet No More.* New York: Disney/Hyperion Books, 2009.
Seuss, Dr., *The Sneeches.* New York: Random House, 1961.
Vassel, Jennifer and Penny Webber. *I Am Unique.* Chino Hills, CA: BuddingRose Publication, 2015.
Whitcomb, Mary. *Odd Velvet.* San Faancisco, CA: Chronicle Books, 1998.
Zobel-Nolan, Allia and Miki Sakamoto. *What I Like About ME.* New York: Readers Digest Children's Books, 2005.

Preparing the Ground: Buy-In for Class Meetings

Animal Kingdom

OBJECTIVE:
- To help students understand that we are all different.
- To then move beyond understanding to see how our differences become assets we can embrace and celebrate.

MATERIALS:
- Four flip chart sheets prepared in advance (one for each animal) See samples on following pages
- Four marking pens
- Pictures of a lion, an eagle, a turtle, and a chameleon (or stuffed animals of each)

COMMENTS FOR TEACHERS:
- This is a profound and important activity. It brings forward a non-intuitive awareness about differences and how we work together in a community. It takes the classroom beyond awareness and invites a deeper understanding and ability to celebrate and embrace our diversity as human beings.
- It is important to be sure that students will be helpful, not hurtful, before you begin this activity.
- The activity can be completed over several days.
- This activity usually generates a lot of laughs and a lively discussion with children from 5 years old to adults.
- Place or post one picture of each animal in 4 different areas of the room. (Note: You or a student may have to describe a chameleon, because many students are not familiar with that animal.)
- Post each prepared chart beside the appropriate picture.

DIRECTIONS:

1. **Introduce the concept.** Ask your students to respond, inviting a show of hands:
   - "Raise your hand if you think there is always a right answer or a wrong answer."
   - "Raise your hand if you think there's always one right way to do things."
   - "Raise your hand if sometimes you don't speak up because you think your idea might be wrong or unpopular."

   State, "We are going to do an activity that will help us see how there are many different ways to look at things."

2. **Choose an animal.** Ask the students, "If you could be one of these animals for one day, which one would you like to be?" (See tip #3 on following page)

3. **Move to their choice.** Have them move to the chart and picture for their chosen animal. (See tip # 3 on following page)

4. **Fill in Charts.**
   Have each group of students
   - List all the characteristics they like about their animal under "Why we want to be [their animal]."
   - List all the reasons they don't want to be the other animals under "Why we didn't choose…"

5. **Share charts.**
   - Have all charts posted next to each other.
   - Have each group (one at a time) come to the front and have one person read why they wanted to be their animal. Another person from the group will then read from the other 3 charts, why others did not want to be their animal.

6. **Reflect:** After all the lists have been presented ask students what they notice.
   - Someone will usually notice that what one person likes, another person might not like. <u>In the rare event that this does not come up, it is important to draw it out.</u>
   - Students may react when hearing negative comments about the animal they chose and liked. Within reason, allow students to experience, express, and share their reactions.
   - Ask if our different opinions make one person/group right and another wrong.

---

* Activity previously known as "**It's a Jungle Out There.**"

Positive Discipline in the School and Classroom Manual
by Jane Nelsen, Lynn Lott, Teresa LaSala, Jody McVittie, and Suzanne Smitha

Preparing the Ground: Respecting Differences

- If your students are not yet fluent writers, invite older students or adults to the classroom to be scribes.
- We have included (below) a story and some examples from other classes so you can have an idea about what kinds of things will come up.

7. **Continue the discussion:** Seek comments to the effect that people see the world in different ways. Sometimes we agree and sometimes we don't, even with the same set of circumstances. Possible questions for the discussion include:
   - "What if we all chose the same animal? What would that look like in our classroom?"
   - "How did it feel when comments were made about "your" animal?"
   - "What would a classroom be like if every person in it had the same ideas? What would the plusses and minuses be?"
   - "If we only had one way of solving a problem (because we all thought the same way), what would we do if that solution didn't work?"
   - "We've been talking about animals, but now let's connect the activity to our classroom and to us. How might we be different in how we look, in how we feel, and in where we come from each morning?"
   - "How are our differences an advantage for our class and how we learn together?"
   - "How could our differences be helpful at a class meeting when we are problem solving?"
   - "How can we learn more about each other and how we see the world?"
   - "How might we learn more about the differences that make us uncomfortable, so we can work together?"
   - "How can we begin to recognize and celebrate all of our individual differences?"
   - "How can we include other people who we see as 'different' in our school and community?"
   - "What do we need to learn about them so we can honor who they are?"

8. **Moving it forward.**
   - Identify times when different points of view have been helpful. This might include: different ways to solve math problems, social problems, history lessons, etc.

SAMPLE CHART

Make 4 charts, one for each animal, with the other 3 animals listed on the lower half. For example:

Why we want to be a *Chameleon*		
Why we didn't choose to be a		
Lion	Eagle	Turtle

■ Tips

1. This activity is easier with 5 and 6 year olds if you invite a few older students to come help each group scribe.
2. There are specific reasons as to why these four animals were chosen for this activity and you are encouraged to use the activity as it is. Most students enjoy this activity so much that they don't mind doing it year after year with the same animals.
3. Depending on the age and make-up of your classroom, you may want to have students privately choose their animal by writing it on a slip of paper before describing the full activity. Have the Lions hold up their slip and move to their chart, and so forth with each of the other animals. This eliminates peer pressure to move with friends.
4. Be sure to read the short article below about how the teacher divided her students into small groups to explore solving problems from separate perspectives.

Examples:

Example of the chameleons' choices

Why we want to be a *Chameleon*		
can change - flexible - adaptable - cute - hide easily to watch things - harmless		
Why we didn't choose to be a		
Lion	Eagle	Turtle
loud - power hungry meat eaters - lazy want to be king	lonely - looks bald unapproachable live in a rocky places	they hide - avoid things slow - they bite have to carry their house everywhere

Example of the turtles' choices

Why we want to be a *turtle*		
always have our house with us - safe inside our shell - sturdy - can live on land or water can lay in sun - old and wise - patient - slow and steady - lay eggs and go we are gentle - don't hurt or bother anyone - trusting - relaxed		
Why we didn't choose to be a		
Lion	Eagle	Chameleon
fierce - gruesome - violent destructive - ruthless arrogant - kings - lazy predatory - loud - hunted	power hungry loners	moody - volatile phony - inconsistent not very strong sneaky - unpredictable

Preparing the Ground: Respecting Differences

Example of the eagles' choices

Why we want to be a *eagle*
observe - have keen eyes - can fly & soar - great view from up here - we have freedom & strength & long lives - control our own destiny - protected, beautiful, faithful, aware - respected by Indians we are gentle - don't hurt or bother anyone - trusting - relaxed

Why we didn't choose to be a		
Lion	Chameleon	Turtle
dangerous - macho aggressive - lazy loud live in hot, dry, arid places	too changeable run from problems blend in too much	slow, weak - they hide have a hard, heavy shell to carry around - not attractive

Example of the lions' choices

Why we want to be a *lion*
king of the jungle - playful, especially with our children - proud, passionate, strong nice warm environment - independent, respected - sociable - good looking; great hair people respond to the roar passionately

Why we didn't choose to be a		
Chameleon	Eagle	Turtle
too small, insignificant always blending in no courage	lonely life who wants to fly??? bald	underfoot shy slow

Preparing the Ground: Respecting Differences

Here is one teacher's story about using this activity:

Implementing Positive Discipline Class Meetings:
Lions, Eagles, Turtles and Chameleons, Oh My!
Melissa Walsh, March 21, 2008

I am in the process of implementing Positive Discipline class meetings in my kindergarten, first and second grade classroom. I have used class meetings every year of my fifteen-year career, but never in the capacity presented in my Positive Discipline class and in my reading of the Positive Discipline book, Positive Discipline in the Classroom. Although I have always emphasized active and respectful listening and giving acknowledgements, the eight building blocks for class meetings have given my class a much stronger and more nuanced foundation. The most challenging aspect I have found is staying committed to working with all the building blocks before attempting to use class meetings to tackle actual problems. As I write this, I have a full page of agenda items filled in by students, and three more building blocks to go! Thank goodness for the wheel of choice, which students have been using in the meantime. Despite the sense of urgency, I feel that the time I am spending now will be more than returned in the efficient and effective meetings we will soon be able to conduct together.

One reason I feel this confidence in the process is the result of the "Lions, Eagles, Turtles and Chameleons Activity" used to teach the skill of respecting differences. I decided to depart from the lesson as presented in the book by having the students pick the animal they would like to be and write about why they picked it and why they did not pick the other animals as a homework assignment. I chose to do this so that they would not influence the choice of their close friends; in other words, so that one animal would not become popular based on who was picking it. I got a very good return on the homework and the candor that students expressed affirmed that it was a good idea to send it home. Instead of having the students in small groups, I did a full group lesson. I made a large chart at the front of the room with a box for each animal. I made a plus column and a minus column in each box, writing the plus items in green, and the minus items in red. This allowed the students to clearly see that the very reason some individuals chose a particular animal was the exact reason other individuals did not choose that particular animal. This fascinated the students. They nearly jumped out of their chairs as I wrote each plus and minus in the boxes. They smiled and pointed each time a pro matched a con.

From the beginning, they wanted to know who chose to be an eagle, who chose to be a chameleon, etc., but I waited to reveal this until the end of the lesson. We talked about people who wanted to fly, and people who would hate to fly, and how both kinds of people were right. The students really seemed to grasp this concept quite deeply. Their eyes were shining with recognition.

After we filled in all the pros and cons, I asked the students to go to the four corners of the room to stand with the kids who had chosen the same animal they did. Many students were surprised to see who their "birds of a feather" were. When they were all in place, I also participated by walking to the lion corner, and the students who normally like to please me all the time experienced the freedom of having a difference of opinion from me. We then turned to look at the students in the other corners, silently acknowledging and celebrating our differences. It was a moving experience.

Finally, I had the students get in heterogeneous groups of at least one turtle, one lion, one eagle and one chameleon. Their task was to begin brainstorming solutions to a problem in the role of the animal they chose, not with sound effects or clawing, but with the sensibility of a person who would choose a particular animal. This was eye-opening for them, and now we have a common language. When different perspectives emerge in the classroom, we can say to each other, "ah, this is just like the chameleon, turtle, eagle and lion".

It is just this sort of intentionality and fine-tuning that I have needed in my discipline plan in my classroom, and I am full of hope as we continue to prepare for full-fledged class meetings.

Experiencing Differences
By Molly Henry

OBJECTIVE:
- To help participants understand that not everyone experiences or interprets things the same way.

MATERIALS:
- Cloth Bag (pillow case will work)
- Two Flip Chart Sheets and markers
- Unusual item (e.g. squishy, multicolored, unusually shaped ball) – *something that doesn't feel the way it looks is ideal*

COMMENTS FOR TEACHERS:
- It's interesting to note that sometimes a participant will think they recognize the object by touch and will list colors or attributes that aren't correct because of past experience with a similar object. This is a great opportunity to bring preconceptions, assumptions, etc., into the discussion.

DIRECTIONS:

1. **Divide the group in half.**
   - Have the groups move into separate spaces – separate rooms if possible.
   - Do not let either group see what is taken to the other group.

2. **Take the "Mystery Item" to first group.** (Keep it completely enclosed in the bag.)
   - Allow each person to reach into the bag for a few seconds and touch the item.
   - Do not let anyone in this group see it.
   - Leave the group to brainstorm adjectives that describe the item and list them on the flip chart.
   - Take the object with you.

3. **Take the "Mystery Item" to the second group.** Remove it from the bag and place it carefully on a table in full sight of the group.
   - Do not let anyone in this group touch the item.
   - Leave the item out for about 15 seconds and then remove from view.
   - Ask this group to brainstorm adjectives that describe the object and list them on the flip chart..

4. **Bring groups together.**
   After both groups have had time to make their list of adjectives, bring them together.
   - Have a representative from each group read their list.
   - Place both lists side-by-side at the front of the room.

5. **Reflection.**
   - Ask if they think they were describing the same thing. Since the descriptions are based on two different experiences (seeing and touching), the lists often differ.
   - Reveal that they were both describing the same object.
   - Ask if they know why the lists are so different. If they don't figure it out, explain that one group felt the object and one group saw the object.

6. **Moving it forward.**
   - Bring up real life examples and discuss how we experience things differently (e.g., parent-teen, boy-girl, a playground accident where there are differing opinions on whether a person fell or was pushed, etc.).

You Decided

OBJECTIVE:
- Practice respecting differences

MATERIALS:
None

COMMENTS FOR TEACHERS
- We keep forgetting that all people do not see things the same way or make the same decisions about what they experience.
- Having different perspectives is very helpful when problem solving.

DIRECTIONS:

1. **Set the stage:**

Ask participants to pretend they have just learned their best friend didn't make the basketball team or, for younger students, that their best friend got a new pet snake.

2. **Divide into small groups.**

Have them get into groups of four and share with each other the answers to these questions:
- "How do you feel?"
- "What would you be telling yourself?"
- "What would you do?"

3. **Come back together and discuss.**
- "Did everyone have the same thoughts and feelings?"
- "Did you assume everyone would think the same as you?"
- "Were you surprised at some of the responses?"
- "How could having different points of view be helpful in our class?"

■ Extension

Use the above as an introduction to a book of your choice about a person who saw the world differently and acted on their perceptions in a way that might have surprised their family or peer group. Refer to list on face sheet for suggestions.

Buy-In for Class Meetings
Preparing the Ground: Face Sheet

Concept: Buy-in

- "Buy-in" is the commitment of interested or affected parties to a decision. Students buy-in to the concept of class meetings when they understand how class meetings will be useful to them and when they are part of the process of getting them started. *Though it may seem counter-intuitive, this should be the last Preparing the Ground section you do with your students.*
- There are decisions that teachers must make (curriculum, grading) and there are decisions in which students can collaborate. Be clear in your own mind about this before you start any of the activities below. As long as behavior standards are met, teachers often let students have power over seating, classroom jobs, effective classroom noise levels, etc.

Why buy-in is important

- Buy-in, the agreement to support class meetings, is the key to cooperation.
- Cooperation is critical for learning the skills to have successful class meetings.
- Without this cooperation, it is more challenging for the class to move forward.
- Students will be unskilled when they are first starting class meetings. Being unskilled can lead to uncomfortable feelings, which, for some students is enough to invite misbehavior. Participation in Preparing the Ground and the Building Blocks can mitigate misbehavior.

What else are students learning?

These activities begin the process of working toward a common goal. Students learn about cooperation, solving problems together, and how power can be helpful rather than hurtful. The class is a team and all are needed for success and the creation of a win/win environment.

Recommended order for teaching buy-in for class meetings

It is recommended that this be the *last* preparing the ground step that you teach.

- ***Exploring Power: Win/Win*** (For grades 3 and up.) This is similar to the activity **Exploring Power: Building Cooperation** and sets the frame for collaborative problem solving.
- ***Why have class meetings?*** Or ***Introducing the Class Meeting.*** (For grades K-2.)
- ***Middle School/ High School Buy-In***

When you finish this section, you will have completed the Preparing the Ground Steps for Class Meetings. You and your class are ready to move on to working on the Essential Skills for Class Meetings.

Notes

Exploring Power: Win/Win

OBJECTIVE:
- To help students see the value of win/win solutions before they begin class meetings.

MATERIALS:
- Board
- Blank chart to make notes (see below)
- Materials for poster (optional)

COMMENTS FOR TEACHERS:
- Class meetings are a form of shared power. Lifting out the power dynamic before beginning class meetings helps all involved.
- Working together with shared power to resolve issues is more satisfying for both teachers and students.
- This activity is similar to the activity **Exploring Power: Building Cooperation.**

OPTIONAL POSTER

> We work together for Win/Win Solutions

DIRECTIONS:

1. **Discuss the role of power in relationships in school.**
   - Adult power:
     - "Does it work in a classroom if the teacher has all of the power and students have no power?"
     - "What would that look like and sound like?"
     - Write down their examples.
   - Student power:
     - "Would it work in a classroom if the students had all the power and the teacher had no power?"
     - "What would that look like and sound like?"
     - Write down their examples.
   - Shared power:
     - Ask students to brainstorm what it would be like to be in a classroom with shared power and respect for everyone.
     - "What would that look like and sound like?"
     - Write down their examples.

2. **Reflect.**
   - For each column ask students what the adults might be feeling, what the students might be feeling.

3. **Label.**
   - On the chart, label the first two groups (adult power, student power) as win/lose situations and the third group (shared power) as a win/win situation.

4. **Explain.**
   For Class Meetings to be safe, everyone must work together to find win/win solutions. No one has power over another, but people work together to find solutions all can live with.

5. **Moving it forward.**
   If appropriate for your age group, ask a volunteer to make a poster about win/win solutions. (See sample, left).

Adult power Looks like / sounds like	Student power Looks like / sounds like	Shared power Looks like / sounds like

Preparing the Ground: Buy-In for Class Meetings

Introducing the Class Meeting

OBJECTIVE:
- To introduce class meetings.

MATERIALS:
- Board

COMMENTS FOR TEACHERS:
- Teachers often handle classroom issues themselves, thereby missing opportunities to involve students in learning how to think, how to solve problems, how to contribute, and how to help each other.
- Class meetings teach students the skills to take on problems by themselves.

DIRECTIONS:

1. Setting the stage.
- Ask students, "What happens in the classroom, cafeteria, halls, or playground that causes problems or makes it difficult to learn?"
- List their concerns on the board.
- If they have trouble thinking of things, get them started by asking, "What about fights over playground equipment, other students bothering you in some way, etc.?"

Note: Especially in upper grades there are some problems that are not appropriate for class meetings. For example, talking about gang-related problems may put some students at risk. You know your community. Keep this in mind as you move to step 2.

2. Proposing collaborative problem solving.
- Ask, "How many of you think that by working together, we can come up with positive and helpful solutions to these concerns?"
- Get a show of hands.
- If some seem doubtful, ask, "How many of you would be interested in learning skills that would make you better helpers to each other?"

3. Setting up practice. Let your class know:
- "We all will work together to learn how to use class meetings to solve problems by focusing on solutions."
- "We'll begin by using "practice" problems to ensure that the class is skilled at suggesting helpful solutions."
- "We'll also make time to practice real problems that impact everyone."

Why Have Class Meetings?

OBJECTIVE:
- To introduce four purposes for class meetings.

MATERIALS:
- Board

COMMENTS FOR TEACHERS:
- Steps 1 - 3 are better for K-5. The modifications suggest another way to introduce class meetings with older students.
- This is meant to take only 10 to 15 minutes - a quick give-and-take between you and your class.

DIRECTIONS:

1. **Discuss the four purposes of class meetings.**

Tell your class that before starting class meetings, you want to help them understand more about why and how they are used.

- Compliments (Note: There are several lessons to teach compliments later in the manual. This is a brief introduction meant only for the students to share what they already know.)
    - Define compliments.
    - Ask for examples.
    - How does it feel to give or receive them?
- Helping each other
    - Ask for examples of ways people help each other in school
    - "How does it feel to help or be helped?"
- Problem solving
    - "What are some examples of problems people can have in school?" (Use descriptions rather than names.)
    - "Who typically solves the problems?"
    - "What are some ways people currently solve problems?"
    - "How do you feel when you help solve a problem?"
- Planning for events and activities
    - "What classroom activities or events have students helped plan in the past?"
    - "What might you feel when you are part of the planning?"
    - "What do people learn from helping to plan things?"

2. **Connect above topics to class meetings.**

Tell students that class meetings are a way for students and teachers to get more practice with:

- Giving compliments or appreciations,
- Helping each other,
- Solving problems by focusing on solutions, and
- Planning events and activities.

3. **Moving it forward.**

Ask for a show of hands. "How many of you would be willing to learn how to hold class meetings?" If a majority agrees, tell them you'll be happy to help them, since you can see they are committed to learning. Remind them that there will be some mistakes made along the way, and we will all learn together.

Positive Discipline in the School and Classroom Manual
by Jane Nelsen, Lynn Lott, Teresa LaSala, Jody McVittie, and Suzanne Smitha

Preparing the Ground: Buy-In for Class Meetings

▪ Tips

It rarely happens, but if you do not have majority agreement for #3 above, you should:

- Ask if they would be willing to respectfully support the rest of their classmates anyway, while the group gets started on the process.
- Go visit another class to watch their class meeting and come back and discuss.
- Ask those who are apprehensive what they would need to know to give it a try.

▪ Modification

For students in grade 5 and up, you can introduce the idea of class meetings in a social studies lesson on different forms of government. You might compare specific countries or the actual forms. A sample chart to complete might look like:

Form of Government	Who makes decisions?	Who or what limits those decisions?	What responsibilities do the leaders have in this form of government?	What responsibilities do the people have in this form of government?
Dictatorship or Authoritarian	Dictator	Only the power of the dictator, as held perhaps through an army	Responsible to self & those who help them hold on to power	None; someone else makes all the decisions so they just have to survive
Democracy	Elected officials	The people & legislative, executive & judicial parts of government	Listen to their electorate; make informed decisions in the best interest of the majority	Inform self for educated voting; participate in community
Anarchy	Everyone or no one; anyone who wants to do so	Nothing except individuals who may decide to try to limit decisions made by others	There are no leaders chosen by the group; leaders may eventually rise but have no obligation to answer to the people	Each takes care of his or her own needs and desires; there is no obligation to community needs

Draw a comparison between these three forms of government and ways a classroom community might operate. What form of government would students prefer for this classroom? If they want an authoritarian form, you as teacher will handle everything without their input. If they want a more democratic classroom, the best way to achieve that would be to implement class meetings.

Middle School/High School Buy-In

OBJECTIVE:
- To get "buy-in" from students for the process of class meetings.

MATERIALS:
- Board

COMMENT FOR TEACHERS:
- When students decide it's what they are willing to try, there will be more trust and involvement, and it's less likely they will sabotage the process.
- Allow time for this process and for the sharing of experiences as they come up.

DIRECTIONS:

1. **Begin the discussion.**

   Ask the class for a show of hands in response to the following questions:
   - "How many of you would like to share ideas or be part of the 'decision making process' on some aspects of how this classroom is run each day?"
   - "How many of you have been in a situation before where you have felt controlled and/or manipulated?"
   - "How many of you have ideas about things we could do in our classroom or here at our school to help each other feel connected and to learn better?"

2. **Exploring control vs. collaboration.**

   Lead and model a conversation/discussion around some or all of the following questions:
   - "Has anyone ever experienced the feelings of being controlled or manipulated in school?"
   - "Would anyone be willing to share how it felt?"
   - "How do those experiences influence our classroom? Our relationships? How we learn? The decisions we make?"
   - "Does anyone have ideas about how we can handle problems that come up in our classroom or school?"
   - "Based on our conversations, would you be open, interested and willing to make some changes and work on a new system?"

3. **Moving it forward. Introducing class meetings.**
   - Explain that you have learned about a process called class meetings, where students and staff work together to solve problems, share ideas and plan activities in a manner that allows everyone to feel heard and respected.
   - Ask students to raise their hands if they would be willing to work together to implement/use class meetings.
   - If the entire class does not raise their hand, ask those who did not what assurance or information they would need in order to give it a try. Or, ask if they would be willing to respectfully support the rest of their classmates for a few weeks while they start the process.

Notes

8 Essential Skills for Effective Class Meetings: Laying the Foundation
Face Sheet

A Positive Discipline class meeting is a regular, 15 to 20-minute gathering in a circle *that follows a very specific format and uses an agenda.* Class meetings use an object chosen by the class as a talking stick and begin with compliments. After compliments, previous solutions are reviewed and new problems that have been written on the agenda are addressed by the class. Classrooms that are skilled have student led meetings.

The big idea: Class Meeting Essential Skills

This section includes activities used to teach students the formal structure of class meetings *after* they have been taught foundational concepts from *Preparing the Ground*, which focuses on building students' ability to:

- Manage emotions and behavior long enough to sit in a circle for 10 to 15 minutes,
- Understand how to be helpful, not hurtful, and
- Use "I-messages" and listen to others.

This next section, Essential Skills for Effective Class Meetings, helps students learn how class meetings are structured: they *always* follow a specific process and an agenda. This takes practice for both students and adults.

Why the essential skills are important

These essential skills teach the specific structure and process of class meetings. In addition, they introduce a variety of tools for effective problem solving, which include:

- Establishing a helpful environment,
- Focusing on solutions,
- Creative brainstorming,
- Role-playing, and
- Building a deeper understanding of why people do what they do.

Learning and following structure and process is an important investment. The practice students get in class meetings requires them to integrate the socials skills they have learned with their problem-solving skills. This process leads to an orderly classroom where everyone can focus on academic progress.

Essential Skills for Class Meetings

What else are students learning?

Class meetings invite students to learn by doing. They provide the practice arena for all of the skills necessary to grow citizens who are responsible, respectful and resourceful members of the community.[1] Students learn:

- To use their voice,
- To practice looking at issues from multiple points of view,
- That mistakes are opportunities to learn,
- To see strengths in themselves and others,
- How collaboration can change things,
- That they have influence in a socially useful way, and
- What it feels like to set goals, plan and be able to carry out the plan.

Recommended order for teaching the *8 Essential Skills for Class Meetings*

1. *Forming a Circle*
2. *Practicing Compliments and Appreciations*
3. *Respecting Differences* (covered in depth in *Preparing the Ground* activities)
4. *Communication Skills* (covered in depth in *Preparing the Ground* activities)
5. *Focusing on Solutions*
6. *Brainstorming and Role-playing*
7. *Using the Agenda and Class Meeting Format*
8. *Understanding and Using the Four Mistaken Goals*

---

[1] In workshops, participants identify the skills and character traits that they wish for their students. These often include things like: respect for self and others, responsibility, self-esteem, patience, perseverance, generosity, passion for learning, curiosity, the ability to take appropriate risks, common sense, good judgment, listening skills, relationship skills, problem solving skills, self-advocacy, work ethic, a willingness to give to the community, a sense of their own capability, a love of learning, empathy, compassion, internal motivation, ability to set own goals, a sense of belonging, hope, etc.

Essential Skills for Class Meetings

A class meeting story:

Early in the spring, students in a Seattle 5th-grade class started bringing some silly putty to school, using it to occupy their hands instead of fidgeting. One week later, the silly putty became a bit of a problem. Some of the silly putty (being used inappropriately) got put in time out on a shelf. And then it disappeared. This was stressful for Liz (not her real name) as she had saved her money to buy the silly putty.

At their class meeting, the students talked about how embarrassing it would be to admit that you had taken the silly putty. They talked about mistakes being opportunities to learn and that no one would be punished. Nothing happened. Then Clyde (not his real name), prime suspect #1, "found" the silly putty in a cupboard – but denied having taken it. The class was suspicious but the teacher set very clear expectations that no one would be blamed without evidence. The next morning, shortly before their scheduled class meeting, as students were working in small groups Clyde blurted out, "Alright, I did it!" Not everyone heard this but Liz did. She asked to meet with Clyde and the two of them found a quiet place to talk.

The teacher had some concerns. He knew that Clyde's name was on the agenda for another problem. He didn't know whether Clyde would be willing to come to the class meeting after his confession and didn't think that it would be a good idea to tackle the next problem when Clyde was feeling vulnerable. He decided to have the class meeting but only do compliments.

Liz and Clyde arrived just as the class meeting started and found places to sit in the circle. The student leader started the meeting and announced that compliments would be given as "give or get." Clyde was sitting three spaces away from the leader, curled over himself. He sat up when he got the talking stick and complimented Liz for being a friend and listening to him. Liz was about 4 students later and complimented Clyde for being a good friend and listening to her. Two students later James (who had put Clyde on the agenda for the other problem) complimented Clyde for being a good friend. Then another student and another complimented Clyde. One compliment was "I compliment you for being a friend and I trust you." Clyde began to uncurl his body and a tear ran down his right cheek. Several students asked for a compliment and picked the student to give a compliment. Clyde began to partly raise his hand to volunteer to give a compliment. He was invited to give the next compliment. This was followed with more compliments for Clyde. The last one was from a boy who said, "I compliment you for being open with your emotions, the happy ones and the unhappy ones."

No adult prompted or commented on the abundance of compliments for Clyde. It just happened. To conclude the meeting, the teacher reminded the students that as a class, over the year they had had several struggles and each time they had been up to the challenge – and he felt they had once again met a significant challenge successfully. They ended with a brief fun rhythm activity.

After the meeting, one of the students remarked under his breath, "Clyde got nine compliments!" (From a class of 28.) The teacher saw this meeting as a watershed meeting for his class; partly because of how they welcomed Clyde back in, partly because James initiated the repetitive compliments – James who had been struggling with Clyde all year. He recognized the courage modeled by Clyde and Liz. The teacher also understood that if he had not "prepared the ground" by teaching about mistakes, about differences, compliments, and encouragement, these students would not have had the skills they needed to come together, forgive and welcome Clyde back into their community.

Notes

Forming a Circle
Essential Skill #1: Face Sheet

Concept: Forming a circle
- A circle is the structure of the class meeting process because it facilitates listening, taking turns, and expressing oneself effectively and respectfully.
- Everyone can be seated in chairs, on the floor, or when necessary, even on desks.
- Teachers are seated at the same level as the students (on the floor or on chairs).
- Meetings work best when students do not have anything in front of or with them.
- The process of getting into and out of a circle requires practice and will become a familiar classroom routine. With practice, students can get into (or out of) a circle in less than 60 seconds even when moving furniture. They enjoy this challenge.

Why forming a circle is important
- Class meetings are held in a circle so everyone can be seen and heard.
- Having everyone at the same level models horizontal relationships and shared responsibility.

How class meetings use the circle
- The circle is used for every class meeting.
- A talking stick/object is passed around the circle once for compliments.
- The talking stick/object is passed around the circle once for brainstorming solutions for each problem.

What else are students learning?
- How to collaborate and work together to move desks/tables/chairs,
- How to sit comfortably in full view of peers, and
- How to project their voice to be heard by all.

Recommended order for teaching forming a circle
- ***Forming a Circle – Quickly, Quietly, Safely***
- If your students have in previous years done **Quickly, Quietly, Safely**, you can extend their skill by using the variation at the end of the activity.

Essential Skills for Class Meetings: #1 Forming a Circle

■ General tips

- Forming a circle *takes practice*. Teachers will often practice forming a circle with a timer several times before proceeding to have a meeting in a circle.
- When students are fluent in forming a circle, the circle can be used for other classroom activities (talking about academic subjects, celebrations, etc.).

> *They drew a circle that shut me out -*
> *Heretic, rebel, a thing to flout.*
> *But love and I had the wit to win:*
> *We drew a circle that took him in.*
>
> from "Outwitted" by
> Edwin Markham, American Poet, 1852 - 1940

Essential Skills for Class Meetings: #1 Forming a Circle

Forming A Circle - Quickly, Quietly, Safely

OBJECTIVE:
- To create a democratic atmosphere where win/win solutions can take place, where all feel safe, and where everyone has equal rights to speak and be heard.

MATERIALS:
- Board
- Stop watch or timer that can record seconds

COMMENTS FOR TEACHERS:
- A circle contributes to a democratic atmosphere by allowing all to be seated at the same level, where everyone can see and be seen (including the teacher).
- It is also a reminder that class meetings are a different and special part of what we do at school.
- When students are used to being "told" how things will be done, it takes a while to help them feel comfortable thinking and sharing. Trust the process; it is worth the wait!
- Some teachers give up on the process because of crowded space. Be creative. Desks can be in the middle (clear desktops), or in a U shape (to sit upon). In one science classroom, the class used a combination of sitting on desks and tables.

DIRECTIONS:

1. **Introducing the circle.**

Using curiosity questions, discuss why it is important for *all* to sit in a circle:
- "What is the advantage of sitting in a circle?"
- "How does being able to see each other help us?"

2. **The circle in your classroom.**
- Everyone needs to sit at the same level (including the teacher).
- With students, come to an agreement on how the circle will be formed to ensure that the needs of every person are addressed. (For example, if someone cannot sit on the floor how will you make a circle where everyone is at the same level?)

3. **Quickly, quietly, safely.**
- Write the following headings on the board: Quickly, Quietly, Safely.
- Ask, "How can you form your circle quickly?"
- Record ideas on the board or flip chart.
- Repeat for *quietly* and for *safely*.
- Help them be specific. If furniture needs to be moved be specific about how and where it will be moved.

4. **Review the lists with students.**
- "Are any ideas in the *quickly* column not safe or quiet?"
- "Are any ideas in the *quietly* column not safe or quick?"
- "Are any ideas in the *safely* column not quick or quiet?"
- "Do we need to remove any ideas that are not practical or respectful?"

5. **Buy-In.**
- Ask, "Are we all in agreement with the guidelines on how we're going to move into a circle together?" If all agree, proceed.
- If someone does not agree ask, "What would you change so you and everyone else can agree?"
- If agreement is not reached at this point, ask, "Would everyone agree to try it as written for one week? After one week, we can re-visit our decision and ask how it's working."

6. **Estimate how long it will take.**
- Ask the students to guess how long it will take to form the circle using the agreed-upon guidelines.
- Write several guesses on the board.
- Ask for a volunteer to use a stopwatch or clock with a second hand to keep track of how long it takes.

Positive Discipline in the School and Classroom Manual
by Jane Nelsen, Lynn Lott, Teresa LaSala, Jody McVittie, and Suzanne Smitha

Essential Skills for Class Meetings: #1 Forming a Circle

7. Practice.
- Have the group form a circle while your timekeeper is monitoring the time.

8. Reflection.
After the circle is formed, process by asking:
- "How long did it take us?"
- "How successful were we?"
- "What did you learn that would help us improve next time?"
- "Is there anything we should try differently?"
- "Were we quiet and safe?"
- "As we move the chairs back to where they were, what do we need to do?"

9. Moving back.
Have your timekeeper time the process of going back to the original class set-up.

10. Practice, practice, practice.
Practice as many times as needed for the group to feel they have done their best at forming and un-forming the circle quickly, quietly and safely.

■ Variation

If your students have done **Quickly, Quietly, Safely** in previous years, you can have the students pick three new words that describe an effective way to move into class meetings. Replace step 3 and 4 above with:

- Ask the group to suggest three words that would best describe ways they think the class should move into a circle so that everyone feels comfortable. Some examples might include: efficiently, carefully, or respectfully.
- List these words on the "Chart Form" provided and ask the students to volunteer words that describe how the three words look, sound, and feel.
- Allow the group to add, delete, or change any words until the chart represents the group's perception of how they will move together.

Chart Form

Our words:	Looks Like	Sounds Like	Feels Like

Practicing Compliments and Appreciations
Essential Skill #2: Face Sheet

Concept: Giving and receiving compliments and appreciations

- A compliment or appreciation is a formal act of civility, courtesy and respect.
- Compliments and appreciations express gratitude and recognize the good qualities of someone or something.
- *Positive Discipline Class Meetings always start with compliments and appreciations.*

Why compliments and appreciations are important

- They assist the class in making a clear transition into the class meeting and set class meetings apart from other discussions.
- They set a positive tone for the meeting.
- They teach students the importance of noticing the positive aspects in each other and foster connections between students and teachers.
- They enhance students' sense of belonging.
- Problem solving is much easier in an atmosphere of positive regard.
- The entire classroom climate changes when everyone gives and receives compliments freely.

How class meetings use compliments and appreciations

- *Every* class meeting starts with compliments or appreciations. It is an important part of the routine.
- Compliments and appreciations set the tone for the class meeting and clearly set it apart from "discussions" or other meetings.

What else are students learning?

- How to look for, notice and acknowledge the positive in others.
- How to speak directly to another when offering a compliment.
    - "Jenae, I'd like to compliment you for playing with me at lunch today." (The student says this while looking directly at the recipient.)
    - Instead of, "I would like to compliment Jenae because she played with me at lunch today." (Saying this while looking at the teacher.)
- How to receive and respond to a compliment by saying, "Thank you."

Essential Skills for Class Meetings: #2 Compliments and Appreciations

Recommended order for teaching *compliments and appreciations*
- ***Compliments and Appreciations 1: Introducing the Format & Process - Giving and Receiving***
- ***Compliments and Appreciations 2: Sharing Compliments***
- ***Compliments and Appreciations 3: Give, Get or Pass***

■ Tips
- Giving compliments takes practice.
- Limiting compliments to things that happen at school helps avoid problems that arise from students feeling left out of social situations (parties, play dates, etc.).
- Occasionally students give each other "backhanded" compliments, statements that may have both helpful and hurtful components. Examples include:
    > "Jose, I'd like to compliment you for helping me, *because you usually don't.*"
    > "Diana, I'd like to appreciate you for sharing today *because you never share!*"

    If this happens ask the student to rephrase the compliment in a way that is helpful, not hurtful.
- A common concern is that some students don't get compliments. Our experience is that students notice this and address the issue themselves. This challenge is a wonderful early class meeting agenda problem. They often come up with creative solutions to the problem. Another option is to challenge your students to compliment someone they have not complimented before.
- Early in the process students tend to compliment others about superficial things (like their new shoes, their clothes etc.). After the students get the rhythm of compliments it is important to challenge them to "kick it up a notch." Introduce the difference between "inside" and "outside" compliments. An "inside" compliment is about something the person does or who they are; an "outside" compliment is about appearances or possessions. In the process, they will learn that "inside" compliments are more meaningful.
- It will take practice for students to directly compliment others. Continue to insist on the format, [Name] I would like to compliment you for _____."
- Another common concern is that students want to compliment all of their friends, listing several names. We recommend that students compliment no more than two people at a time. If more than two people are recipients, no names are used and the compliment would be worded: "I would like to compliment all the people who... (for example, "helped me with my project" or "played with me at recess").
- To vary compliments,
    ° At the beginning of a particular lesson for example, math, ask students to be prepared to later give a compliment about something that happened in math.
    ° If you as the teacher notice a kind or helpful act taking place in the classroom, you can privately encourage a student to remember it and give the compliment during the class meeting.
    ° Invite students to compliment someone at home and report back what they noticed.
    ° Invite students to compliment someone who doesn't usually get compliments at school and report back what they noticed.

Story

Middle school students at Unity Charter School in New Jersey created a community compliment booth as a group project. They designed a physical booth out of a big cardboard box with a sign about how to respectfully give compliments and some ideas about what compliments might be given for. Inside the booth they placed a tablet. Those who want to offer a compliment to anyone in the school community can participate. To give a compliment they go up to the booth, press the start button on the tablet, and their video compliment to another person is recorded. At the end of the day the technology teacher reviews them to make sure that the compliments are appropriate and posts them on the TV monitors in the school hallways.

Essential Skills for Class Meetings: #2 Compliments and Appreciations

Compliments and Appreciations 1:
Introducing the Format and Process of Giving and Receiving

OBJECTIVE:
- To teach, learn, and practice the process of giving and receiving compliments.
- To present the format for giving and receiving a compliment.
- To boost self-esteem, foster class connections, and enhance awareness of the good students do for each other, the class, and the classroom.
- To start the class meeting on a positive note.

MATERIALS:
- Talking Stick Item

COMMENTS FOR TEACHERS:
- At first students may feel uncomfortable or think giving compliments is silly. If you have faith in the process, teach the skills and give them opportunities to practice, their awareness and comfort levels will grow, as will good feelings in the classroom.
- In some cultures, asking for a compliment is not an acceptable practice. If this is an issue move to "Compliments and Appreciations 2".
- It is the teacher's job to ensure safety. See tip on the face sheet regarding backhanded compliments.
- Students complimenting one another should speak in the first person while making eye contact directly with the person they are addressing.

DIRECTIONS:

1. **Introducing compliments and appreciations.**
   Brainstorm and dialogue with students by asking:
   - "What is a compliment?"
   - "How do you feel when you get a compliment?" (Some students will share that it feels good, others may acknowledge that it feels uncomfortable.)
   - "What happens in the classroom or school each day that we appreciate and could acknowledge with a compliment?"
   - "What are things we do each day to help each other that we appreciate?"

   (Examples might include: lending another student something, saying a kind word, helping with an assignment, cleaning up, or listening.)

2. **Teach students the format for compliments and appreciations.**
   - When you give a compliment, say, "[Name], I would like to compliment/appreciate you for [what]."
   - When you receive a compliment, say, "Thank you, [Name]."

   (Many teachers post this written format on the wall.)

3. **Getting ready to practice.**
   - Acknowledge that initially it can feel awkward to give and receive compliments.
   - To ease the process of creating a compliment, allow a minute or two for students to think of something they have done in class or at school for which they would like to receive a compliment. (Option: Ask them to close their eyes, think of a compliment for themselves, then open their eyes as a signal that they are ready.)
   - Ask if there are any students unable to think of a compliment. If yes, ask the class, "Who has noticed something _____ has done for someone else, or some improvement _____ has made that deserves a compliment?" Have them share.

4. **Giving compliments.**
   - Begin passing the "talking stick" item around the circle. The student who has the "talking stick" shares what they thought of for which they would like to receive a compliment.
   - The student on their left gives that compliment.

© Positive Discipline Association ■ www.PositiveDiscipline.org

Essential Skills for Class Meetings: #2 Compliments and Appreciations

- Be aware that students tend to look at the teacher and speak in the third person when giving a compliment.
- It is also important to teach how to respond gracefully to a compliment.
- Many teachers who have class meetings regularly share that students complain when a meeting is called off because nothing is on the agenda. They say, "Well, we could at least do compliments and appreciations."

For example:

<u>Asking student</u>: Jasmine says, "I would like a compliment for not talking out of turn during class."

<u>Giving student</u> (to the left): Zack, makes eye contact and says, "Jasmine, I would like to compliment you for not talking out of turn during class."

<u>Response:</u> Jasmine, while looking back at Zack, says, "Thank you, Zack."

- Then Jasmine passes the talking stick to Zack who shares something for which he would like to be complimented.
- Repeat this process until everyone in the circle has had a turn giving and receiving a compliment.

5. Moving it forward.

- Invite students to start noticing positive things about each other and tell them that you will practice compliments again at the next meeting.
- When you observe positive things happening in the classroom, be sure to recognize them and ask students to remember the compliment for the next meeting.
- As students become more proficient, challenge them to compliment and acknowledge themselves or others for who they are and what they do, not on how they look. *These are what we call "inside" compliments.*

Tips

See Practicing Compliments and Appreciations Face Sheet.

Essential Skills for Class Meetings: #2 Compliments and Appreciations

Compliments and Appreciations 2: Sharing Compliments

OBJECTIVE:
- To teach, learn, and practice the process of giving and receiving compliments.

MATERIALS:
- Talking stick item

COMMENTS FOR TEACHERS:
- Positive Discipline class meetings start with compliments. This is an intentional part of the routine and structure of class meetings.
- The talking stick/object goes around the circle one time.
- Limit the compliments to what happens at school. This is important for building your classroom community.

DIRECTIONS:

1. **Review.**
   - "What is a compliment?"
   - "What do we give compliments for?"
     - things that happen at school
     - things we appreciate about another person (sharing, helpfulness, accomplishments).
   - "How does it feel to give or get a compliment?"

2. **Reflection.**
   Have students sit quietly and think of someone in the class they would like to compliment. Ask, "What did that person say or do that you appreciated or noticed as being special?"
   (**Option:** ask them to close their eyes, think of something and open their eyes as a signal that they are ready.)

3. **Practice.**
   - Pass the talking stick/object around the circle, giving each student a turn to share a compliment.
   - Each "receiver" responds with "thank you"; they do not need the talking stick/object to reply.
   - Students always have the option to "pass" (to say nothing) when the talking stick/object comes to them.

■ Tips

See Practicing Compliments and Appreciations Face Sheet.

Variations

Once a class gets really skilled at compliments, it is helpful to occasionally add variety to the process. Variations include:

- Students compliment the person sitting next to them.
- Students draw a name ahead of time and compliment that person.
- Students draw a name and have a compliment buddy for the week or the next day. Buddies notice actions that are worthy of acknowledgment and then share a compliment at the class meeting.
- Ask students to plan to compliment someone outside the classroom. At the class meeting the next day, they can share who they complimented and how that person reacted.
- Ask students to plan to compliment someone they have never complimented before.
- Ask students to pay attention during a specific class/time and plan to give a compliment to someone about something they did during that class/time.

Essential Skills for Class Meetings: #2 Compliments and Appreciations

Compliments and Appreciations 3: Give, Get or Pass

OBJECTIVE:
- To practice another approach for compliments.
- To introduce the meaning of "Give, Get or Pass."

MATERIALS:
- Talking stick item

COMMENTS FOR TEACHERS:
- This is a third step in the process of teaching compliments and appreciations.
- In this step, when a student asks to "get" a compliment, it may interrupt the flow. For this reason, we suggest students be comfortable and aware of what's taught/practiced in **Compliments and Appreciations** 1 and 2 before introducing this lesson.
- Asking classmates for a compliment can be very empowering to students.
- As always, the talking stick gets passed around the circle one time.
- In some cultures, asking for a compliment is not an acceptable practice. If this is an issue, use **Compliments and Appreciations 2**.

DIRECTIONS:

1. **Introduce "Give, Get or Pass."**
   Explain "Give, Get or Pass."
   - Give: Students can choose to give a compliment as they have learned previously.
   - Get: Students can choose to get a compliment for something they have done for which they would like recognition (i.e., they may ask for a compliment).
   - Pass: The student may choose to pass. They say, "pass" and give the talking stick object to the next student.

2. **Teaching the process.**
   - *Give:*
     - If a student chooses to "give" a compliment, they should look at the person they are complimenting and say, "[Name]_, I would like to compliment/appreciate you for [what]."
     - The receiving student responds by saying, "Thank you, [Name]." (No talking stick is needed.)
   - *Get:*
     - If the student chooses to "get" a compliment, they say, "I would like to be complimented for_____."
     - The meeting leader or teacher asks, "Who would like to compliment _[Name]_ for ____?"
     - Willing students raise their hands and the meeting leader or teacher chooses one.
     - The chosen student, while looking at the receiver, says, "_[Name]_, I would like to compliment you for_____." (The talking stick remains with the student who asked for the compliment. After they have said, "thank you," it is passed to the next student in the circle.)
   - *Pass:*
     - If the student chooses to pass, they say, "pass" and pass the talking stick/object to the next person.

3. **Practice.**
   - Invite the students to think for a moment and decide whether they want to give, get or pass. (Option: Ask them to close their eyes, think for a moment, and then open their eyes as a signal that they are ready.)
   - Start the object around the circle letting the students give and get compliments (or pass).

Respecting Differences
Essential Skill #3: Face Sheet

Respecting Differences is also covered in *Preparing the Ground* with five activities for teaching this skill.

As you prepare for class meetings, it is important to review the information about respecting differences. Class meetings are a wonderful way for students to learn about the benefits of differences through problem solving.

Concept: Respecting differences

- Respecting differences highlights the fact that each person sees and interprets the world in their own way, and no one's perception is necessarily the "right" one.
- We are often drawn to spend time with people who are similar. This can appear to be exclusive and limits our ability to learn from each other's differences. This is not right or wrong, but in problem solving it is helpful to be inclusive, work together and learn from each other's perspectives.
- We each make meaning of the events around us in the context of our own experiences.
- Differences can be a challenge for students, but they are a powerful and rich asset to any community.

Why respecting differences important

- Students often see differences as bad or as, "I am right, you are wrong." Some students who perceive themselves as different begin to believe that they are bad or that something is "wrong" with them. These perceptions can be compounded by systemic structures that may intensify inequity.
- Embracing differences contributes to respect and compassion for self and others.
- Different points of view are extremely useful in problem solving.
- The ability to see the world from another person's (different) point of view is also one of the key skills needed for the development of empathy.
- Understanding differences is essential to continuously build cultural responsiveness (the ability to effectively interact with people across cultures).
- New data on community resiliency also demonstrates that diverse communities are much more resilient. http://www.stockholmresilience.org/

What else are students learning?

- The skills to be equitable, inclusive, and respectful in relationships with others they perceive as different (culture, race, physical, gender, learning styles, socio-economic class, religion, emotional differences),
- How to celebrate and share their own identities while holding space for classmates to do the same, and
- How to share safely their own life experiences. *For example,* in one classroom, after discussions about differences, one student felt comfortable enough to teach her classmates about her physical tics and Tourette Syndrome. This helped her classmates understand her behavior, addressed their fear of the unknown, and gave her the opportunity to speak for herself. She gained a sense of belonging in the classroom and the other students gained empathy, knowledge, and understanding.

Essential Skills for Class Meetings: #3 Respecting Differences

Recommended order for teaching these *respecting differences*
- **It's Not Fair!**
- **Rhythm Band Warm-Up**
- **Step Into my Shoes** - This activity is not appropriate for younger students.

Note: There are additional activities in the Preparing the Ground, Respecting Differences section of this manual.

■ Tip

In class meetings, students may need to be reminded that:
- There is more than one way of perceiving a problem.
- The variety of suggestions they have brainstormed is a benefit of having so many different perspectives and creative minds in the circle.

LITERATURE CONNECTIONS
Adler, David A. *A Picture Book of Jackie Robinson.* New York: Holiday House, 1994.
Byers, Grace. *I Am Enough.* New York: Harper Collins Children's Books, 2018.
Cannon, Janell. *Stellaluna.* New York: Scholastic Inc., 1993.
Choi, Yangsook. *The Name Jar.* New York: Knopf, Borzoi Books, 2001.
DeRolf, Shane. *The Crayon Box That Talked.* New York: Random House, 1966.
Dismondy, Maria and Kim Shaw. *Spaghetti in a Hot Dog Bun.* Wixom, MI: Making Spirits Bright, 2008.
Giles, Andreae and Guy Parker-Rees. *Giraffes Can't Dance.* New York: Orchard Books, 2001.
Jeffers, Oliver. *Here We Are: Notes for Living on Planet Earth.* New York: Philomel Books, 2017.
Lionni, Leo. *Little Blue and Little Yellow.* New York: Alfred A. Knopf, 2009.
Lobel, Arnold. *Frog and Toad Together.* New York: Harper Festival, 1999 - 1972. (Note: Many of the Frog and Toad books teach about different perspectives.)
MacLachlan, Patricia. *Through Grandpa's Eyes.* New York: Harper & Row, 1980.
Munch, Robert. *The Paper Bag Princess.* Toronto, Canada: Annick Press Ltd., 1995.
Parr, Todd. *It's Okay to Be Different.* Boston: Little, Brown & Company, 2001.
Rappaport, Doreen. *Eleanor, Quiet No More.* New York: Disney/Hyperion Books, 2009.
Seuss, Dr. *The Sneeches.* New York: Random House, 1961.
Vassel, Jennifer and Penny Webber. *I Am Unique.* Chino Hills, CA: BuddingRose Publication, 2015.
Whitcomb, Mary. *Odd Velvet.* San Francisco, CA: Chronicle Books, 1998.
Zobel-Nolan, Allia and Miki Sakamoto. *What I Like About ME.* New York: Readers Digest Children's Books, 2005.

"Say there was a problem that I had like years beyond now, I might not exactly remember the class meeting format but I could relate some of the problems that the other students had and use some of their solutions."

– 5th Grade student
Lakeridge Elementary, Renton, WA

"I feel comfortable about this class. I feel like I could tell any one of the teachers or any one of the students how I feel about something. I feel like this right here is trustworthy school you got some trustworthy teachers."

– 5th Grade student (in her 4th school, in 2 years)
Lakeridge Elementary, Renton, WA

Essential Skills for Class Meetings: #3 Respecting Differences

It's Not Fair!

OBJECTIVE:
- To help students understand that everyone is different and that "being fair" does not mean treating everyone the same.

MATERIALS:
- A pencil
- Tape to hold it to the wall

COMMENTS FOR TEACHERS:
- Students arrive in your classroom with different skills and abilities, which requires you to teach and relate to them differently.
- It is hard for students to understand that "being fair" does not mean treating everyone the same. It is important to illustrate and teach it explicitly.

DIRECTIONS:

1. **Before class.**
   - Tape a pencil high enough on the wall that your tallest student could reach it, but one of your shorter students could not reach it without assistance.

2. **Ask for volunteers.**
   - Ask one of the tallest and one of the shortest persons in class to help you with a demonstration.
   - Explain that you will ask them to do something that might not seem fair.

3. **Do the activity.**
   - Have the volunteers come to the wall where the pencil is taped.
   - Say, "The objective is to get the pencil off the wall. You may not help or hurt each other or use any object to help get the pencil down."
   - Say, "Go!"
   - The taller student will get the pencil down (unless the shorter student talks the tall one out of it, which is an interesting possibility).
   - Thank the volunteers.

4. **Process the activity.**
   Ask volunteers and then the class:
   - "What did you notice? Was this fair?"
   - "Who was this task easy for? Hard or impossible for?"
   - "Does either person have control over how tall they are?"
   - "What would have made this fairer?"
   - *Optional:* Did either of these two students use any different talents or skills to try to get the pencil? (For example, did the shorter person use negotiation skills to get help from the taller one?)

5. **Take it deeper. Discuss/compare the activity to school life.**
   - "What makes it harder or easier for some people to learn a particular subject?"
   - "Do we choose if it is easy or hard for us to learn something like reading or math?"
   - "What about sports?"
   - Draw from your discussion with your students that we have different talents and abilities.
   - "Should the teacher treat all students the same during every class? Is it even possible to treat everyone the same during every class?" "Is 'same' equivalent to 'fair'?"

For an image that illustrates this concept go to:
http://interactioninstitute.org/illustrating-equality-vs-equity/

Positive Discipline in the School and Classroom Manual
by Jane Nelsen, Lynn Lott, Teresa LaSala, Jody McVittie, and Suzanne Smitha

Essential Skills for Class Meetings: #3 Respecting Differences

Rhythm Band Warm-Up

Inspired by an activity presented by Judi Fitzgerald, Pastor, Matthews United Methodist Church, Matthews, NC

OBJECTIVE:
- To realize we all can contribute in different ways to reach a harmonious outcome.

MATERIALS:
- 4 or 5 rhythm band instruments (sand paper blocks, tambourines, sticks, bells etc.)

(If rhythm band instruments are not available, rhythms can be generated with hands and feet.)

COMMENTS FOR TEACHERS:
- This activity can be challenging for the youngest students.
- Our differences can make what we create together more interesting.
- To benefit from our differences, we have to listen to each other. If we aren't paying attention to what others are doing, the result may be chaos.
- *Zin, Zin, Zin!* Is a book that can supplement this activity.*

*Moss, Lloyd. *Zin, Zin, Zin!* New York: Simon & Schuster Books for Young Readers, 1995.

DIRECTIONS:

1. **First rhythm band practice – everyone different.**
   - Invite 4 or 5 students to come to the front of the room and give each one of them a rhythm band instrument.
   - Have each person think of their own short rhythm pattern that can be repeated over and over.
   - Have them all play their own pattern at the same time.
   - Process: "Could you hear each rhythm? Each instrument? What did you notice?"

2. **Second rhythm band practice – everyone the same.**
   - Ask one student (preferably the student with the loudest instrument) to play his or her pattern.
   - Have the other band members listen and then copy as exactly as possible the rhythm of the first instrument.
   - Stop the band when the rhythm has been established.
   - Process: "What was different? Is this as creative?"

3. **Third rhythm band practice – everyone different but with an order.**
   - Ask the first instrument (from above) to begin the same rhythm again, but this time have the band members join in one at a time (to your signal) with a rhythm that is different but compliments the first rhythm.
   - Process: "What did you notice this time?"

5. **Discuss to establish a connection to problem solving.**
   - "What did you notice?"
   - "What happened when there wasn't any order?"
   - "What happened when everything was exactly the same?"
   - "What did the different rhythms add to our music?"
   - "What was needed from each person to work together?"
   - "How do our differences help our classroom? How might they help us in a class meeting?"

▪ Extension

Include the rest of the class
- Before the discussion, invite the rest of the class to join in by adding their own complimentary rhythm using their hands or feet to make sounds.
- Have the leader begin with the same rhythm again, signal each instrument to enter with their rhythm, and then invite groups of students (e.g., according to seating, or color of clothing) to add their individual, complementary rhythm.

Essential Skills for Class Meetings: #3 Respecting Differences

Step into My Shoes
By Melanie Miller and Aisha Pope

OBJECTIVES:
- For students to become aware of their classmates' "worlds."
- To encourage understanding and appreciation of differences.
- To build empathy.

MATERIALS:
- Six to eight prepared "shoe boards" from the options below. (Make sure you include the "I belong" and "I matter" shoe boards.)

COMMENTS FOR TEACHERS:
- This activity is not appropriate for younger children.
- Through the metaphor of shoes, students learn that they can move in and out of roles. When a role doesn't fit them anymore, they can change to something more encouraging. They can find their own personal power, or ask for help to change what isn't working anymore.
- Use your judgment about which boards to include for your students.

DIRECTIONS:

1. Prepare students for the lesson. Explain that:
- We all see the world differently because we have had different experiences.
- Cards with shoes on them are placed in a circle around the room. Each volunteer will have a chance to stand in someone else's shoes.

2. Read the "shoes."
- Walk around the circle reading each title out loud.

3. Ask for volunteers.
- Explain that you will ask for volunteers to come stand in the "shoes" and pretend that they are that person.
- You will ask them to rotate so that they can try on "different shoes."
- Explain that you will do the activity more than once, so more than one group of students can participate.
- Ask for as many volunteers as you have shoe boards.
- Instruct participants to find one shoe board to stand on.
- Remind all students (participants and audience) that this is a quiet activity. There is to be no talking.

4. Stepping into someone else's shoes.
- Ask participants to stand on their shoe board and silently read what is written.
- Invite them to really feel or experience the person in those "shoes."
- Say, "Notice what you are feeling, thinking or deciding about yourself and others. Notice what it is like to step into this particular pair of shoes."
- Say, "When you are ready, step off your shoe board, and rotate onto the next shoe, when that person has stepped off."

5. Sharing.
- Invite the students to return to their seats.
- Ask them to share what they learned or noticed doing this activity.
- The activity can be repeated until all of the students who want a chance have participated.

6. Moving it forward.
Ask students:
- "How might standing in some of these shoes change how you see the world?"
- "How might it influence your behavior?"
- "What are some situations where we might exclude others because we perceive they are different?"
- "How could you tell if a pair of shoes no longer fits?"
- "What do you do then?"

Positive Discipline in the School and Classroom Manual
by Jane Nelsen, Lynn Lott, Teresa LaSala, Jody McVittie, and Suzanne Smitha

Essential Skills for Class Meetings: #3 Respecting Differences

■ Follow up Activity

Invite students to create the pair of shoes that they would like to wear.

Sample shoe board

Sometimes I Need to Feel Powerful Shoes

I like to feel powerful.

I feel powerless.

I need to look cool.

I feel discouraged.

My brother is mean to me.

My parents overreact and yell a lot.

Sometimes I'm intimidated by other kids' abilities.

My friends think I'm funny.

Tough is better than weak.   Don't you dare…I'll get even.   What? I didn't do anything.

"I feel like I belong" shoes: My school classroom is friendly and helpful. I have friends who support me and watch out for me. My teacher encourages me when I struggle to learn something new. Others listen to me. Others notice me and include me.

"I matter" shoes: I have good ideas. I am unique and bring unique perspectives to our discussions. I know useful things. I can teach others some of the things I know. My help is appreciated. I'm proud of my cultural heritage. I can have a positive impact on others.

"My parents are getting a divorce" shoes: I feel alone. No one else is dealing with this. I feel angry. I feel confused. I'm tired of my parents arguing. Is it my fault? I miss my friends when I go to my dad's house. Everyone in my family is so angry. I just wish my parents would get back together. It's hard to concentrate at school.

"I'm overscheduled" shoes: I have too much to do. My parents get mad if I don't get "A's. I have to go from basketball to piano to scouts. I never have time to play. We're always going somewhere in the car. I feel stressed. I feel alone. I feel tired.

"I'm always picked on" shoes: I don't have any friends. Kids make fun of me. I feel scared. I don't like school. I wish adults would take me seriously. I try to fit in. I sometimes do wrong things because people tell me to just make a friend. I feel alone. I wish I could disappear.

"Bystander" shoes: I want to be a part of the cool group. If I tell an adult, will I be bullied next? I feel worried. I feel confused. Sometimes the teasing is funny. I belittle people. I join in. I want to have friends. I don't want to be the next victim. The power feels good. At least I'm not the one getting picked on.

"New kid at school" shoes: I just moved here and don't know anyone. The teachers are mean. I sit alone at lunch. No one asks me to play at recess. I miss my old friends and school. I feel alone. I feel depressed. No one understands. Other kids look at me and talk behind my back.

"Excluded kid" shoes: I walk up to a group and they walk away from me. Others spread rumors about me. No one invites me into their group. When I sit down at lunch, others move away from me. I feel alone. I feel embarrassed. I wish someone would notice me, talk to me. Kids laugh at me. They do things behind my back.

"Perfect student" shoes: I have to get perfect grades. I want people to like me. I'll do anything to impress others. I feel nervous and anxious. If they only knew what my life is really like. My parents expect me to get really good grades. I have to be the best athlete. There is no room for anything that isn't perfect in my family. My parents don't understand. I feel so much pressure. I can't keep up much longer.

"I'm not perfect but I'm doing the best I can" shoes: I have my good days and bad days. Sometimes I get along well with my friends and sometimes we get in fights. We usually work things out. I have fun at school and usually can learn things pretty quickly, although math has always been tough.

Notes

Communication Skills
Essential Skill #4: Face Sheet

The practice of communication skills is covered in *Preparing the Ground* with five activities for teaching.

As you prepare for class meetings, it is important to review this skill. Class meetings are a wonderful way for students to practice.

Concept: Communication skills

Communication is the process of sharing information with at least one other person.

- There is a sender, a message and a receiver. The skills of communicating involve learning to be an effective "sender" as well as an effective "receiver."
- Listening to another and expressing desires and feelings effectively and respectfully are skills that need to be taught and take practice.

Why communication skills are important

- They give students a sense of both connection and autonomy.
- They help students express thoughts, feelings and ideas in a respectful manner and empower them to influence the world around them.

What else are students learning?

- Patience
- Projecting voice
- Public speaking skills
- There is a connection between feelings and thoughts
- The power of words and communication can influence and make changes in the world
- Communication takes practice

How class meetings enhance communication skills

Class meetings teach communication skills in many ways. In class meetings, students:

- Practice giving and receiving compliments,
- Listen as one person talks while an object is passed around the circle,
- Choose how to deal with a problem: 1) share feelings while others listen 2) discuss without fixing or 3) ask for problem solving help,
- Practice speaking in public by articulating their suggestions for classmates, and
- Experience the power of their voice by witnessing the changes in their relationships, classroom and school.

Essential Skills for Class Meetings: #4 Communication Skills

Recommended order for teaching *communication skills*

Lessons are listed here again, from the earlier section Communication Skills, Preparing the Ground: Essential Skills for a Positive Discipline Classroom. There are activities to practice "sending" and "receiving" communication.

- **Sending: *Bugs and Wishes, I-Messages.*** All children can learn "I-messages" but for younger children (10 and under) who are not fluent in speaking about emotions, Bugs and Wishes is an easier first step.
- **Receiving: *Listening 1, Listening 2*** depending on the skill set of your class.
- You can also use **Four Problem-Solving Suggestions, Wheel of Choice** and/or **Solution Table** from Essential Skill #5: Focusing on Solutions in the next section.

Recommended review lesson for *communication skills*

- ***Listening 2***, including the guidelines your class created for effective listening. These can be adapted for class meetings.

▪ Tips

- In class meetings, students will sometimes look at the adult instead of the student to whom they are talking. It is important to remind students to look at the person to whom they are talking.
- Communication skills need continual practice and review.

LITERATURE CONNECTIONS

Binko, Howard. *Howard B. Wigglebottom Learns to Listen.* Marina Del Ray, CA: Thunderbolt Publishers, 2005.
Lester, Helen and Lynn Munsinger. *Listen Buddy.* Boston, MA: Houghton Mifflin, Harcourt, 1995.
Moss, Pegg. *Say Something.* Gardiner Maine, Tillbury House, 2004.
Scheuer, Karen. *A Bug and a Wish.* Houston, TX: Strategic Book Publishing and Rights Co, 2014.
Williams, Barbara. *Albert's Impossible Toothache.* Cambridge, MA: Candlewick Press, 2003.

Focusing on Solutions
Essential Skill #5: Face Sheet

Concept: Focusing on solutions

- *Positive Discipline is a restorative practice.* The focus is on fixing mistakes and repairing harm. The regular practice of sitting in a circle, listening to each other and solving problems builds connection, empathy, trust, and community.
- The word "solution" comes from the Latin *solvere:* to loosen, free or release. Students gain a sense of freedom and power from repairing mistakes and resolving challenges.
- The Positive Discipline curriculum empowers people to learn from and repair their mistakes by focusing on ways to make things better, instead of relying on traditional approaches that make people "pay for" or feel shame and pain for mistakes. This may involve making amends or contributing to the community.
- All solutions are consequences (something that is linked to or follows something else closely). Not all consequences are solutions.
- Solutions allow students to release their moral burden from having made a mistake.
- Adults often see inappropriate behavior as "intentional" without understanding that the behavior is an unskilled or mistaken method of solving another problem. This is addressed in the section on Understanding and Using the Four Mistaken Goals. Solutions and repairs continue to be the mainstay of interventions for harm to others.
- Solutions are REASONABLE, RELATED, RESPECTFUL and *HELPFUL.* It is the "helpful" element that makes this work powerful and radical.
- Positive Discipline challenges the unspoken assumption that people need to "hurt" in some way so they remember not to make the same mistake again.

Why focusing on solutions is important

- People learn and function better when they are allowed to maintain dignity and repair their mistakes.
- By focusing on being *helpful, not hurtful,* students recognize they can support others, *learn from their mistakes* and *learn from the mistakes of others.*
- Solutions become a powerful tool for building a community.

How class meetings encourage focusing on solutions

- The class meeting guidelines teach students to offer only helpful comments and suggestions, or to pass; there is no provision for punishment.
- Emphasis is placed on how to resolve the problem or keep it from happening again, instead of addressing only what happened in the past.
- Regular class meetings give students frequent practice using solutions, thereby integrating solutions into daily classroom life.

Essential Skills for Class Meetings: #5 Focusing on Solutions

What else are students learning?
- A willingness to both make and repair mistakes is an important life skill that enhances engagement and fosters academic success. Rudolf Dreikurs reminds us that we need the *courage to be imperfect.*
- Students must take risks in order to learn. Mistakes are inevitable when we push ourselves to try new things. In fact, fear of making mistakes or "failing" keeps many students from stretching to attempt new skills and areas of learning, inhibiting their growth as learners at school and in the wider world.

Recommended order for teaching *focusing on solutions*

For one-on-one problem solving:
- ***Four Problem Solving Suggestions*** (May have been introduced earlier)
- ***Wheel of Choice*** (Many teachers introduce this earlier, after **Bugs and Wishes**.)
- ***Solution Table*** (Can be introduced after Bugs and Wishes.)

For group problem solving:
- ***Solutions vs. Logical Consequences***
- ***Solutions and Curiosity Questions, not Blame***
- ***The Helpful, Not Hurtful Monitor***

LITERATURE CONNECTIONS

Beaty, Andrea. *Rosie Revere, Engineer.* New York: Abrams, 2013.
Beaty, Andrea. *Ada Twist the Scientist.* New York: Abrams, 2016.
Gray, Monique. *You Hold Me Up.* Custer, WA: Orca Book Publishers, 2017.
Hopkinson, Deborah. *Sweet Clara and the Freedom Quilt.* New York: Alfred A. Knopf Inc., 1993.
Wood, Audrey. *King Bidgood's in the Bathtub.* Orlando, FL: Harcourt Brace Jovanovich, 1985.
Yamada, Kobi. *What Do You Do With a Problem?* Seattle, WA: Compendium. 2016.

Four Problem Solving Suggestions

OBJECTIVE:
- To teach a process inviting students to solve problems outside the class meeting allowing them, rather than the teacher, to take responsibility for their behavior.

MATERIALS:
- "Four Problem Solving Suggestions" sample poster to share with students (next page)

COMMENTS FOR TEACHERS:
- Referring to the poster takes the pressure off the teacher to solve everything immediately.
- When students come to you with a problem, ask if they have tried the problem-solving suggestions. If not, ask them, which one(s) they would like to try.
- This is a simplified version of the Wheel of Choice activity and can be used as students begin to expand their toolbox for solving problems.

DIRECTIONS:

1. **Post the "Four Problem Solving Suggestions"** in the classroom.

2. **Describe/discuss each of the steps.**
   - Refer to chart below and discuss each option by asking students what they think the words mean and how or when they might use each option.

3. **Explain any exceptions you (or your school) require.**
   - Specify the issues you do want students to bring directly to you (for example, illness, fire, blood, bullying, etc.).

4. **Role-play.**
   - Divide the class into groups of 5 or 6.
   - Each group is to come up with a problem they would normally take to the teacher.
   - Have them role-play their problem for the class, using one of the "Four Problem Solving Suggestions" instead.

5. **Moving it forward.**
   - Share what the class has learned.
     - Video some of the role-plays and share them on closed circuit TV with the rest of the school (if your school has this technology available),
     - Share them at an assembly, or
     - Share with a younger class.
   - Teach the Wheel of Choice, which offers an expanded repertoire of options for students.

CHART
The Four Problem-Solving Suggestions

1. Ignore it.
   a. Act by walking away instead of reacting.
   b. Take a positive time out for cooling off.

2. Talk it over respectfully with every person involved.
   a. Share how you feel and listen to how others feel.
   b. Take responsibility for what you did to contribute to the problem.
   c. Share what you are willing to do differently.

3. Agree on a win-win solution.
   a. Brainstorm for ideas.
   b. Choose the solution that works best for all concerned.

4. Put the problem on the class meeting agenda.
   a. Consult with each other and learn from the problem.
   b. Brainstorm with more people to generate more ideas.

Essential Skills for Class Meetings: #5 Focusing on Solutions

Wheel of Choice

OBJECTIVE:
- To provide teachers and students with another tool for problem solving.

MATERIALS:
- "Wheel of Choice" handout
- Flip Chart and pens
- A large, pre-prepared, blank wheel of choice
- Optional: pre-cut wedges that fit onto the wheel of choice (Step 3, option 1)

COMMENTS FOR TEACHERS:
- Students feel empowered when they are included in the creation of choices.
- They then have "ownership" in the process and more enthusiasm and cooperation for a plan they helped create.
- The Wheel of Choice works best when it isn't the only option. It may be more effective to ask children, "Would you like to use the Wheel of Choice, or put this problem on the agenda so we can find a solution later?"
- Some schools give playground supervisors, lunch supervisors and bus drivers pocket-sized copies of a school Wheel of Choice to assist students in thinking of solutions.
- A large Wheel of Choice can be painted on the playground so that students can stand in choices as they think.

DIRECTIONS:
1. **Introduce the Wheel of Choice.**
   - Show your students the sample Wheel of Choice on the next page.
   - Explain, "The wheel is a tool for problem solving that anyone can use when they feel "stuck" and can't think of solutions."
   - Explain, "We will create choices for our own wheel."

2. **Brainstorm ideas for the Wheel of Choice.**
   - Brainstorm and record possible solutions for typical problems such as fighting or not taking turns.
   - Ensure you agree that each option is respectful *and* helpful.
   - Vote to choose 8 to 12 solutions to use for your Wheel of Choice.

3. **Build the wheel of choice.**
   Option 1:
   - Divide the class into small groups, one for each solution.
   - Give each group a wedge of the pie; have them write their solution on the wedge and illustrate their choice.
   - Have students paste the wedges carefully on the template for a completed wheel of choice.

   Option 2:
   - Write the solutions directly onto the pie chart leaving room for symbols or pictures.
   - Have small groups of students illustrate each segment.

4. **Practice.**
   - Ask, "Who would like to role-play students who are having a problem (e.g., a fight over sports equipment)?"
   - In the middle of the role-play, ask a student to present the completed Wheel of Choice and invite the role-players to choose a solution.
   - Repeat this for different problems and choices.

5. **Moving it forward.**
   - Laminate the wheel of choice and post it over the solution table, or where it can easily be seen.
   - Keep a small version available with a spinner attached.
   - Refer to the Wheel of Choice when students are solving problems during class meetings. "Are there any ideas on the Wheel of Choice that might be helpful for this problem?"

* You can purchase "The Wheel of Choice: A Problem-Solving Program" by Jane Nelsen and Lynn Lott at positivediscipline.com

Essential Skills for Class Meetings: #5 Focusing on Solutions

Wheel of Choice Sample

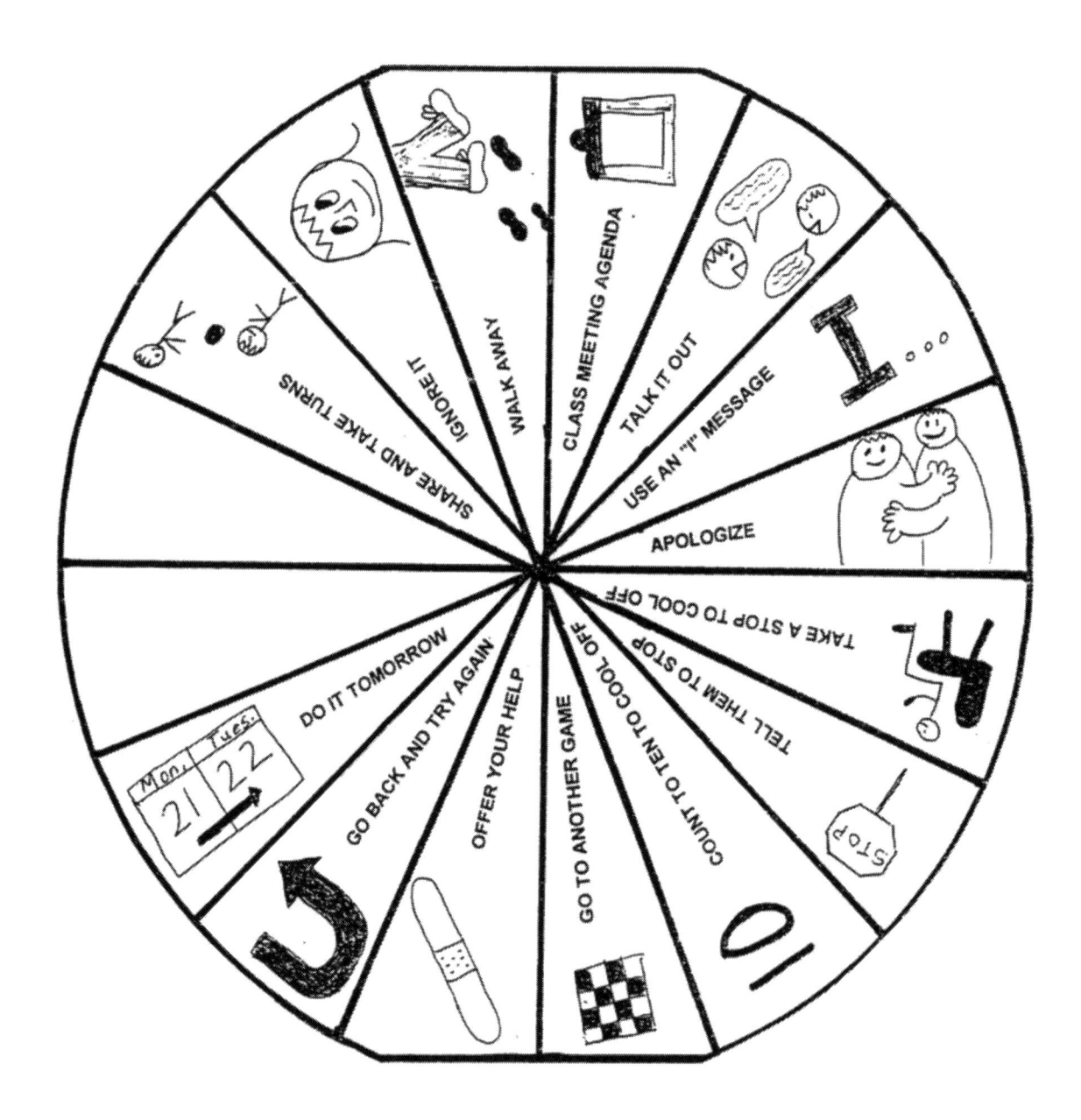

Appreciation is expressed to Dina Emser for sharing this wheel, created by 5 and 6-year-old students at Blooming Grove Academy in Bloomington, Indiana.

Wheel of Choice Sample

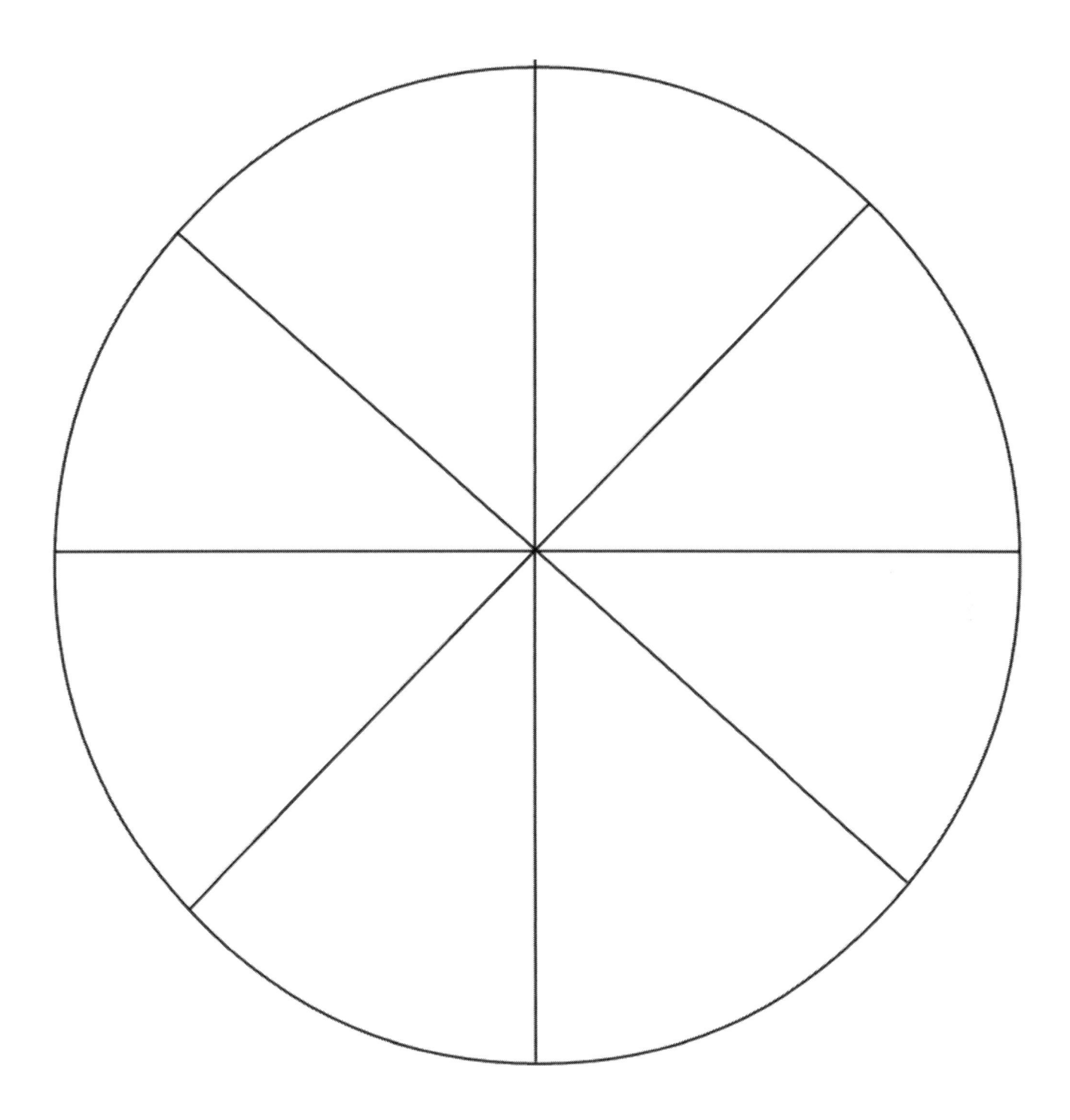

Essential Skills for Class Meetings: #5 Focusing on Solutions

Solution Table
By Stacy Lappin

OBJECTIVES:
- To establish a space in the classroom where students can solve problems with each other.
- To establish a clear and safe process for problem solving.

MATERIALS:
- A space for problem solving
- Sentence strips as appropriate for your students (See examples below)

COMMENTS FOR TEACHERS:
- It is important that students already have learned "Bugs and Wishes" or "I-Messages" before creating a solution table.
- A solution table is a place where students can discuss and solve problems.
- Physically, it can be a small table, desk or mat somewhere inside the classroom.
- It is helpful to have the steps written out so students have a format to follow while at the solution table.
- It is also helpful to have two students (of different genders) who have the job of being problem solving guides.

Sample sentence strips or posters to help students remember what to say both for "bug" and the response.
- "It bugs me when ____ and I wish _____." (bug and wand picture)
- "I heard you say ____" (This might be too much for many kindergarteners.)
- "I'll stop." (picture of a stop sign)
- "I'm sorry." (heart)
- "I'll do ____ instead." (stick figure with hand up)
- "I didn't know/mean to_____."

DIRECTIONS:

1. **Review problem solving language.**
   - Review **Bugs and Wishes** and/or **I-Messages** lesson(s). Focus review on the appropriate responses (**Bugs and Wishes**, step 6, **I-Messages**, step 5). These responses will include:
     "I'll stop."
     "I'm sorry."
     "I'll do ____ instead."
     "I didn't know/mean to."
   - Older students can learn to use reflective listening: "I heard you say_____" and repeat what they heard the person with the problem say.
   - *Move forward only when your students are skilled at helpful responses.* If not, go back and re-teach and practice the lessons.

2. **Setting up the problem-solving space.**
   - Involve students in the decision process (if there is choice) about location of the problem-solving site. It can be a small table, a mat on the floor under the posted guidelines, or a pair of chairs next to the posted guidelines.
   - Eventually your solution table (or mat/chairs) will have a variety of props. In the younger grades, it is helpful to add them one at a time so that students can use new ones as they are added. These might include:
     - A bug and a wand (see **Bugs and Wishes**)
     - Sentence strips for problem solving cues
     - A Wheel of Choice
     - The names of the students who have the job of "problem solving guides" that week.

3. **Creating guidelines.**
   Brainstorm some simple guidelines for using the solution space/table. Examples include:
   - The space can be used during "free" time; no line after recess.
   - Only the students solving the problem and their "guide" can be at the table at once.
   - Voices are quiet.
   - If someone asks you to come to the table, you come and talk it out even if you don't think it is a problem.
   - If you are stuck, stop and ask for help when the teacher is available or put the problem on the class meeting agenda, etc.

Essential Skills for Class Meetings: #5 Focusing on Solutions

4. **The problem-solving guides.**
   - Add "problem solving guide" to your weekly class job list (two students with the job each week).
   - The guides' job is:
     - To be an observer of the problem-solving process.
     - To make sure that each problem solver is listening and being helpful, not hurtful.

5. **Practicing in the space.**
   - Invite 3 volunteers to practice using the space. One has the problem, one is the person they have the problem with, and one is the problem-solving guide.
   - Choose a simple problem, such as one has taken a pencil without asking the other.
   - Allow them to choose one of the problem-solving props or suggestions (as in #3 above) and practice using it.
   - Ask the problem-solving guide what they noticed. Did the two students listen to each other? Were they helpful, not hurtful?

6. **Moving it forward**
   - Have the students use the solution table for a week and then ask them how it is going.
   - "Do the guidelines need to be changed?"
   - "Do you need more tools?"
   - "What have you learned?"

Essential Skills for Class Meetings: #5 Focusing on Solutions

Solutions vs. Logical Consequences

OBJECTIVE:
- To help teachers and students see the value of focusing on solutions instead of consequences.

MATERIALS:
- Flip Chart
- Marking Pens
- Poster:

> Solutions are:
> Reasonable
> Related
> Respectful
> AND
> Helpful

COMMENTS FOR TEACHERS:
- Using solutions creates a paradigm shift within a classroom. This is how students learn to be helpful, not hurtful and where they begin to deeply understand that mistakes are opportunities to learn.
- Though not intended as punishment, logical consequences often are perceived as such and break relationship bonds.
- The practice of using solutions instead of consequences is a shift, and some may question its application for the "real world." In a school environment, the focus needs to be on teaching and being helpful not hurtful.
- "Where did we ever get the crazy idea that in order to help students do better, first we have to make them feel worse? Students (and adults) do better when they feel better."
  – Jane Nelsen

DIRECTIONS:

1. **Set up scenario.**
   - Ask students to pretend that two names have been put on the agenda for coming in late from recess. (You can ask your older students to pretend that they are 4th graders for this activity.)
   - Have them think of consequences for these students. "What should we do to these students because they have been late?"
   - Record ideas on a flip chart/board. A typical list might include:
     Make them write their names on the board.
     Stay after school that many minutes.
     Take away minutes from tomorrow's recess.
     No recess tomorrow.
     Give them detention.
     The teacher could yell at them.

2. **Introduce solutions.**
   - Have a discussion about how we teach people by trying to make them "get it." This usually looks like hurting them in some way or "making them pay." We do this so often it may feel like the right thing to do.
   - Explain, "In our classroom, we will focus on solutions instead of consequences (helpful, not hurtful)."
   - Hold up the solutions poster and ask the class to share their understanding of each word: Reasonable, Related, Respectful and Helpful.

3. **Practice solutions.**
   - Using the example of the students who are tardy, ask the students now to brainstorm a list of solutions.
   - A typical list might look like:
     Someone could tap them on the shoulder when the bell rings.
     The student could have a job (line leader, collect equipment).
     Everyone could yell together, "Bell!"
     They could play closer to the building.
     They could watch to see when others are going in.
     They could play with a buddy.

   (**Note:** If students offer ideas that sound more like consequences, gently ask, "Can you help me understand how that is helpful?" Then help the student reframe the suggestion into a solution.)

4. Reflection.

Ask the students to reflect and have a dialogue.
- "What differences did you notice between the two lists?"
- "If you were one of the late students, which list would invite you to feel a greater sense of belonging in the group?"
- "Which list invites you to come in on time?"
- Ask one or two students, "Which solution would you choose if this were a real problem for you?"
- "For secondary students: How does this apply to being late in the morning, or being late for a class?"
- "Did it feel different when you brainstormed for solutions than when you brainstormed for consequences? How was it different?"
- "What did you learn from this activity?"
- "How can this approach help us as we problem solve during Class Meetings?"

Essential Skills for Class Meetings: #5 Focusing on Solutions

Solutions and Curiosity Questions, not Blame

OBJECTIVE:
- To introduce the concept of focusing on solutions instead of blame.

MATERIALS:
- Board
- Solutions poster (sample at the end of the lesson) or materials for students to create a solutions poster

COMMENTS FOR TEACHERS:
- Asking "why" someone did something invites blame.
- Asking curiosity questions invites solution-focused problem solving.
- **Stop the blame game:** Looking for blame or judging who is "right" or "wrong" gets in the way of solving the problem. Students can revert to blame easily. In the second part of the activity, your job is to interrupt the blaming and bring them back to solutions.

DIRECTIONS:

1. **Student reflection.**
   - Ask your students if they have ever been blamed for something.
   - What did they feel?
   - What did they learn?

2. **Using role-play to explore blame.**
   - Ask for volunteers to role-play one or more of the following situations using blame. Ask the blaming student to use "why" questions and accusing statements. ("Why did you do that? Why do you always get in my stuff?" "You never pay attention. You never think!")
     ○ A student takes someone else's lunch by mistake.
     ○ Two students argue over a pencil.
     ○ A student makes excuses for not turning in an assignment.
     ○ A student bumps into another student in the hall.

   Hint:
   - Remind students that this is a *role-play*. No one is really being blamed.

3. **Learn from the role-play.**
   - Ask each student in the role-play what they were feeling, thinking and learning.
   - Did you feel like you were about to flip your lid? (See **Brain in the Hand**)
   - Ask the group if there was much opportunity to repair the problem.

4. **Student reflection.**
   - Ask students, "What might have been different if the 'blaming' student was interested in solving the problem instead of figuring out who was 'right or wrong?'"
   - What kinds of statements might they have heard?

5. **Using curiosity to find solutions.** Explain to students, "One way to find a solution is to use curiosity questions. Most curiosity questions start with 'what' or 'how.'" Invite them to brainstorm curiosity questions beginning with 'what' or 'how' that might work for their role-plays. These might include things like:
   - "What just happened?"
   - "What do you think is going on?"

- "How did you feel about that?"
- "What might you do to change this?"
- "What did the other person say?"
- "What else could you have done?"
- "What other ideas do you have?"

6. **Practicing solutions**
   - Divide the class into small groups.
   - Ask each group to rewrite the original role-play(s) using curiosity questions and brainstorming to find a solution.
   - Allow several groups to share their new role-play.
   - Discuss what students are learning.

7. **Moving it forward.** Ask a volunteer to hang the pre-made poster or make a poster to hang in the room.

> We are **Looking for Solutions…**
> …not **blame!**

> We use curiosity:
> What….?
> How…?

Essential Skills for Class Meetings: #5 Focusing on Solutions

The Helpful, not Hurtful Monitor

Inspired by a 5th grade class at the Evergreen School, Shoreline, WA

OBJECTIVE:
- To give students practice and enhanced awareness of when suggestions are helpful, not hurtful.

MATERIALS:
- Equipment to make some kind of reversible "helpful/hurtful" sign
- A popsicle stick and paper plates work

COMMENT FOR TEACHERS:
- This activity is best after students have been problem solving in class meetings for several weeks. It is an advanced tool.
- This activity may not be necessary if students are successful at giving helpful solutions.

DIRECTIONS:

1. **Student reflection.**

   Ask students, "How are we doing at making problem solving suggestions in class meetings that are "helpful, not hurtful?" (You can use thumbs up/sideways/down.)

2. **The helpful, not hurtful monitor.**
   - Let the students know you would like to have a "helpful, not hurtful monitor" for class meetings so you aren't the only one paying attention to whether suggestions are helpful, not hurtful. This job would rotate like other classroom jobs.
   - That person would silently share their opinion by holding a sign that says "helpful" on one side, and "hurtful" on the other side.

3. **Thinking ahead.**
   - Ask students to brainstorm things that were said that weren't meant to be hurtful but were.
   - Ask students to brainstorm what to do if the monitor indicates that something was hurtful. Ideas might include offering a different solution, rephrasing what was said, withdrawing the suggestion, or asking for clarification.
   - Some classrooms need to practice this in role-plays to ensure students understand the monitor is offering a chance to make things better, instead of calling them out as "bad" or "wrong."

4. **Moving it forward: Make the sign.**
   - Have a small group of students make a "helpful, not hurtful" sign to use during class meetings.
   - Have the monitor use it during class meetings. This may take practice to do well.

A STORY

One fifth-grade class was having a problem with a game at recess. Students would get warm from running around, take off their coats and put them in a pile by the door. Some other students thought it was fun to take the coats and run with them, which started a game of chase. At the class meeting, one student asked that the class solve the problem because not everyone liked having their coat taken. The talking object was passed around the circle and suggestions were given. Every time a student talked about coats being "stolen," the helpful/hurtful monitor turned her sign around. The student giving the suggestion then gave the suggestion again using different words. The solution that the students eventually chose was to make two piles of coats: one for students who wanted to play the "chase the coat" game and one for students who didn't want to chase their coats. It was a surprising solution to the adults in the room, but it made perfect sense to the students.

Notes

Brainstorming and Role-playing
Essential Skill #6: Face Sheet

Concept: Brainstorming and role-playing

Brainstorming and role-playing are two tools that help students deepen their understanding of others and improve their ability to problem solve.

Brainstorming is a creative process for generating a list of possible solutions to a problem. Sometimes, even a crazy idea may stimulate useful ones. There are two main ways to brainstorm:

- By giving everyone a turn in order (structured), or
- By letting ideas flow quickly and spontaneously from anyone (popcorn).

There are advantages to each approach. **Class meetings use structured brainstorming** (each person gets a turn as the object is passed around the circle). There are several reasons for this:

- Each person exercises the option of deciding to speak or not speak, which encourages attention and participation.
- Quieter students have an opportunity to speak (and other students have an opportunity to hear their often very wise comments).
- There is a clear beginning and end.

Role-playing is a process by which students take on the role (real or imaginary) of another person to act out problems or practice solutions.

- Role-playing deepens students' understanding of each other's perspectives.
- Students do best when they *see and experience* both problems and possible solutions.
- It is important to remind students to exaggerate and have fun in the process.
- Adults are sometimes more uncomfortable than students with this process. Students benefit enormously from role-playing.

Why brainstorming and role-playing are important

Brainstorming is important because:

- Students learn that they can find solutions without adult help.
- They begin to recognize that "many minds are better than one."
- It teaches them to begin to reach for new possibilities and to listen to others.

Role-playing is important because:

- It allows students to get in another person's shoes and recognize that not everyone sees the world the same way (respecting differences).
- It offers students the opportunity to practice solutions. They learn that thinking about doing something (asking someone to stop bugging them, for example) is very different than actually doing it or watching someone else do it.

Essential Skills for Class Meetings: #6 Brainstorming and Role-playing

How class meetings teach role-playing and brainstorming
Class meetings use brainstorming and role-playing regularly. Students learn through practice. (Use it!)

What else are students learning?
- Problem solving
- Empathy
- Compassion
- Seeing the world through other people's eyes.

Recommended order for teaching *brainstorming and role-playing*
- *Paper Clip Activity*
- *Brainstorming*
- *Role-playing*
- *Role-playing and Brainstorming: Working with Guest Teachers*

Essential Skills for Class Meetings: #6 Brainstorming and Role-playing

Paper Clip Activity

Armelle Martin and Beatrice Sabate

OBJECTIVE:
- To give students an opportunity to explore and use the skills of brainstorming.
- To help students recognize that working together helps generate ideas.
- To help students recognize that shifting perspectives can generate more ideas.

MATERIALS:
- Paperclips or other object such as a clothespin, or pipe cleaner (one per student)
- Paper and pencils
- Pictures of persons or characters, a different one for each group

COMMENTS FOR TEACHERS:
1. This activity will need to be adapted for younger children.
2. Brainstorming and generating ideas is a powerful learning and academic tool.
3. Time invested in giving students the opportunity to practice helps them develop problem solving skills, creativity, appreciation for the perspective of others, solutions and collective responsibility.

DIRECTIONS:

1. **Individual brainstorming.**
   - Give each student a paperclip.
   - Tell them to work in silence, making their own list of all the possible uses they can imagine for that paperclip.

2. **Groups brainstorming.**
   - Have students move into groups of 4 with each member taking responsibility for a job: a timekeeper, a moderator (who keeps the group on task), a scribe, and a spokesperson.
   - In the small group, each person shares their ideas from Step 1 and the scribe records them.
   - The group continues to brainstorm additional ideas for a total of 5 minutes.

3. **Brainstorming with additional information.**
   - Give each group a picture of a person or character (any cartoon character, actor, actress, political figure, unknown people, whoever). Each group has a different picture.
   - Ask the groups to think about new ideas the picture may give them for using the paper clip.
   - Give groups 3 more minutes and again, record ideas.

4. **Process.**
   - Give each group 5 minutes to discuss what they noticed about brainstorming during this activity.
   - Have each group summarize the discussion into one or two sentences for the scribe to record.
   - Give them 3 more minutes to discuss what helped their group work efficiently. Summarize and record.
   - Have the spokespersons share what they recorded with the whole class.
   - Optional: Record the learning on chart paper.

5. **Draw connections to the classroom.**
   - Ask, "What did you learn from this activity that might be helpful in our classroom or class meetings?"
   - Ask, "From what we learned what will help us work together better as a group?"

Essential Skills for Class Meetings: #6 Brainstorming and Role-playing

Brainstorming

OBJECTIVE:
- To help students get into a rhythm of sharing ideas and solutions without judging or analyzing.
- To provide a structured process, giving space for each student to use his/her voice.

MATERIALS:
- Flip Chart/ Pens
- Talking stick object

COMMENTS FOR TEACHERS:
- When students know their idea will not be judged, it frees them to offer suggestions instead of playing it safe for fear of looking foolish.
- Using the process of passing the talking object around the circle invites quieter students to speak up. Others are often surprised by their wisdom.
- If a student makes an inappropriate but not hurtful comment, write it down and wait to use the process in number 2 to eliminate it.
- If a **student makes a hurtful comment,** it needs to be addressed right away. Say, "Help me understand how that comment is helpful, not hurtful." Invite the student to change it into a helpful comment. It only takes doing this a few times for students to understand that they don't get power or "juice" from hurtful comments and these comments gradually disappear from the circle.

DIRECTIONS:

1. **Teach brainstorming.**

   Share with students:
   - Brainstorming is a process we will use to think of as many ideas as possible in a short period of time, without criticizing or analyzing any suggestions.
   - When brainstorming in class meetings, the object is passed around the circle giving every person a chance to make a comment or suggestion, or to pass.
   - Only the person with the talking object speaks.
   - When brainstorming, it is fun to think "out of the box" or offer different ideas to start creative juices flowing.
   - The suggestions are meant to be helpful, not hurtful. (Refer to class guidelines, **Charlie** or **Respect for Self and Others** activity).
   - We are interested in how to repair mistakes, rather than who made them. (We are looking for solutions, not blame.)
   - Every suggested solution will be written down. Writing a brainstorm suggestion down doesn't mean it will work; it is just a suggestion. There will be time later to eliminate suggestions that are impractical or disrespectful, or do not follow class or school guidelines (see teacher comments).

2. **Practice brainstorming.**
   - Pick a group problem or a "pretend group problem" for practice.
   - Pass the object around the circle, giving each person an opportunity to offer a solution or pass.
   - Write the solutions on the board/flip chart (or have a student scribe for you).
   - Ask the students if they see any items listed that need to be eliminated because they are not helpful, reasonable, respectful, related to the problem, or go against school policy. If a suggestion is not appropriate put it in parenthesis.

3. **Pick the solution.**
   - Because it is a group problem, ask the students to vote on a solution that might work. (Note: Later, when working with problems involving individual students, voting is not used.)

Role-playing

OBJECTIVES:
- To learn and practice role-playing, a skill that will increase the effectiveness of problem solving.
- To deepen students' understanding of each others' perspective.

MATERIALS:
- Flip Chart Paper
- Markers

COMMENTS FOR TEACHERS:
- Role-playing is fun, especially for students.
- Role-playing brings greater understanding of the feelings involved in interactions.
- Role-playing gives students a chance to practice the problem-solving tools they are learning.
- Students love to role-play and sometimes beg to replay the scene over and over. They especially like playing the part of the teacher and watching the teacher pretend to be one of the students.
- Adults are often uncomfortable with role-playing. Because of the discomfort, this powerful tool is under-used.

DIRECTIONS:

1. **Getting ready.**
   - Choose a general problem that lends itself to role-playing and that will not be identified with any one particular student. Possibilities include cutting in line, yelling out in class, or not being prepared for class.

2. **Teach role-play.**
   - Ask how many students have ever role-played before.
   - Point out that role-playing is like putting on a play where class members will pretend to be different people involved in the problem they want to solve.
   - Engage students in thinking about role-playing by asking if they can guess three rules for role-playing.
   - Acknowledge the students' guesses.
   - Then share the three important rules:
     1. You have to exaggerate.
     2. You have to have fun.
     3. Keep it short.

3. **Getting ready to practice.**
   - Invite the students to help you set up a role-play. Describe a time the problem occurred. (Do not use names.)
   - Give enough detail that other people in the class will know how to role-play the different parts.
   - If additional details are needed, ask some of the following questions: "What happened? Then what happened? What did you do? What did the other person do? What did you say? What did the other person say?"
   - Review the lines and actions and ask for volunteers to play out the scene.
   - Play the scene in the middle of the circle.

4. **Learn from the role-play.**
   - It is important to process feelings and decisions after each role-play so students understand how each person sees the problem. This is where the greatest learning takes place.
   - Ask each of the players, "What were you thinking, feeling, or deciding to do as the person you were playing?"

5. **Moving it forward: role-playing the solution.**
   - Brainstorm some solutions for the problem.
   - Invite the students to role-play the solution they chose.
   - Process the solution role-play by asking the questions listed above.

Essential Skills for Class Meetings: #6 Brainstorming and Role-playing

Role-playing and Brainstorming: Working with Guest Teachers (Substitutes)

OBJECTIVES:
- To teach and/or practice brainstorming and role-playing.
- To increase student ownership and readiness for guest/substitute teachers.

MATERIALS:
- Flip Chart Paper
- Markers

COMMENTS FOR TEACHERS:
- This is an application of brainstorming and role-playing that teaches by "doing." It can be preceded or followed by the role-playing and brainstorming activities.
- Though many class meeting agenda items get role-played at the "problem" stage, this activity only uses a role-play at the solution stage.
- Sometimes it is helpful to play the same scene a second time with different actors so that students can integrate what they have learned.

DIRECTIONS:

1. **Getting ready.**
   - Have students think about a time when there will be a guest/substitute teacher in the room.
   - Say, "Think about what you could do to help the guest teacher feel welcome and to make it a good day for teaching and learning."

2. **Brainstorm ideas.**
   - Give students a moment to think. Then pass the object around the circle so that each student can offer a suggestion or pass.
   - Scribe all of the suggestions.
   - Ask, "Are there any suggestions that wouldn't work because they are disrespectful, don't follow school guidelines, or cost too much?" Put a parenthesis around those.

3. **Set up role-play.**
   - Pick one or two of the ideas to role-play. Usually the class offers an idea that includes some kind of welcome or introduction of the guest teacher.
   - Ask for a volunteer to be the guest teacher.
   - Ask for a volunteer to be the introducing student.
   - Ask the student if they need any suggestions for things to say to introduce themself to the teacher or the teacher to the class. (Offer or invite ideas from the class as appropriate.)

4. **Action.**
   - Have the students "perform" the role-play.

5. **Process the role-play.**
   - Ask the "guest teacher" how it felt to be welcomed. Ask, "Were you thinking or deciding anything about our class?" "Were you thinking or deciding anything about yourself?"
   - Ask the "student" what they were feeling. Ask, "Were you thinking or deciding anything about the guest teacher?" "About yourself?"

6. **Moving it forward.**
   - Ask the class what they learned from this activity. (Students often reflect on how they can help the guest teacher.)
   - Make a plan for how the rest of the solutions will be implemented. (Some classes talk about creating a routine book, having jobs to help the guest teacher, having maps, having student guides etc.)

Using the Class Meeting Format and Agenda
Essential Skill #7: Face Sheet

Concept: The Class Meeting Format and Agenda

The *class meeting format* provides a structure and process for safely solving problems in a Positive Discipline Class Meeting. In Positive Discipline Class Meetings, the agenda is the list of issues or problems that have been written down before the meeting starts.

The class meeting format is a specific process for how each class meeting is conducted. The order is as follows:

CLASS MEETING FORMAT

1. Compliments
2. Follow up on prior solutions
3. Agenda items:
    - Share feelings while others listen *or*
    - Discuss without fixing *or*
    - Ask for problem solving help
4. Closing Activity or class planning (field trips/parties/projects)

Compliments (#1): The talking object is passed around the circle for compliments or appreciations.

Following up on prior solutions (#2): All solutions are reviewed after an agreed-upon time period (usually one or two weeks) to see if the solution worked.

- If it is working, the leader says, "Thank you."
- If the solution to a group problem is not working, the leader invites the person with the problem to put it back on the agenda for a future meeting.
- If the solution to an individual problem is not working the students can put it back on the agenda or, after the meeting, they can look at the list of solutions from the previous meeting and see if there is another they would like to try.

Agenda items (#3): The leader first addresses any problem unfinished from the previous meeting and then takes new agenda items in order.

- The leader asks if the problem is still an issue.
    - If the answer is "no," the student is asked if they would like to share the outcome or solution.
    - If the answer is "yes" (it is still a problem), then problem solving begins.

Essential Skills for Class Meetings: #7 Using the Class Meeting Format and Agenda

- The student chooses how to solve the problem (share feelings while others listen, discuss without fixing, or ask for problem solving help).
- The student shares their perspective/feelings. With an individual problem, the second student also shares their perspective/feelings. (They don't have to agree.)
- If the student chose "share my feelings, while others listen," (because the student shared their perspective/feelings) the chairperson says, "Thank you," and moves on to the next problem.
- If the student chose "discuss without fixing," the leader passes the talking object around the circle giving each participant an opportunity to offer a comment, a suggestion or pass.
- After the object goes around, the chairperson says, "Thank you, I hope this was helpful." and moves on to the next problem.
- If the student chose "ask for problem solving help," the leader passes the talking object around the circle giving each participant an opportunity to offer a solution or pass.
- All brainstormed solutions are recorded.
- The method for choosing a solution is dictated by the type of problem.
    - If it is a **group problem**, all students vote. The vote is typically by majority.
    - If it is an **individual student problem**, the student with the problem chooses the solution that will work best for them.
    - If it is a **problem between two or more students**, the student who put it on the agenda chooses the solution they think will work for all of them. The other student(s) involved then either agree or suggest another solution that will work for everyone. The students will learn to think about what might work for the other person as they agree on one solution. (This should not be a negotiation. If they can't agree quickly, either have them meet after the meeting and pick a solution from the list to try for a week or put it back on the agenda for more solutions at another meeting.)

Closing activity or class planning (#4): Classrooms use this time to plan parties, field trips, and curriculum. This is not done at every meeting, but may be included when planning is necessary and/or when there are no other agenda items. It is helpful to finish meetings with a short closing activity. See list of Class Meeting Closers in the Handout section of this manual.

The Agenda. All Positive Discipline Class Meetings use an agenda.

- All problems to be solved in a class meeting must be on the agenda before the meeting starts.
- Problems are put on the agenda (by students and the teacher) as they arise between meetings.
- The physical agenda looks different in different classrooms.
    - It may be a clipboard, a notebook or a box.
    - An effective agenda system tracks who had the problem, a brief summary of the problem and some way of marking the order in which it was submitted.
    - When a student approaches a teacher with a problem that could be solved in a class meeting, the teacher can respond by saying, "Have you tried the four problem solving suggestions?" "Is this a problem that the class could help you with in a class meeting?"

Essential Skills for Class Meetings: #7 Using the Class Meeting Format and Agenda

Why the class meeting format and using an agenda are important

The class meeting format:

- Creates a regular process for addressing problems, and
- Offers students a predictable and safe way to approach their problems.

The agenda helps students:

- Articulate and document their problem,
- Think about how they would like to solve the problem, and
- Have time for cooling off. (Problems are rarely addressed the day they occur.)

What else are students learning? Class meetings look like they are about problem solving but they are the laboratory for practicing Positive Discipline, a comprehensive social and emotional learning curriculum. Students are practicing all of their SEL skills. They are learning how to feel included and valued in a learning community. Through the class meeting process students learn how to:

- Become a community
- Self-regulate
- Use effective communication skills
- Mutual respect
- Demonstrate mutual respect
- Build cooperation, connection and empathy
- Experience mistakes as opportunities to learn
- Encourage and compliment others
- See differences as assets and listen to others' ideas
- Focus on solutions and be helpful, not hurtful
- Brainstorm

They also learn:

- How people can work effectively together to solve problems
- A respectful and safe structure can help us tackle very difficult issues
- How to wait to solve problems
- How to articulate a problem so that others can help
- A solution doesn't always fix something forever, and problems can be re-solved

Recommended order for teaching the class meeting format and using the agenda:

1. **Introducing the Class Meeting Format**
2. **We Decided: Guidelines for Class Meetings**
3. **Our Class Meeting Agenda** (Review sample agendas following lesson before teaching.)
4. **Introducing the Class Meeting Format - Group Problems**
5. **Class Meeting Agenda Using Individual Problems**

General tips

- Class meetings are suggested 3-5x /week in elementary schools and 1-2 x/week in secondary schools. Students need to practice this regularly to develop their skills.
- In middle and high schools, class meetings are best offered in the advisory period and comprise an excellent social learning curriculum.
- If you have options, be intentional about what time of day you schedule your class meetings.
- Some classrooms suggest steps before putting items on the agenda like letting the other person know that the item is on the agenda, and first using one or two other problem solving tools (e.g. Solution Table, Wheel of Choice, Four Problem Solving Steps, or Bugs and Wishes).
- Using student names as part of the problem-solving process can feel daunting to many teachers. However, by the time the "Preparing the Ground" steps have been taught and students have the skills to be helpful, not hurtful, using names empowers students to do real problem solving.
- Occasionally one student ends up "on the agenda" repeatedly. This can be discouraging for the student. It can be helpful for the teacher to ask the class to give the student an agenda break so that they can work on the solutions already generated.
- Resist the temptation to handle all classroom issues yourself. You will miss opportunities to involve students in learning how to think critically, how to problem solve, how to contribute, and how to help each other.
- Though teachers need to review the agenda to ensure that the problems are class meeting appropriate, it should be set primarily by students.
- Students have an easier time accepting solutions when there is a clear time frame. For example, "We will try this for one week, until our meeting next Friday."
- Time and timing of class meetings:
  - Class meetings should be limited to 15-20 minutes (depending on student age).
  - Teachers often hold meetings just before an event with a clear starting time, such as recess, lunch, or the end of class.
  - If an agenda item is not finished, it becomes the first item for the next meeting. Typically, the solutions are read and the object is passed around the entire circle for additional solutions.

OTHER RESOURCES

Building Classroom Community – a video of a 5th grade class doing a class meeting. It can be purchased at https://www.positivediscipline.com/products/building-classroom-community-dvd

Essential Skills for Class Meetings: #7 Using the Class Meeting Format and Agenda

Positive Discipline Class Meetings Overview

Inspired by the work of Jane Nelsen and Lynn Lott
Sound Discipline

This is meant to be a quick guide or can be used as a checklist for your class meetings.

Classroom
___ Class meeting format is posted/ visible in the classroom

The Circle
___ Getting in a circle: quickly, quietly, safely
___ Everyone sitting at the same level in the circle (including the teacher)
___ Students leave the circle quickly, quietly, safely

Compliments
___ Object is passed
___ Compliment is given directly to the person "Name, I compliment you for _____"
___ Compliment is acknowledged, "Thank you, Name."
___ Compliments are inside vs. outside compliments (long-term goal)
___ Compliments are smooth (e.g. had think time and can move through process)

Review previous solutions
___ Object is passed
___ Previous solutions reviewed
___ If still a problem, student has choice to put back on agenda

Current agenda
___ Written agenda is used
___ Object is passed
___ Student chooses one of the 3 ways to solve the problem
      o Share while others listen
      o Discuss without fixing
      o Ask for problem solving help
___ If it is a group problem, class votes
___ If it is an individual problem, the students involved solve the problem
___ Solutions are helpful, not hurtful
___ The teacher is part of the meeting but doesn't take over or make lots of comments
___ Teacher steps in if hurtful

Planning or closing activity

Other:
___ Item always goes around the circle (compliments, brainstorming)
___ Students are listening to each other
___ Meeting is 20 minutes or less
___ Students have basic skills (listening, mistakes are opportunities, helpful, not hurtful)

More advanced:
___ Student-led meeting
___ Student takes notes
___ Role-play is used

Essential Skills for Class Meetings: #7 Using the Class Meeting Format and Agenda

Introducing the Class Meeting Format

OBJECTIVE:
- To talk through the format for class meetings.

MATERIALS:
Poster of the Class Meeting Format (see below)

COMMENTS FOR TEACHERS:
- The routine of this consistent structure is helpful to students and teachers. Not following the routine is one of the most common mistakes in implementing class meetings.
- Teachers often handle classroom issues themselves, missing opportunities to involve students in learning how to think, problem solve, contribute, and help each other.
- If needed, review Introducing the Class Meetings (in the "Buy-In" section).
- Details about the Agenda will be dealt with in "Our Class Meeting Agenda."

CLASS MEETING FORMAT

1. Compliments
2. Follow up on previous solutions
3. Agenda items:
   - Share feelings while others listen
   OR,
   - Discuss without fixing
   OR
   - Ask for problem solving help.
4. Closing Activity or class planning (field trips/parties/projects)

DIRECTIONS:

1. **Post the poster: Class Meeting Format.**

2. **Sitting in a circle.**
   Explain, "Class meetings are always held in a circle and have an object ready to pass."

3. **Using poster, share overview of steps.**
   Step 1. "We begin by sharing compliments and appreciations."
   Step 2. Prior solutions.
   - The leader asks if the solution is working.
   - If the solution is working, the leader says, "Thank you."
   - If it is not working, the leader invites the person with the problem to put it on the agenda for a future meeting *or* to privately review other solutions and try a different approach.

   Step 3. Agenda items.
   - Agenda items are addressed in order.
   - The leader of the meeting first asks the person who put the problem on the agenda if it is still a problem.
   - If it is still a problem that person can either:
     a. Share his or her feelings while others listen, *or*
     b. Ask for discussion without fixing, or
     c. Ask for problem solving help.

   Step 4. Planning or fun activity.
   - "On occasion, time will be saved at the end of our meeting for planning. "
   - Planning might include details for a field trip, equipment for recess, due dates for projects or curriculum choices when available.
   - It is helpful to close the meeting with a short, fun activity. See: Class Meeting Closers in the Handout section of this manual, for ideas.

4. **Set the stage.**
   Tell the class:
   - "We will talk more about the agenda and the options for problem solving."
   - "We will all work together to learn how to use class meetings to solve problems by focusing on solutions."
   - "We'll begin by using "practice" problems to ensure that the class is skilled at suggesting helpful solutions."
   - "We'll also make time to practice real problems that impact everyone."

Essential Skills for Class Meetings: #7 Using the Class Meeting Format and Agenda

We Decided: Guidelines for Class Meetings

OBJECTIVE:
- To create guidelines for class meetings.

MATERIALS:
- Board
- Materials for a poster

COMMENTS FOR TEACHERS:
- This is an activity that is done *after* students have an idea of what class meetings are, but *before* class meetings have started.
- It is assumed that the class already has guidelines for how students treat each other in the classroom. (See **"Beginning the Almost Perfect School Year"**.) Some classrooms find that their classroom agreements are sufficient in the class meeting circle as well. The class can help you decide whether additional agreements are necessary.
- The safety of the class meeting circle is extremely important. If a problem occurs that is not addressed by the guidelines, suggest the class consider a revision of the guidelines.

DIRECTIONS:

1. **Brainstorm.**
   - Ask, "What do you need from each other to be able to work together and feel safe in a class meeting?" Common examples include: Listen while others talk, tell the truth, help each other, look for solutions, keep your hands to yourself, take turns, etc.
   - Write all of the suggestions on the board.
   - Ask, "Do our classroom guidelines cover this or do we need a few more guidelines to make sure that our class meetings are helpful, not hurtful?"
   - Proceed if the class decides that extra guidelines are needed.

2. **Vote.**
   - Ask students to vote for the three that they think are the most important.
   - Tally the votes and use the top 3 – 5 ideas.

3. **Make a poster and sign on.**
   - Have student volunteers make a poster to display chosen guidelines. Use their words, for example:

     OUR CLASS MEETING - WE DECIDED

     Listen while others talk

     Help each other

     Look for solutions

   - Have each student sign the poster as acknowledgment of their agreement.

4. **Moving it forward (the follow through).** After the poster has been made, review, pause and reflect at meetings:
   - "Show me with a thumb up, sideways or down how we are doing on [guideline]? ("Show me how you think we are doing on our 'listen while others talk' guideline.")
   - "Think of one small thing YOU can do to help us meet this guideline better. Please do it now."
   - It is important to do this when things are going well so students can see their progress.
   - Non-judgmental observations help students become more aware. For example: "I can tell you are excited about the field trip tomorrow and it is harder to listen while others talk."

Positive Discipline in the School and Classroom Manual
by Jane Nelsen, Lynn Lott, Teresa LaSala, Jody McVittie, and Suzanne Smitha

Essential Skills for Class Meetings: #7 Using the Class Meeting Format and Agenda

Our Class Meeting Agenda

OBJECTIVES:
- To agree on how to record items for the agenda and possible solutions.
- To establish agreement about how the agenda is used.

MATERIALS:
- Board
- Sample agenda slips (see Sample Agendas in this section)

COMMENTS FOR TEACHERS:
- Before beginning problem solving and using the agenda, students must be skilled at being helpful, not hurtful. In some groups, this takes quite a bit of time.
- Positive Discipline Class Meetings use an agenda. The items are addressed in order. If an item is not on the agenda in advance, it is not discussed. This means that as the teacher, you too use the agenda.
- It is important to keep agenda items in order so that there is a sense of fairness and so that parties involved have a chance to cool down before problem solving.
- Students are not always used to helping each other or coming up with solutions. They may be afraid to use the agenda if they are not confident that their peers will be helpful, not hurtful.
- Investing time in setting up the process for using a class meeting agenda saves time and avoids confusion later. Keeping track of all proposed solutions can become a valuable resource for students working on solving new problems.
- The agenda should be primarily for student problems. Teacher's problems can be put on the agenda sparingly.

DIRECTIONS:

1. **Setting the stage.**
   - When the class is ready, let them know they are now skilled enough at being helpful, not hurtful to begin class meetings. (If this skill is missing, they are not ready for problem solving.)
   - One remaining step is to figure out how to keep track of the problems that they want to solve and how to keep track of the solutions they propose.

2. **Invite reflection. Ask,**
   - "Why is it important to keep track of the items on the agenda?" (It is fair to keep items in order and we have a chance to cool down before problem solving.)
   - "Why might it be helpful to keep track of the solutions you come up with? "(To remember what you have decided, use them as a resource for solving other problems, to be able to follow up and see if they are working.)
   - Invite the class to think of ways to do both respectfully.

3. **Share what other classrooms have done.**

   It may be helpful to offer options for ways to place items on the agenda and to keep track of solutions. Options include:
   - **Box.** When someone has a problem, they fill out a piece of paper and put it in the box. The class keeps a separate notebook for meeting notes and solutions.
   - **Notebook.** The class keeps blank agenda slips in the notebook and writes solutions on the back of the agenda slip.
   - **Clipboard.** Agenda items are written on paper kept on the clipboard. The class keeps a separate notebook for meeting notes and solutions.
   - **Flip chart** or **dry erase board.** The class keeps a separate notebook for meeting notes and solutions.

4. **Discuss and make decisions.**
   - "Which type of agenda will be chosen from the options above?"
   - "How will we keep track of the order in which items were put on the agenda?"
   - "How will the group keep track of solutions?"
   - "What sort of agenda slip is best for the group?"
   - "Make a clear plan about where the agenda will be kept and when it can be used."

© Positive Discipline Association ■ www.PositiveDiscipline.org

5. Share.

- Say, "At first we will use the agenda only for problems that involve the whole class" (group problems).
- "As our skills develop, we will move on to solving problems that involve fewer people. You might want to ask for help on a problem that you are having by yourself or with one or two other people."
- "We know we are better problem solvers when we are cooled off. One of the reasons we use the agenda is so we remember to solve the problem. We won't solve the problem immediately. We solve it after we have had a chance to cool off."

Modifications

When students can't yet write:

- Use the sample drawing agenda pages in this section.
- Use a clipboard with a pencil tied to it, and allow students to write what they can (maybe only their name) and then bring it to an adult who will write down the problem.
- Give each student a clothespin with their name on it that they keep in their cubby; when they want to put an item on the agenda, they clip their clothespin to the side of the agenda clipboard, or drop it into a basket. (Note: When they don't write the problem down, they sometimes forget what it was. That's okay; learning still happens!)

SAMPLE AGENDA SLIPS

Agenda Item

Name _____

Date _____ Time _____

I have tried the following problem-solving tool(s):

1. ____ Ignored it
2. ____ Talked it over respectfully with the other person
3. ____ Agreed upon a win/win solution
4. ____ Bugs and wishes
5. ____ Wheel of choice

I would like help from the class to solve this problem (state the problem):

_____

At the class meeting I think I would like to:

__Share my feelings while others listen

__Discuss without fixing

__Ask for problem solving help

Solutions from class:

Essential Skills for Class Meetings: #7 Using the Class Meeting Format and Agenda

Sample Kindergarten Agenda

Name _____ Date _____ Time _____

The Problem is:

_____

_____

The solution I chose is: _____

_____

Essential Skills for Class Meetings: #7 Using the Class Meeting Format and Agenda

Sample Primary Grade Agenda

Stacy Lappin

Name _____ Date _____ Time _____

Describe the problem:

_____
_____
_____

Who are you having the problem with?

_____

Circle the words that describe the problem:

cutting in line	hitting	pushing
name calling	stealing	lying
not playing fair	fighting	
not listening		

Circle how you tried to solve the problem:

deep breath	bugs & wishes	take a break
use quiet signal	ignore	walk away
talk it out	put on agenda	count to 10

Picture of the problem (on back of page):

Solutions:

Essential Skills for Class Meetings: #7 Using the Class Meeting Format and Agenda

Sample Agenda Slip for Older Students

Name _____ Today's Date _____ Time _____

BRIEF description of problem:

_____
_____
_____
_____

I have already tried to solve this problem by:

_____
_____
_____
_____

I think I will want to (check one)

__ Share my feelings while others listen

__ Discuss without fixing

__ Ask for problem solving help

Solutions we brainstormed: _____ Follow up date: _____

Introducing the Class Meeting Format – Group Problems

OBJECTIVES:
- To focus on the three ways problems are handled in class meetings.
- To practice with group problems before beginning to solve individual problems.

MATERIALS:
- Poster of the Class Meeting Format (below)
- An "object" that can be passed around the circle to indicate who has permission to speak
- Tools for recording solutions (flip chart/notebook)

COMMENTS FOR TEACHERS:
- This activity is best done in a circle so it models the class meeting process.
- This activity builds on previous skills and gives some structure and predictability to the methods used to problem solve.
- As students practice using the agenda format, *one of the teacher's jobs is to make sure that comments remain helpful, not hurtful. Some classrooms use "practice" problems until it is clear that the students can be both respectful and helpful. Other classrooms use real problems but handle only whole group problems until the students are more skilled.*
- If your students still struggle finding helpful solutions, review the lesson, **Solutions vs. Logical Consequences**.
- This activity teaches the process with group problems. The process of choosing a solution is different for individual problems. See **Class Meeting Agenda Using Individual Problems**.

DIRECTIONS:

1. **Post and review the "Class Meeting Format" chart.**
   - When an agenda item is addressed, the person who put it on the agenda chooses one of three ways to handle the issue. They can:
     a. Share feelings while others listen
     b. Discuss without fixing
     c. Ask for problem solving help

2. **Explain the options:**

A. *Share feelings while others listen.*
   - The person with the problem shares with the group. No object is passed.
   - Briefly discuss:
     o "What might a person learn from this option?"
     o "What is the role of the rest of the class?" (respectful listening)

B. *Discuss without fixing.*
   - The person shares with the group.
   - The object is passed around the circle so each person has an opportunity to make a comment about the issue, offer a suggestion, or pass.
   - No solution is chosen.
   - Briefly discuss:
     o "What might a person learn from this option?" (Sometimes just sharing ideas about a problem is enough.)
     o "What is the role of the rest of the class?" (sharing ideas)

C. *Ask for problem solving help.*
   - The person shares with the group.
   - The object is passed around the circle so each person has an opportunity to offer a solution, or pass.
   - A solution is chosen (by vote for class problems).
   - Briefly discuss:
     o "What might a person learn from this option?" (There may be many options for solving a problem.)
     o "What is the role of the rest of the class?" (brainstorming respectful solutions)

Essential Skills for Class Meetings: #7 Using the Class Meeting Format and Agenda

> **CLASS MEETING FORMAT**
>
> 1. Compliments
>
> 2. Follow up on previous solutions
>
> 3. Agenda items:
>   - Share feelings while others listen, *or*
>   - Discuss without fixing, *or*
>   - Ask for problem solving help.
>
> 4. Closing Activity or class planning (field trips/parties/projects)

3. **Practice using different ways to solve problems.**
   - Ask the class to brainstorm some minor problems that could occur in school that would affect most students. (Examples: cafeteria noise, loud hallways, forgotten recess equipment, talking during quiet work time.)
   - Write a few of these where all students can see them.

A. *Sharing feelings:*
   - Have a volunteer pick one of the problems to demonstrate how to share feelings while others listen.
   - It is important for students to use "I-statements" rather than blaming or accusing others. *This is the time to ensure that the class understands that "sharing feelings" does not involve blaming others.*
   - Thank the volunteer.

B. *Discuss without fixing:*
   - Have a volunteer pick one of the problems and begin the "discuss without fixing" process by sharing the problem with the class.
   - Pass the object around the circle giving each person a chance to "discuss without fixing," to make a comment or a suggestion, or to pass.
   - Thank the volunteer.

C. *Ask for problem solving help.*
   - Have a volunteer pick one of the problems on the list and begin the "ask for problem solving help" process by sharing the problem with the class.
   - Pass the object around the circle, giving each person a chance to offer a solution or pass.
   - Solutions are recorded.
   - Solutions are read after the object has gone around the circle once.
   - Since the practice problem is a "group problem," the person leading the meeting asks the class to vote on a solution to try for the next week.

Class Meeting Agenda Using Individual Problems

OBJECTIVE:
- To learn and practice how to solve individual or small group problems using class meetings.

MATERIALS:
- Talking stick/object
- Book for recording solutions
- Poster of class meeting format

COMMENTS FOR TEACHERS:
- This activity is to be taught after "Introducing the Class Meeting Format - Group Problems".
- Classrooms are ready for individual problem solving when the teacher is confident that students can be helpful, not hurtful.
- Names are used in problem solving. (Students know who the person is anyway).
- The class will become comfortable using students' names in a respectful way and teachers must support this practice.
- Many teachers are concerned about using student names. It is our experience that using names is helpful, *and* it is extremely important that the class be prepared.
- The students (and teacher) must be skilled at being helpful, not hurtful, which requires teaching and practice.
- It is important to have the student choose how the problem will be solved.
- Notice that before problem solving both students involved have an opportunity to share their perspectives without name calling or blaming. They do not need to agree.

DIRECTIONS:

1. **Reflection.**

Reflect with your classroom about what kinds of solutions they have found for group problems.

- "What is working?"
- "What could work better?"
- "How has focusing on solutions helped our class?"

2. **Introducing individual problem solving.**

Explain that your students now know how helpful it can be to solve problems as a group.

- Let them know they now have the skill to do this respectfully.
- Remind them that mistakes are an opportunity to learn.

3. **When is it okay to put items on the agenda?**

Often there are problems between two or more students. Some students may still feel embarrassed if their name shows up on the agenda. Ask students:

- "If you have a problem you haven't been able to solve with another student and you know that we are all here to help both of you respectfully, would you use the class meeting to get some help?"
- "Is it important that you give that person an opportunity to solve the problem with you another way?" (**Solution Table, Wheel of Choice, Bugs and Wishes,** and the **R's of Recovery** are examples.)
- "If you have a problem with another student that you can't solve by yourselves, is it important to let them know ahead of time that you will be asking the class for help with the problem?" (Yes, no one wants to be surprised.)
- Support your class in figuring out whether it is important to write what they have already tried on your agenda forms. (Note: This can change over time, as students get more skilled and comfortable.)

4. **Using solutions.**

Remind your class about solutions: They are reasonable, related, respectful and helpful.

5. **Practice.**

It is important to practice with imaginary individual problems before asking students to try it with a real problem.

- Say, "We are going to practice with an imaginary problem so everyone knows how it works. We will assume that the students have already tried other ways to solve the problem."

Positive Discipline in the School and Classroom Manual
by Jane Nelsen, Lynn Lott, Teresa LaSala, Jody McVittie, and Suzanne Smitha

Essential Skills for Class Meetings: #7 Using the Class Meeting Format and Agenda

- Use a relatively simple problem: one student takes a pencil without asking.
- Ask for two students to be volunteers. One student will have put the problem on the agenda; the other student will be the one who took the pencil.

Choose how the problem will be solved

- Ask the first student how they would like to solve the problem. (Share feelings while others listen, discuss without fixing, or ask for problem solving help.)

Begin problem solving:

- Ask the first student to share their perspective on the problem without name calling or blaming.
- Ask the second student to share their perspective on the problem. They do not need to agree.
- If the student picked "share feelings while others listen," the process stops after both students have shared their perspectives/feelings.
- If the student chose "discuss without fixing" pass the talking object so students can make a comment or suggestion, or pass.
- If the student chose "ask for problem solving help," pass the object around for solutions.

Role-play (optional):

- Students may choose to role-play the problem (at the beginning) and/or the solution (after it is chosen).

Choosing the solution:

When a student puts an item on the agenda about another student and asks for problem solving help, the process for picking a solution is as follows:

- The student with the problem (who put it on the agenda) is asked to choose from the list of solutions, thinking about one that will work for them and the other student(s) involved.
- The other student involved is then asked if they would be willing to try that solution for a week. If they answer "yes", the solution is noted in the agenda book. If they answer "no", they are asked to pick a different solution that might work for all parties. This usually goes quite quickly.

Following up:

- Explain to students that one week later, during the class meeting, the chairperson will ask the volunteers if the solution that they chose worked. If not, they will be given the option of trying a different solution (from the saved list), or to put it back on the class meeting agenda (to be handled in turn).

6. Moving it forward.

Tell students that from now on, when they come to you with a concern (that doesn't involve someone being sick, someone about to be hurt or something dangerous), you will remind them about their problem-solving tools. After trying a problem-solving tool, they can put the problem on the meeting agenda.

Understanding and Using the Four Mistaken Goals
Essential Skill #8: Face Sheet

Concept: Understanding and using the four mistaken goals (the belief behind the behavior)

Positive Discipline uses a framework for helping people understand that the "problem we see is often a solution to another problem" that might not be as apparent. It is an advanced concept, so many teachers teach this skill last.

Why the belief behind the behavior is important

- It is helpful for students to understand that what behavior looks like on the outside might not be what it means on the inside.
- When students understand that misbehavior can be a way to feel "I fit / belong" or "I matter," they can help each other find better ways to be part of the classroom community.
- Seeing beyond what "behavior looks like" to guess what might be "behind the behavior" can help students develop a sense of compassion and improve their ability to problem solve.
- Students develop an understanding of why people do what they do.
- Students gain insight into their own behaviors.

How class meetings teach the belief behind the behavior

- As students get more practice at problem solving, they begin to develop curiosity about the "why" of behavior.
- As students develop skills for seeing the world through another's eyes they become more skilled problem solvers.
- The class meeting leader can invite students to think about the belief behind the behavior as they look for solutions.

Example: In one 4th grade classroom, students were discussing how to behave when a student from another class seemed aggressive. Appropriately, they were talking about things that they could do that were respectful. Halfway around the circle one boy remarked, "I know that Joey seems pushy, but I think it is his way of saying, 'I want to be your friend.'" This student was able to see beyond the behavior and make a guess about what might be going on inside. After the student made that observation, the other students were able to generate ideas for more useful ways to help Joey make friends in the future.

What else are students learning?

- That people usually are doing the best they can at that moment.
- Compassion for others.

Essential Skills for Class Meetings: #8 Understanding and Using the Four Mistaken Goals

Recommended order for teaching *understanding and using the mistaken goals*

This is an "advanced" concept and can be extremely useful. We suggest using these four activities in the following order:

- **Introduction to the Four Reasons People Do What They Do.** (Optional and powerful) This activity requires an additional book (listed below and easily available). The activity can be used alone for a simple introduction to the concepts.
- **The Mistaken Goal Chart.** The primary activity used for teaching this concept.
- **Mistaken Goals and Us.** This helps students apply the ideas to their own life.
- **Encouragement Using Mistaken Goals.** This activity takes the concept one step further so that students can problem solve and begin to respond usefully.

LITERATURE RESOURCES

Kent, Jack. *There's No Such Thing as a Dragon.* New York: Random House, 2005.

Introduction to The Four Reasons People Do What They Do

OBJECTIVES:
- To introduce the "Four Mistaken Goals of Misbehavior."
- To help children understand that misbehavior is sometimes a solution to other problems.

MATERIALS:
- Kent, Jack. *There's No such thing as a Dragon.* New York: Random House, 2005.

COMMENTS FOR TEACHERS:
- This activity helps students develop empathy and understanding, and supports the problem-solving process.
- Although the book is written for young children, it is powerful for any age.
- Misbehaviors are unskilled solutions, but the best the person can do in the moment.

DIRECTIONS:

1. **Read** *There's No Such Thing as a Dragon,* by Jack Kent, to the class.

2. **Discuss the story.**
   - "How did the dragon misbehave?"
   - "Was the dragon trying to hurt anyone or be mean?"
   - "How do you think Billy, Mr. Bixby, and Mrs. Bixby felt about what happened?"
   - "What happened at the end when Billy told his parents there was a dragon, and patted the dragon on the head?"
   - "What did the dragon want all along?"
   - "What do you think we might learn about people from this story?" (Sometimes people do things for reasons they are not aware of, in order to be accepted or included in a group.)

3. **Process.**
   - "How many of you want to feel like you belong and are important in your family, with your friends, or in the classroom?"
   - "When we don't feel like we 'fit in' as part of a group, or when we feel like we are not important in that group, we sometimes do things without knowing why, just like the dragon did."
   - "We call these 'hidden reasons.' The hidden reasons we do things are based on wanting to belong and feel important in a group, like our classroom or our families."

4. **Moving it forward.**

Tell the class you will do another activity soon that builds upon this story and discussion (Mistaken Goal Chart Activity).

The Mistaken Goal Chart

OBJECTIVE:
- To help students understand the Mistaken Goal Chart

MATERIALS:
- Prepared chart (see model below)
- Markers

COMMENTS FOR TEACHERS:
- Many teachers are uncomfortable teaching "the reasons why people do what they do." It can be reframed as *one* powerful way of understanding why people do what they do.

DIRECTIONS:

1. **Prepare ahead.**
   - The mistaken goal chart with the columns filled in.

2. **Tell students:**
   - "Think of a time when you felt unloved or left out, thought you were not special, or felt you didn't belong."
   - "Try to remember exactly what happened, what you felt, and what you decided to do."

3. **Reflection.**
   - Give students a little time to mentally relive the situation.
   - Post the five-column chart from the materials list.
   - Tell students, "Look at the chart and note if any of the feeling words apply to the situation you were thinking about. If you were not able to think of a situation, you can think of a time you had any of the feelings on the list."

4. **Sharing.**
   - Ask for a student to share his or her example.
   - In the second and third columns of the chart write what the volunteers were thinking and what they did when they had those feelings. (A chart completed by a third-grade class is provided as an example.)
   - Find an example for each of the groups of feeling words.

5. **Discuss columns 4 and 5.**
   - Use the completed chart (below) as a guide.
   - For column 4 you can say, "This is a guess at the hidden belief behind the behavior and might explain why a person does what they do."
   - For column 5 you can say, "This is what we call a hidden belief."

6. **Teaching.**
   - After filling in the chart, explain to students, "Everyone gets discouraged at times. When we are discouraged, we have these feelings, think these thoughts or act these ways."
   - "For example, when a student doesn't have a sense of connection or importance and thinks it is because s/he is not getting enough attention, s/he may seek undue attention by making funny noises when the teacher is not looking."
   - We all find different ways to reconnect or feel important based on what we "mistakenly" believe about the world around us. Those are called mistaken goals.

7. Moving it forward.
- Remind students that this is not to label people but to understand "where they are coming from."
- Invite students to notice their own feelings when other people behave inappropriately to see if they can notice how others try to belong and/or feel important.

Tips

You'll notice that in the feelings column, "angry" shows up in both the goal of misguided power and revenge. If a student feels angry, it might be helpful to ask, "Are you feeling more hurt or more challenged?"

Blank Chart

Feeling	Thinking/Deciding	Behavior	Possible belief (out of awareness)	Mistaken Goal
Irritated Worried Annoyed			I belong when I'm the center of attention.	Undue attention (to be noticed)
Challenged Defeated Provoked Angry			I'm important when I'm the boss. You can't make me.	Misguided Power (to be the boss)
Hurt Disappointed Upset Sad Angry			I feel hurt and I feel better when I hurt you back.	Revenge (to get even)
Hopeless Helpless			I don't think I'll ever be able to do it. Leave me alone.	Assumed Inadequacy

Sample Chart

Feeling	Thinking/Deciding (examples)	Behavior (examples)	Possible belief (out of awareness)	Mistaken Goal
Irritated Worried Annoyed	Teacher only pays attention to the smart kids.	I make funny noises and make fun of the teacher when she is not looking.	I belong when I'm the center of attention.	Undue attention (to be noticed)
Challenged Defeated Provoked Angry	The playground supervisor tells me I have to eat lunch or I can't play.	I pretend to eat my sandwich but I hide it in my pocket.	I'm important when I'm the boss. You can't make me.	Misguided Power (to be the boss)
Hurt Disappointed Upset Sad Angry	Someone called me "Fatso."	I said, "You're ugly." I cried so no one could hear me.	I feel hurt and I feel better when I hurt you back.	Revenge (to get even)
Hopeless Helpless	I'll never be able to do multiplication.	I said, "I hate math and I think it is stupid." I threw my paper in the garbage.	I don't think I'll ever be able to do it. Leave me alone.	Assumed Inadequacy

Essential Skills for Class Meetings: #8 Understanding and Using the Four Mistaken Goals

Mistaken Goals and Us

OBJECTIVES:
- To have students consider the possibility that they have used the "Four Mistaken Goals of Misbehavior."
- To help them understand their "hidden" reasons for doing what they do.

MATERIALS:
- Board
- Prepared chart of mistaken beliefs (the one the class made for the Mistaken Goal Chart activity)

COMMENTS FOR TEACHERS:
- This activity follows The Mistaken Goal Chart Activity
- We call the four mistaken goals "hidden reasons" for doing what we do because we are not consciously aware of them.

DIRECTIONS:

1. **Brainstorm group misbehaviors.**
   - "What are some things students do that make it difficult for a group to work well together?"
   - Invite the students to brainstorm quite a long list.
   - Write each suggestion so it is visible to the class.

2. **Explain,** "Everyone would like to be part of the group and be successful, but not everyone believes they can. Sometimes, people try to be part of a group in ways that don't work very well or that bother other people."

3. **Review Mistaken Goal Chart made previously by class.**
   - This private logic usually falls into one of four groups of mistaken beliefs (show chart).
   - Review the Mistaken Goal chart that the class made.
   - Ask the students if, since learning about beliefs behind the behavior, they have observations or experiences that they would like to share (no names).

4. **Identify mistaken beliefs.**
   - Go back to the brainstormed list (#1 above) and ask students to help you guess which belief or beliefs might go with each behavior.
   - Beside each behavior, write a letter, **A**, **P**, **R**, or **I**.
     - o **A** for **Attention:** "I belong when I'm the center of attention."
     - o **P** for **Power:** "I feel important when I have power. You can't make me!"
     - o **R** for **Revenge:** "I feel hurt and want to get even (and then I'll feel better)."
     - o **I** for **Inadequacy:** "I don't think I can do it well enough so I will give up or won't even try."

   (There may be more than one way of looking at a behavior, so there may be more than one letter beside each behavior.)

5. **Move it forward**
   Ask students:
   - "What did you learn by doing this?"
   - "How might this information be useful?"
   - "What other behaviors might come from mistaken beliefs?"
   - "Would you be willing to notice your behavior and think about whether it might be due to a hidden belief?"
   - "How can understanding these ideas help us be more empathetic?"
   - "How might we help someone feel more belonging in our classroom?"

© Positive Discipline Association ■ www.PositiveDiscipline.org

Essential Skills for Class Meetings: #8 Understanding and Using the Four Mistaken Goals

Encouragement Using Mistaken Goals

OBJECTIVE:
- To help students grow encouragement skills based on new knowledge about beliefs behind behaviors.

MATERIALS:
- Prepared chart (see model below)
- The chart created in "Mistaken Goals and Us", or "Mistaken Goal Chart" Activity
- Markers

COMMENTS FOR TEACHERS:
- This is a follow-up activity *after* the mistaken goals have been introduced.
- This activity gives students ideas about how to respond to someone's behavior in an encouraging way.

DIRECTIONS:

1. **Prepare ahead.**
   - A chart for organizing the brainstorming (sample below). Have the class' chart from **Mistaken Goals and Us** or **Mistaken Goal Chart Activity** ready to use.

2. **Review.**
   - Briefly review the mistaken goals from either the **Mistaken Goal Chart Activity** or **Mistaken Goals and Us**.

3. **Reflection.**
   - Tell students, "Look at the class-generated chart and think about what might help people in these situations get a better sense of connection or value in the group."

4. **Brainstorm and record.**

   Ask the following questions and record answers on the prepared chart.
   - "If someone believes they belong only if they are being noticed or are the center of attention, what might help?"
     ○ "How could a person get attention in constructive ways instead of annoying ways?"
     ○ "What would encouragement for this person look like and sound like?"
   - "If someone believes they count only if they are the boss, what would help them feel powerful in a useful way?"
     ○ "How could a person use his or her power in useful ways, to help others instead of to defeat others?"
     ○ "What would encouragement for this person look like and sound like?"
   - "What would be encouraging for someone who feels hurt and feels the need to hurt others?"
     ○ "How could a person handle hurt feelings without hurting themselves or others?"
     ○ "What would encouragement for this person look like and sound like?"
   - "What might motivate students who believe it is better not to try because they worry about doing things the "right" way?"
     ○ "How could a person get help learning a skill or learn that it is okay to make mistakes?"
     ○ "What would encouragement for this person look like and sound like?"

5. **Moving it forward.**

   Post this list for a week, and ask students to be prepared to share about times they were encouraged or were able to encourage someone else. This could be done in a group setting or as a writing prompt.

Essential Skills for Class Meetings: #8 Understanding and Using the Four Mistaken Goals

Blank Chart

Undue attention	Misguided power	Revenge	Assumed Inadequacy

Sample Chart

Undue attention	Misguided power	Revenge	Assumed Inadequacy
• Walk to school with them. • Sit by them at lunch. • Laugh at their stories. • Talk to them.	• Ask for their ideas. • Let them be a line leader. • Put them in charge of a project. • Ask for their help to tutor another student.	• Listen to their feelings. • Acknowledge their feelings. "It seems like you feel hurt." • Be their friend. • Spend time with them.	• Let them help someone else with something they are good at. • Have another student work with them. • Play with them. • Tell them math was hard for you, too.

Positive Discipline Principles
Face Sheet

A quick summary

Positive Discipline developed by Jane Nelsen, Ed.D. is based on the work of Alfred Adler (1870-1937) and Rudolf Dreikurs (1897-1972), both Viennese psychiatrists. Adler's theory and practice were influenced by living in a poor neighborhood in highly class-structured society, by his indigent patients and his experience as a psychiatrist for the Austrian Army during World War I. After the war, Adler initiated a series of child guidance clinics to teach parents and teachers more effective methods for working with young people, using the democratic principles of dignity and respect. He believed that children needed both order (structure and responsibility) and freedom in order to grow into responsible, contributing citizens of their community. Dreikurs was a student of Adler's and led one of the guidance centers.

Adler saw human behavior as movement toward or striving toward a sense of belonging (connection) and significance and from a sense of "less than" to a sense of wholeness. He argued that most misbehaviors were really solutions to a different problem (usually a sense of being less than), and that understanding the problem would offer insight into helping the person find more effective and socially useful solutions. He understood that growing and learning as a human being requires the courage to be imperfect. A deep believer in respect and dignity for all, Adler spent a significant amount of his professional time working with people who were part of Vienna's "underclass" and was an advocate for safe working conditions.

Adler observed that we have a deep longing to be part of a community and learning the skills to contribute to the community, to have "social interest," is an important component of long-term mental health. Though he developed his philosophy almost a century ago without the aid of modern technology, current brain science supports his theories, which were based on his careful observation of human behavior.[1]

Why the theory is important

One of the strengths of Positive Discipline is its strong theoretical framework. As a practitioner, one doesn't need to remember a long set of tools or rules about what behaviors might be acceptable or whether a response to an inappropriate behavior is "right." Instead, by returning to theory and asking a few simple questions, one can decide for oneself.

- Is it respectful to the other person? Was it respectful to me?
- Did it lead to a better sense of connection?
- Did it invite the student to have a sense of value, meaning or a sense of "I am capable?"
- Was it encouraging? Did it help bring out the other person's best self?
- Will it be helpful long-term?
- Does it invite a sense of social interest and community? Does it work toward the common good?

---

1   Source: Terner, J., & Pew, W. L. *Courage to Be Imperfect,* New York: Hawthorn Books, 1978

Positive Discipline Theory

In her book, Positive Discipline, Jane Nelsen shared Four Criteria for Positive Discipline, and later added the 5th criteria.

> ## 5 Criteria for Effective Discipline
> Jane Nelsen
>
> 1. *Helps children feel a sense of connection. (Belonging and significance.)*
>
> 2. *Is mutually respectful and encouraging. (Kind and firm at the same time.)*
>
> 3. *Is effective long - term. (Considers what the child is thinking, feeling, learning, and deciding about himself and his world – and what to do in the future to survive or to thrive.)*
>
> 4. *Teaches important social and life skills. (Respect, concern for others, problem solving, and cooperation as well as the skills to contribute to the home, school or larger community.)*
>
> 5. *Invites children to discover how capable they are. (Encourages the constructive use of personal power and autonomy.)*

In addition to the work of Adler, Positive Discipline has been shaped by the work of Jane Nelsen and Lynn Lott. Several of their significant contributions include:

- The recognition that human beings learn new patterns of behavior best through playing with the material and discovering meaning through experience and contrast instead of by just reading or thinking.
- Moving beyond logical consequences to solutions, which are reasonable, related, respectful and helpful.
- An enormous generosity of spirit which has empowered thousands of passionate men and women to be able to take this work to their own communities around the world with the expectation that their work is honored and done well, but without expecting to be paid every time it is used.

And finally, this work has been shaped by many students of Jane and Lynn who, while remaining true to Adlerian principles and the experiential nature of the work have drawn the links to brain science, adapted it to their own culture and language and have added their creative ideas. As a result, the community and work continues to grow around the world and expand the tools and practices that we all need to invite more respect and peace in the world.

Positive Discipline Theory

In this section, you will find:

- A Brief Introduction to the Thought of Adler: A one-page summary of Adlerian theory, as well as a chart comparing Adlerian practices with common school practices
- Developing Relationships with Children Along the Dimensions of Kindness and Firmness
- Positive Discipline: Big Ideas
- Positive Discipline: Your Perspective Is Important
- Applying Positive Discipline: A Scaffolded Approach

Moving it forward

If learning about Positive Discipline in the School and Classroom has left you yearning for a deeper understanding of theory:

- Utilize some of the many resources at the end of this manual.
- Join the Positive Discipline community by becoming a member at PositiveDiscipline.org.
- Follow the Positive Discipline Association on Facebook.
- The North American Society for Adlerian Psychology (NASAP) has an annual conference with a track for educators (www.AlfredAdler.org) and there is also a two-week international summer conference, ICASSI, sponsored by the Rudolf Dreikurs Summer Institute (www.icassi.net).

Positive Discipline Theory

A Brief Introduction to the Thought of Alfred Adler
Terry Chadsey

Core ideas
1. Behavior is purposive
2. The goal of behavior is belonging (sense of connection) and meaning (significance). Mis-behavior is from a "mis"-taken belief about how to find belonging/meaning.
3. People are continually making decisions based on how their world is perceived.

   Perception ⟶ Interpretation ⟶ Belief ⟶ Decision (Private logic)

4. Horizontal relationships: Everyone is worthy of equal dignity and respect.

Implications
- The "problem" is really a "solution" to another problem that is unstated or out of awareness. The mis-behaving child is a discouraged child.
- Gemeinshaftsgefuehl (Community feeling)
    - Being part of a community (belonging/connection)
    - Being able to make a contribution to the community (significance/purpose)

Basic tools and principles that flow from Adler's thoughts
1. Teach life skills.
2. Pay attention to the power of perception.
3. Focus on encouragement (Connection and presence, not rah-rah).
4. Hold the tension of kindness AND firmness at the same time.
5. Look to mutual respect.
    - Respect for yourself and the situation (firmness).
    - Respect for the needs of the child and others (kindness).
6. Assume mistakes to be opportunities to learn.
7. Look to solutions rather than punishment.

Developing Relationships with Children According to the
Dimensions of Kindness and Firmness
Terry Chadsey

Kindness

Permissive (Freedom, no order)	Authoritative/ Democratic (Freedom and Order)
Neglect (No order, no freedom)	Authoritarian (Order, no freedom)

Firmness

Two Opposing Schools of Thought on Human Behavior
Chart by Terry Chadsey and Jody McVittie

	Dominant and Traditional Practice in American Schools	**The Democratic (Solution Focused) Approach**
Theory based on:	Common practice, Pavlov, Thorndike, Skinner.	Adler, Dreikurs, Dewey, Glasser, Nelsen, Lott, Dinkmeyer, Albert.
Behavior is motivated by:	People respond to rewards and punishments in their environment.	People seek a sense of belonging (connection) and significance (meaning) in their social context.
We have most influence on the behavior of others:	At the moment of response to a specific behavior.	In an ongoing relationship founded on mutual respect.
The most powerful tools for adults are:	Control, rewards, and punishments.	Empathy, understanding the perspective of the student, encouragement, collaborative problem solving, kind *and* firm, follow through.
"Respect" is:	Obedience and compliance in relationships in which dignity and respect of the adult is primary.	Mutual, in relationships in which each person is equally worthy of dignity and respect.
"Appropriate" response to inappropriate behavior:	Censure, isolation, punishment.	Naming without shaming and blaming, identifying the belief behind the behavior, focus on solutions, follow through.
"Appropriate" response to dangerous and destructive behavior:	Censure, isolation, punishment.	Maintaining safety for all, holding the student accountable for their action, followed, at a later time, by solution-focused planning and clear follow through.
Student learning is maximized when:	The adult has effective control over student behavior.	The student feels belonging and significance in the classroom.

Positive Discipline: Big Ideas

Behavior is movement toward a sense of "I belong" and "I matter." Misbehavior is a coded message.

Courage (from the root word *cor* – Latin, heart) is the small step you take towards being more of who you truly are, when it might be easier to take a step in another direction. When you ***encourage*** someone, you are creating a space for him or her to take that step toward his or her best self.

The Courage to be Imperfect

Children sometimes "learn" that they "are" a mistake and feel shame, instead of understanding that everyone "makes" mistakes. When mistakes are opportunities to learn, children are better able to take appropriate risks in school.

Recovery from a Mistake

(Repair is critical!) (adapted from Jane Nelsen, *Positive Discipline*):

- Re-gather: *Self-calm and find your rational self before starting the "repair."*
- Recognize: *"Whoops, I made a mistake."*
- Reconcile: *"I'm sorry."*
- Repair *"How can I fix this?"*

> *"A misbehaving child is a discouraged child."*
> -Rudolf Dreikurs

Respect

Mutual respect is respect for the dignity of others and respect for oneself.

Results of Punishment

(from Jane Nelsen, *Positive Discipline*)

- Resentment: "This is unfair. I can't trust adults."
- Revenge: "They are winning now, but I'll get even."
- Rebellion: "I'll do just the opposite to prove I don't have to do it their way."
- Retreat:
    from others: "I won't get caught next time."
    or from one's self: "I'm a bad person."

Solutions: Reasonable, Respectful, Related AND Helpful
All solutions are consequences, but not all consequences are solutions

> "The essentials for living in a democratic society can be simply stated...*The principle implies mutual respect, respect for the dignity of others, and respect for oneself.* The principle is expressed in a combination of firmness and kindness. Firmness implies self-respect; kindness, respect for the others."
> - Dreikurs, Social Equality: *The Challenge of Today* (emphasis in original)

Positive Discipline: Your Perspective is Important
The Development of Self-Control

Laurie Prusso Hatch

The Teacher's Role

It is the role of the teacher to teach children skills and provide them with many opportunities to practice and master the skills that they will need to become successful; this includes the skills of self-control.

Your beliefs influence your thoughts and feelings…
Your thoughts and feelings influence your decisions…
Your decisions determine your actions…
What you do has a direct effect on a student.

Which student do you know?

Trouble Maker	Inquisitive and curious
Disrespectful	Outspoken
Boastful	Confident
Destructive	Creative
Hyperactive	Energetic
Bossy	Leader
Rebellious	Independent
Stubborn	Persistent
Non-compliant	Self-directed
Picky	Sensitive
Defiant	Decisive

Seeing a student through the lens of his or her strengths

- Is encouraging to the student,
- Invites behavior that is more helpful than hurtful,
- Helps students redirect their behavior to become more socially useful, and
- Makes it easier for the educator to work with the student to solve problems more effectively.

> "We must realize that *we cannot build on deficiencies, only on strength.* We cannot help our children – or anyone else – to have faith in themselves as long as we have no faith in them."
> – Dreikurs Social Equality: *The Challenge of Today*, p. 122 (emphasis in original)

**When people face challenges in a supportive environment, growth occurs.
When people face challenges in a non-supportive environment, avoidance occurs.
The teacher's role is to encourage growth.**

Positive Discipline Theory

Applying Positive Discipline: A Scaffolded Approach

Adapted for Positive Discipline from the Response to Intervention (RTI) framework, from Multi-Tiered Systems of Support (MTSS) framework. The tiered model was originally published by Sugai et. al, in 2000.

Solution-focused discipline speaks the same language as RTI (Response to Intervention) and MTSS (Multi-Tiered System of Support).

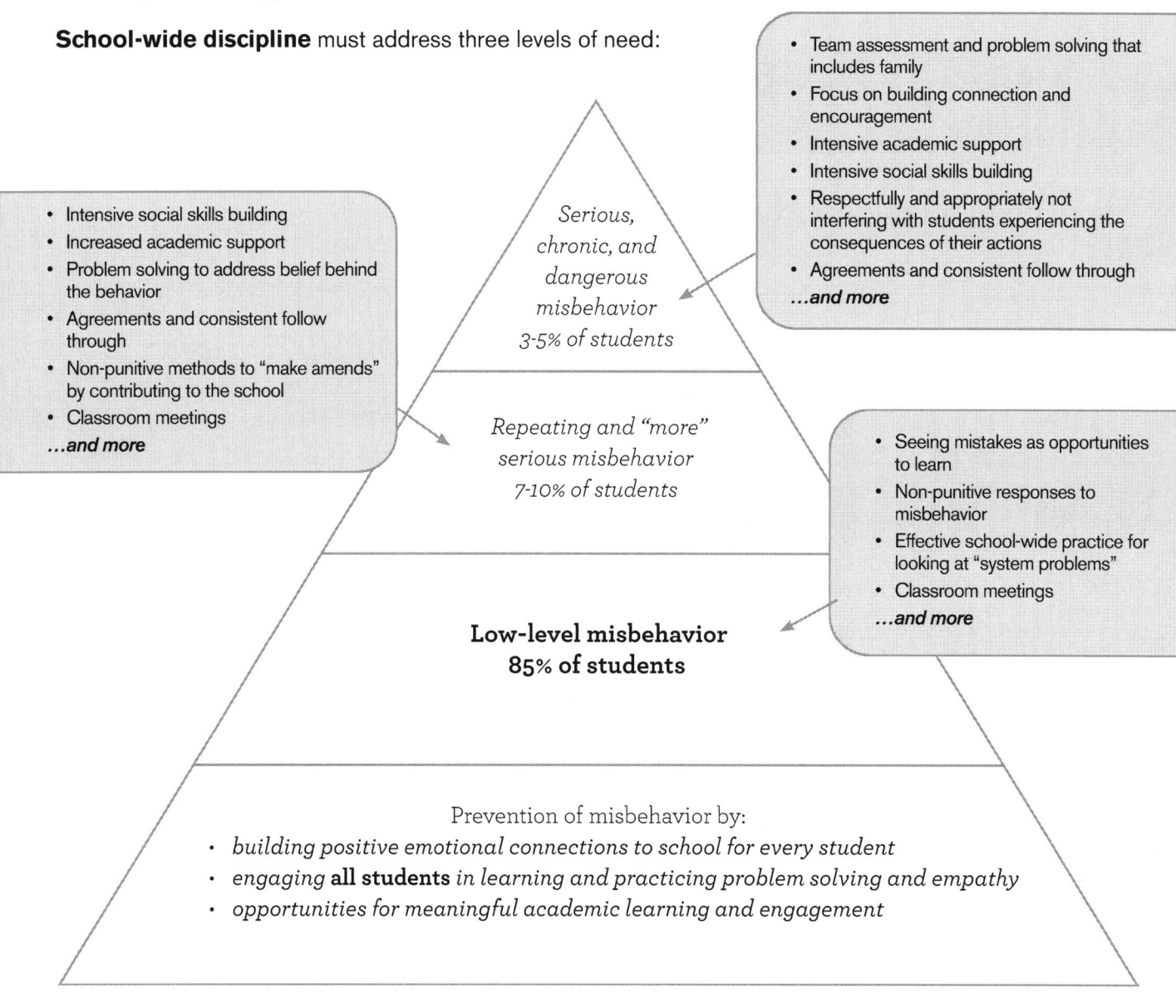

School-wide discipline must address three levels of need:

Serious, chronic, and dangerous misbehavior
3-5% of students

- Team assessment and problem solving that includes family
- Focus on building connection and encouragement
- Intensive academic support
- Intensive social skills building
- Respectfully and appropriately not interfering with students experiencing the consequences of their actions
- Agreements and consistent follow through
- *...and more*

Repeating and "more" serious misbehavior
7-10% of students

- Intensive social skills building
- Increased academic support
- Problem solving to address belief behind the behavior
- Agreements and consistent follow through
- Non-punitive methods to "make amends" by contributing to the school
- Classroom meetings
- *...and more*

Low-level misbehavior
85% of students

- Seeing mistakes as opportunities to learn
- Non-punitive responses to misbehavior
- Effective school-wide practice for looking at "system problems"
- Classroom meetings
- *...and more*

Prevention of misbehavior by:
- building positive emotional connections to school for every student
- engaging **all students** in learning and practicing problem solving and empathy
- opportunities for meaningful academic learning and engagement

Respect throughout:

Respect for self: *What do I need?*
Respect for others: *What does this student need? What do other students need?*
Respect for the situation: *What does the situation demand?*

Handouts for Workshop
Face Sheet

In this section, you will find:
Handouts that accompany most of the activities in the Positive Discipline in the Classroom workshop. You may copy these handouts for your staff as long as the source at the bottom of the page is included.

Kindness and firmness at the same time

CONNECT B4 CORRECT

The "mis" behavior that you see is really the child's unskilled solution to another problem (that you may not see.)

Where did we ever get the crazy idea that in order to make children do better, first we have to make them feel worse? CHILDREN DO BETTER WHEN THEY FEEL BETTER. - Jane Nelsen

The Brain in the Hand*

Your Wrist and Palm: Brain Stem. Responsible for survival instincts: flight, freeze or fight. Autonomic ("automatic") functions.

Your Thumb: Limbic area. The amygdala (the brain's safety radar), memories, emotions.

Your Fingers over **your Thumb:** Cortex. Perception, motor action, speech, higher processing and what we normally call "thinking."

Your Fingernails: Pre-frontal cortex – a primary integration center for the brain, like a "switchboard" that makes sure messages get where they need to go. Documented functions of the pre-frontal cortex are: regulation of body through autonomic nervous system, emotional regulation, regulation of interpersonal relationships, response flexibility, intuition, mindsight, self-awareness, letting go of fears, morality.

What happens when you are stressed, overwhelmed, or trying to deal with traumatic or painful memories? The pre-frontal cortex shuts down; it no longer functions. (This is temporary, thank goodness!) You have "flipped your lid". You can't use most of the nine functions above--and you can't learn without them. To engage and to learn, you need to calm down and bring the pre-frontal cortex back into functioning. To watch Daniel Siegel explain it, internet search for Brain in the Hand, Daniel Siegel.

Mirror Neurons: The "monkey see, monkey do" neurons that play a key role in social interaction, connection and learning. Internet search YouTube, mirror neurons, NOVA to see an excellent 14-minute Nova episode on **mirror neurons**.

Your brain, when the prefrontal cortex is working:

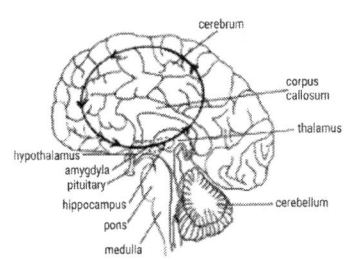

Integrative functioning (the high road)

> Integrative functioning: "A form of processing information that involves the higher, rational, reflective thought process of the mind. High-road processing allows for mindfulness, flexibility in our responses and an integrating sense of self awareness. The high road involves the prefrontal cortex in its processes." Siegel and Hartzell, *Parenting from the Inside Out*.

Non- integrated function (flipping your lid, the low road)

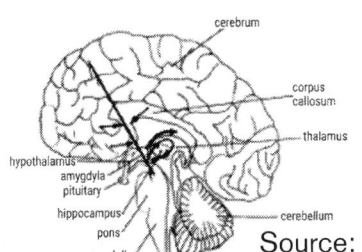

> "Low road functioning involves the shutting down of the higher processes of the mind and leaves the individual in a state of intense emotions, impulsive reactions, rigid and repetitive responses and lacking in self-reflection and the consideration of another's point of view. Involvement of the prefrontal cortex is shut off when one is on the low road." Siegel and Hartzell, *Parenting from the Inside Out*.

Source: Siegel and Hartzell, Parenting from the Inside Out. P. 157

---

* "The Brain in the Hand" is the work of Daniel J. Siegel, M.D., first published in his book, **Parenting from the Inside Out** (2003) and more recently published in **The Whole-Brain Child** (2011). Dr. Siegel is not associated and/or affiliated with, and does not endorse and/or sponsor the Positive Discipline Association and/or its activities.

The Class Meeting
Lynn Lott

Purpose of the Class Meeting

1. Skill building
- The courage to think
- How to think
- Problem solving
- Mutual respect
- Communication skills
- Listening
- Expressing thoughts and feelings
- Respecting differences
- Useful power
- Practice in planning events

2. Self-Reliance
- Self-confidence based on skills
- Self-esteem based on a sense of belonging
- Courage based on the ability to make a difference

3. Problem solving
- Ownership through participation
- Social interest
- Practice in helping each other
- Discipline problems decrease when kids are involved

SIX CRITERIA FOR SUCCESSFUL CLASS MEETINGS

1. Have them regularly (3-5 times per week for elementary school)
2. Form a circle
3. Focus on solutions
4. Pass an item to speak
5. Allow student who put problem on agenda (or student who is focus of the problem) to choose a helpful solution
6. Allow time for all to learn the process.

Adult attitudes and skills necessary to accomplish the above:

- A sincere desire to create an atmosphere of mutual respect for students and adults at all times.
- Faith in the abilities of young people to use wisdom and learn skills. (Act like a broken record.)
- An interest in long-range results for young people rather than short-range. (Replace authoritarian methods with democratic methods.)
- Replacing lectures with questioning skills that draw forth the wisdom of young people. (Ask, "What?" instead of *telling* what.)
- An interest in knowing what students think. (Getting into their world.)
- Giving choices rather than issuing edicts.
- Eliminate punishment and reward in favor of problem-solving, discussion, sharing and sometimes natural or logical consequences.
- Winning cooperation instead of using control.
- Patience. The process takes time.

Class Meeting Closers: Leave 'em Laughing

This is a short list of ideas for closing class meetings.

Look up look down

Have everyone stand up. When the facilitator says, "Look down," everyone looks down. When the facilitator says, "Look up," everyone must look up and stare directly at the face of another person. If two people look up and stare at each other they clap and sit. The rest of the participants who did not make eye contact with another person keep staring until the facilitator says, "Look down," again. Play continues until there are only a few people in the circle.

Trenecsia Bellinger – Lakeridge Elementary School, Seattle, WA

Quick and easies

- Students touch pointer fingers with neighbor and make a doorbell sound (one student goes first and then around the circle).
- Favorite dessert (one student says first, then around the circle).
- Favorite pizza topping (one student says first, then around the circle).
- Favorite recess game (one student says first, then around the circle).

Drew Crandall - Lakeridge Elementary School, Seattle, WA

Undoing a human knot

In groups of 10 or 12, have the students form a tight circle, lift their hands and then, on a signal, grab two other hands (that don't belong to the same person). Tell the group to untangle themselves without letting go of hands.

Four corners

Have 3 or 4 questions prepared. Have the corners of your room numbered. Each question will have 4 possible answers. For example, for a 3rd to 5th grade classroom:
- If this is your first year at our school go to #1, If this is your second year go to #2, If this is your third year go to #3, If you have been here 4 or more years go to #4.
- You can play with favorite recess games, favorite meals, how they get to school (bus, car, walk) etc.

Count to ten

The class tries to count to ten using the following guidelines. The numbers come in order. No one can say two numbers in a row. No one follows a special pattern (e.g. just going around the circle). If two people say the same number you start at one again.

Clapping together

One pair of students starts by facing each other and each clap their own hands, once, at the same time. Then one student turns and faces the person on their other side who faces them, and that pair claps. The "receiving" student then turns to the next person and the sound is passed around the circle. This can be timed. Younger children really have to focus to create their sound at the same time and the practice is helpful. As an extra challenge the first person can "pass the sound" first to a partner on one side, then turn and start the sound going the opposite direction as well.

Curiosity Questions: "What" and "How"

Teresa LaSala

Tone is important. Interest and caring must be expressed through tone.

1. What happened?
2. What would you like to have happen?
3. What or how did you contribute to that outcome?
4. How can you be helpful? What would you like to do to help?
5. What do you think caused that to happen?
6. How did your choices impact the outcome?
7. What were you trying to accomplish?
8. How do you feel about what happened?
9. What did you learn from this experience?
10. What ideas do you have to take care of this problem?
11. What could you do next time?
12. How could you solve this?
13. How can you use what you learned in the future?
14. What do you think will happen if you take that course of action?
15. What is your picture of…?
16. What is your plan for …?
17. How do you see that working…?
18. What is your story about …?
19. What is your understanding of our agreement?
20. What is your understanding of what I just said?

De-escalation Tips: Rx for the Flipped Lid

Jody McVittie

We refer to this as **"having a flipped lid" or "flooding."**

Tips for when YOU have flipped your lid:

1. **Recognize what it feels like physically:** fast heartbeats, pounding head, a sense of urgency, etc. Learn your own body's warning signs.
2. **Recognize what it feels like mentally:** a sense of urgency, thoughts that keep repeating or going in circles, an inability to think calmly and clearly (or do mental math). Learn your own mind's warning signs.
3. **Take a time-out from the situation to calm down.** Recognize that continued engagement isn't going to help.
4. **Focus on your breathing.** Do belly breathing.
5. **Use large muscles:** Walk, do isometrics, do windmills with your arms.
6. **Try to engage your cortex.** Do mental math, spell things backwards, list facts…and slow the pace.
7. **Notice why you are in "survival brain."** "This situation makes me feel vulnerable because. . ." (I'm not being heard, I may not be able to prevent injury, I'm not being respected) and work to not take it personally.

Tips for when the OTHER person has flipped his/her lid (child or adult):

1. **Watch for signs in the other person:** Irrational action, flushed face, intense emotion, disjointed sentences.
2. **Notice your own body.** Remember that mirror neurons work quickly. Don't let the other person's flipped lid "catch" you.
3. **Remember safety.** People who are using their mid-brain and not their cortex do not act rationally and can be physically dangerous. Stay calm, move slowly, and be aware.
4. **Use your mirror neurons.** The more you stay calm and connected, the easier it is for the other person to calm down.
5. **Acknowledge feelings:** Use few words and a calm, empathetic tone.
6. **Don't talk at the person.** Don't touch, and don't make fast movements. If they want to leave (and it is safe) allow it.
7. **Don't crowd.** Don't make demands; don't give complicated directions (a person with a flipped lid cannot process complex verbal statements).
8. **Invite the person to take a time-out (non-punitive) or "cool down time" (CDT).** This works best if it is an option, not a command.
9. **Simple tasks may engage the cortex.** You might ask them to remind you how their name is spelled, to count to ten, ask if they remember how to spell your name.
10. **Ask for his/her help.** After the student has begun to de-escalate, change the subject by asking for his/her help. "I can tell you aren't ready to engage in work yet, but are you calm enough to help me by…?" "I can tell you aren't quite ready to play again, but would you be willing to help me by…?"

Helpful Hints for Empowering vs. Enabling Handout

Jane Nelsen and Lynn Lott

We have become vividly aware of how skilled most of us are at offering enabling responses to students, and how unskilled we are at offering empowering responses.

Our definition of *enabling* is: "Getting between young people and life experiences to minimize the consequences of their choices." Enabling responses include:

- Doing too much for them
- Giving them too much
- Overprotecting/rescuing
- Lying for them
- Punishing/controlling
- Living in denial
- Fixing
- Bailing them out

Our definition of *empowering* is: "Turning control over to young people as soon as possible so they have power over their own lives." Empowering responses include:

- Listening and giving emotional support and validation without fixing or discounting
- Teaching life skills
- Working on agreements through class meetings or the joint problem-solving process
- Letting go (without abandoning)
- Deciding what you will do with dignity and respect
- Sharing what you think, how you feel, and what you want (without lecturing, moralizing, insisting on agreement, or demanding that anyone give you what you want)
- Sticking to the issue with dignity and respect

More hints:

- Enabling responses tend to be easier for most of us than empowering responses. The empowering statements may seem awkward.
- Punishment is enabling, not because of the lack of firmness, but because
    - Control remains with the adult
    - The focus moves from the problem to a power/revenge relationship between the adult and child
    - The young person often believes they have "made the payment" and therefore can drop the problem
    - The young person and adult can shift their focus to resentment instead of problem solving
    - The young person no longer takes responsibility for finding a solution

Empowering/Enabling Statements

Jane Nelsen and Lynn Lott

Enabling Statements

BRIBERY: "You can have a prize from my treasure box if you finish your work by lunch time."

LACK OF FAITH: "Bless your heart. I know that work was too hard for you. Let's get Ms. Jones to help you with it."

MAKING EXCUSES: "You are having a tough week. It's okay with me if you just finish the first page."

PUNISHING: "This is the third time this week you haven't done your homework so you get lunch detention".

PUNISHING: "You didn't get it in again. I'm going to call your coach and tell him that you aren't eligible anymore."

CONTROLLING: "You keep not doing your homework. You can't participate anyway. So go sit in the hall and get it done!"

DOING TO MUCH: "Well, maybe I could help you do that homework."

GIVING THEM TOO MUCH "Let's see, if you get that done quickly, I'll make sure….(ad lib here)."

OVER-PROTECTING "Well, I know you have a lot of sports practices this week. I'll accept it late without a penalty."

RESCUING "Well if you just do the first of the five pages, I'll count that as good enough."

BAILING THEM OUT: "Well, I think you know that material anyway, so you don't need to do it."

RESCUING/LYING: "I'll call your parents and tell them to get off your back and that I lost the paper you turned in. You've had a hard week."

USING JUDGEMENT/BLAMING: "You know if you just kept your papers in order, you wouldn't have this problem."

PERMISSIVE WITH BLAME: "I can't believe you have procrastinated again. What will ever become of you? You can turn it in tomorrow this time, but next time you'll just have to suffer the consequences."

BELITTLING: "How many times have I told you to pay attention and get your work done? Why can't you be more like your brother? Why can't you be more responsible? What will become of you?"

PUNISHING: "I've had it. You had plenty of warning. You can't go on the field trip."

Empowering Statements

EXPRESSING YOUR LIMITS: "I'm available to help with homework before school on Tuesdays and Thursdays. I won't be available to help with last-minute projects."

EXPRESSING YOUR LIMITS: "I'm willing to give you extra time in the library when we come to an agreement in advance for a convenient time, but I'm not willing to get involved at the last minute."

LOVING AND ENCOURAGING: "Do you know that I care about you no matter what – and that you are more important to me than your grades?"

JOINT PROBLEM SOLVING: "What is your picture of what is going on regarding your work? Would you be willing to hear my concerns? Could we brainstorm together on some possible solutions?"

CONNECT FIRST: "I can see that you feel bad about getting that poor grade. I have faith in you to learn from this and figure out what you need to do to get the grade you would like."

LETTING GO OF THEIR ISSUES: "I feel upset when you don't do your work because I value education so much. I think a good education could be very beneficial to you in your life. I really wish you would do your work."

AGREEMENT, NOT RULES: "Could we sit down and see if we can work on a plan regarding class work that we both can live with?"

LISTEN WITHOUT FIXING OR JUDGING: "I would like to hear what this means for you. Can you explain to me why it isn't important to you to do your assignments?"

SHOWING FAITH: "I have faith in you. I trust you to figure out what you need. I know that when it is important to you, you'll know what to do."

RESPONSIBILITY WHERE IT BELONGS: "I am scheduling a meeting with your parent/caregiver. I'll be there while you explain."

CURIOSITY: "What is your plan?"

CURIOSITY: "What is your picture of what is going on regarding your homework?"

Empowering/Enabling Statements for Younger Children

Jody McVittie, Steven Foster and Laurie Prusso Hatch

Enabling statements

"It is clean-up time. Why are you just sitting there?"

"You act like this every day. Is there something wrong with you?"

"All of your friends are able to help. I wonder if you are just a baby, not a big girl?"

"Pick up the toys now, or you will sit on the chair instead of joining us at Circle."

"I am going to set the timer for 3 minutes and these better be picked up."

"We go through this every day! I am tired of it."

"If you want to play with these again, you'd better get them picked up right now!"

"It's okay; Jacob can do it for you."

"Here, I'll do it with you" (and essentially do it for child).

"You can come back and pick them up later."

Empowering Statements

Show faith with a reminder of what the student can do. "I have seen you carry really heavy things before. I know you can do it."

Respond with a question. "I wonder how many ways you can figure out how to do this?"

Acknowledge feelings. "You were really having fun here. It is hard to stop playing to clean up. Which blocks do you want to put on the shelf first?"

Check the child's knowledge or understanding. "What is supposed to be happening now?"

Invite cooperation. "I know you like to be a helper. Do you want to do it and sing at the same time?"

Limited choices. "Do you want to put the big blocks away first or the small blocks?"

Say what you want/mean. Get down at the child's level and with a smile, calmly say, "[name], it is time to put the blocks away now."

Use non-verbal language. Put a gentle hand on his or her shoulder. Look them in the eye (pause to notice the feeling) and with friendly eyes indicate what needs to happen.

Connect and redirect. "It looks like you were enjoying your play and you don't want to stop. How about I pick up the squares and you pick up the rectangles?"

Look for other solutions. "I wonder if one of your friends would come and help you. Who could you ask?"

Connect and redirect. "It is always more fun if we work together. What would you like me to do to help?" (With caution to not do "for")

Encouragement vs. Praise
Rudolf Dreikurs

Encouragement
1. To inspire with courage
(courage < Old French corage, < Latin cor heart)
2. To spur on: to stimulate

Self-evaluation
("Tell me about it.")
("What do you think?")

Addresses Deed
Appreciation, Respectful
("Thank you for helping.")
("Who can show me the proper way to sit?")

Empathy
("What do you think and feel?")
("I can see that you enjoyed that.")

Self-disclosing "I" messages
("I appreciate your help.")

Asks questions
("What is an appropriate noise level for the library?")

Effect:
Feel worthwhile without the approval of others.
Self-confidence, self-reliance.
Self-esteem.

Praise
1. To express a favorable judgment of
2. To glorify, especially by attribution of perfection
3. An expression of approval

Evaluation by others
("I like it.")

Addresses doer
Expectation, Patronizing
("You are such a good boy.")
("Good girl!")
("I like the way Suzie is sitting.")

Conformity
("You did it right.")
("I am so proud of you.")

Judgmental "I" messages
("I like the way you are sitting.")

Should statements
("You should be quiet like your sister.")

Effect:
Feel worthwhile only when others approve.
Dependence on others.
"Other" esteem.

Questions you might ask:
Am I inspiring self-evaluation or dependence on the evaluation of others?
Am I being respectful or patronizing?
Am I helping them discover how to act or trying to manipulate their behavior?
Am I seeing the child's point of view or my own?
Would I make this comment to a friend or neighbor?

Descriptive encouragement: "I notice…" (without value judgments like good, well, or nice)
Appreciative encouragement: "I appreciate…." or, "Thank you for….."
Empowering encouragement: I noticed ….. , with [characteristic] like that…… *"I trust you…", "I know you can…"* (Use your evidence first.)

"Courage (from the root word: *cor* – Latin, heart) is the very small step you take towards being more of who you truly are, when it might be easier to take a step in another direction. When you **encourage** someone, you are creating a space for him or her to take that step toward his/her best self." – Jody McVittie

The Language of Encouragement

Encouragement avoids judgment (words like good, better, best), it isn't always a "positive" statement. It reflects that you are attuned and connected to the other person.

Statements that say, "I see you," or "I notice you".
"You seem to like mysteries a lot."
"How do you feel about it?"
"I can tell you're not satisfied. What do you think you can do?"
"It looks like you enjoyed that."
"I'm noticing that you are working hard."
"I'm noticing that you are having a hard day. Do you want to talk about it?"
"I enjoy your sense of humor."

Statements that say, "I see you are trying."
"You worked hard on that!"
"Look at the progress you've made."
"Looks like you spent a lot of time thinking that through."
"I see you're moving along."
"You may not feel you've reached your goal, but look how far you've come."

Statements that say, "I appreciate you."
"Thanks. That was a big help."
"Thanks for helping me, it made my day easier."
"It was thoughtful of you to do that."
"I really appreciate you helping me. It makes my job go faster."
"I need your help planning the _____."
"You have skill in _____. Would you do that for our class?"
"I really enjoyed our time together. Thanks."
"I learned something new today from you. Thank you."

Statements that show your sense of how capable the person is.
"Can you notice the progress you have made?"
"I trust your judgment."
"That's a tough one, but I think you can work it out."
"I need your help fixing this."
"I think you will figure it out."

Statements that lift up character.
"I saw you shooting hoops until you had to come in. That is persistence."
"I noticed how helpful you were to [name]. Thanks for being sensitive."
"I saw you patiently explain the math problem to [name]. That kind of patience will help you in life."
"I know you didn't agree with [name], but you listened carefully to his explanation. It showed respect for his perception."
"You were in a hurry, and slowed down to help [name]. Your kindness made a difference today."
"You could tell [name] didn't understand so you took time to explain. That showed compassion."
"You noticed [name] was left out; inviting her to join you was a very thoughtful thing to do."

Making Agreements and Following Through Handout

Jane Nelsen and Lynn Lott

The Steps of Making an Agreement

1. Have a friendly discussion with the other person to gather information about what is happening regarding the problem. Start by owning your part of the problem. (Listen and be mutually respectful.)

2. Brainstorm possible solutions. Choose a mutually agreeable solution. This may take some negotiating because each person may have a different favorite. Be willing to learn from mistakes. (Notice that there is no threat or "consequence" here. Consequences undermine the power of any agreement.)

3. Agree on a specific time deadline (to the minute).

4. At the deadline, you simply follow through on the agreement by firmly and respectfully requesting the other person to keep the agreement until it is done.

Four Hints for Effective Follow Through

1. Keep comments simple and concise. ("I notice you didn't _____. Would you please do that now?")

2. In response to objections ask, "What was our agreement?"

3. In response to further objections, shut your mouth and use nonverbal communication (point to your watch; smile knowingly; give a hug and point to your watch again).

4. When the other person concedes to keep to the agreement (sometimes obviously annoyed) simply say, "Thank you for keeping our agreement."

Four Traps that Defeat Follow Through

1. Wanting other people to have the same priorities as you do.

2. Getting into judgments and criticism rather than sticking to the issue.

3. Not getting specific agreements in advance that include a specific time deadline.

4. Not maintaining dignity and respect for the other person and yourself.

Handouts for Workshop

Mistaken Goal Chart

Jane Nelsen and Lynn Lott, www.positivediscipline.com

The Child's goal is:	If the parent/teacher feels:	And tends to react by:	And if the child's response is:	The belief behind the child's behavior is:	Coded messages	Parent/teacher proactive and **encouraging** responses include:
Undue Attention (to keep others busy or to get special service)	Annoyed Irritated Worried Guilty	Reminding. Coaxing. Doing things for the child they could do for themselves.	Stops temporarily, but later resumes same or another disturbing behavior	I count (belong) only when I'm being noticed or getting special service. I'm only important when I'm keeping you busy with me.	**Notice Me. Involve Me Usefully.**	Redirect by involving child in a useful task to gain attention. Say what you will do. (Example: I love you and will spend time with you later.") Avoid special service. Have faith in child to deal with feelings (don't fix or rescue). Plan regular special time. Help child create routine charts. Engage child in problem solving. Use family/class meetings. Set up nonverbal signals. Ignore behavior with hand on shoulder.
Misguided Power (to be boss)	Angry Challenged Threatened Defeated	Fighting. Giving in. Thinking, "You can't get away with it or I'll make you". Wanting to be right.	Intensifies behavior. Complies with defiance. Feels they've won when parent/teacher is upset even if they have to comply. Passive power (says yes but doesn't follow through).	I belong only when I'm boss, in control, or proving no one can boss me. You can't make me.	**Let Me Help. Give Me Choices.**	Redirect to positive power by asking for help. Offer limited choices. Don't fight and don't give in. Withdraw from conflict. Be firm and kind. Don't talk–act. Decide what you will do. Let routines be the boss. Leave and calm down. Develop mutual respect. Set a few reasonable limits. Practice follow-through. Use family/class meetings.
Revenge (to get even)	Hurt Disappointed Disbelieving Disgusted	Hurting back. Shaming. Thinking, "How could you do such a thing?"	Retaliates. Intensifies. Escalates the same behavior or chooses another weapon.	I don't think I belong so I'll hurt others as I feel hurt. I can't be liked or loved.	**I'm Hurting. Validate My Feelings.**	Acknowledge hurt feelings. Avoid feeling hurt. Avoid punishment and retaliation. Build trust. Use reflective listening. Share your feelings. Make amends. Show you care. Encourage strengths. Don't take sides. Use family/class meetings.
Assumed Inadequacy (to give up and be left alone)	Despair Hopeless Helpless Inadequate	Giving up. Doing things for the child that they could do for themselves. Over-helping.	Retreats further. Becomes passive. Shows no improvement. Is not responsive	I can't belong because I'm not perfect, so I'll convince others not to expect any-thing of me. I am helpless and unable. It's no use trying because I won't do it right.	**Don't Give Up On Me. Show Me A Small Step.**	Break task down into small steps. Stop all criticism. Encourage any positive attempt. Have faith in child's abilities. Focus on assets. Don't pity. Don't give up. Set up opportunities for success. Teach skills–show how, but don't do for. Enjoy the child. Build on their interests. Use family/class meetings.

Dreikurs, R., Grunwald, B., B., & Pepper, F., C. (2015). *Maintaining sanity in the classroom: classroom management techniques.* London: Taylor and Francis.

Positive Discipline in the School and Classroom Manual by Jane Nelsen, Lynn Lott, Teresa LaSala, Jody McVittie, and Suzanne Smitha

Handouts for Workshop

The Belief Behind the Behavior – A key for mistaken beliefs

Adapted by Jody McVittie from schema by Steven Maybell and Jane Nelsen

1. Student's Behavior	2. Adult's feeling	3. Adult's mistaken reactions	4. Student's response	5. *The student's belief*	6. Effective prevention (Encouragement)	7. Effective responses (More encouragement)	8. Goal
Nuisance Show-off Clown Disruptive Pesters Blurting out Teacher's pet	• Annoyed • Irritated	Reminding Coaxing	Stops temporarily, but later resumes same or another disturbing behavior	*I count or belong only when I am getting attention, when others notice me*	Spend special time Provide opportunities to contribute. Teach connection skills Set up routines Class meetings	Hear: "Notice me, involve me." "I care about you and _____." (Example: I care about you and will spend time with you later.") Redirect by assigning a task so student can gain useful attention Use problem-solving Touch without words Set up nonverbal signals	Undue Attention
Acts pitiful Acts helpless Acts scared Acts whiny Demanding	• Worried • Guilt • Sorry for • Responsible for	Reminding Taking Responsibility Making excuses for the student Doing things for the student they could do for themselves	Acts incapable or even more demanding often with engaging drama	*I count or belong only when I'm keeping others busy with me. I am special. I'm not sure I can do it for myself, "Do it for me."*	Make room for learning from mistakes. Become "incompetent" Avoid special service or pampering Provide opportunities to contribute Class meetings	Set up routines Use problem solving. Take time for training Allow disappointment and frustration as new skills are learned. Promote autonomy Practice self-respect	Special Service
Defiant Argumentative Passive-aggressive Apathetic Takes over leadership of any group	• Challenged • Defeated • Provoked • Indignation • (Angry)	Fighting Forcing Giving in Thinking "You can't get away with it" or "I'll make you" Wanting to be right Wanting to be in charge/control Punishing	Intensifies behavior Defiant -compliance Feels they've won when adult is upset. Passive power	*I count or belong only when I'm boss, in control, or proving no one can boss me. "You can't make me." "You can't stop me."*	Provide opportunities to contribute in useful ways Set a few reasonable limits (kind and firm) Give choices Develop mutual respect Mutual problem solving. Practice follow through Class meetings	Hear: "Let me help, give me choices" Let routines be the boss Don't fight and don't give in. Withdraw from conflict (leave and calm down) Redirect to positive power by asking for help Be firm and kind Act, don't talk Decide what you will do (vs. what students should do) Use positive time out	Misguided power
Hurtful Vindictive Rude Abusive Self-destructive	• Hurt • Disbelieving • Spiteful • (Angry)	Retaliating Getting even Punishing Play victim - thinking "How could you do this to me?"	Retaliates Intensifies Escalates the same behavior or chooses another weapon	*I don't think I belong (or count) so I'll hurt others as I feel hurt. I can't be liked or loved.*	Teach/ use self-soothing and calming tools Show you care Build relationship Teach/ use "I" statements Avoid blame or shame Encourage strengths Avoid taking sides Class meetings	Hear: "I'm hurting" Connect: acknowledge feelings Emotional honesty Make amends Teach to make amends Avoid acting on hurt feelings Avoid punishment and retaliation Clear and appropriate follow through	Revenge
Withdrawal Indifferent to work Pessimism Hopelessness	• Discouraged • Futility • Helpless (low energy)	Compare student to others Criticize Doing for the student Giving up	Retreats further Passive No response No improvement	*I can't count or belong because I'm inferior to others. It's no use trying because if I did others would find out how inferior I am. I'm not perfect, so I'll convince others not to expect anything of me.*	Give responsibilities Show confidence Show faith Teach routines Teach how to break tasks into smaller pieces Model mistakes: it is okay to be imperfect Class meetings	Hear: "Don't give up on me" Show small steps Remind of past successes and strengths Show faith and confidence Take care of yourself and get support.	Inadequacy or Avoidance of humiliation

© Positive Discipline Association ■ www.PositiveDiscipline.org

Chart of Classroom Interventions by Mistaken Goal
Jody McVittie

Undue Attention Might look like: goofing off clowning annoying behavior distracting behavior helpless behavior incompetence dawdling etc…	Acknowledge student and the expectations of the situation.	"I love you and ____." (Example: "I care about you and will spend time with you later.") Redirect by assigning a task so child can gain useful attention Use secret signal *(nonverbal)* Use an "I-message" Stand close by Pass a written note Encourage Touch without words
	Do the unexpected	Turn out the lights Lower your voice Change your voice Talk to the wall Cease teaching temporarily
	Teach belonging skills	Use class meetings Teach small group skills Teach small group problem solving Set up routines Involve in contributing to the class
	Distract the student	Ask a favor Give choices Change the activity Ask a direct question Change the student's chair
	Minimize attention	Avoid special service Ignore
Misguided Power Might look like: Bossiness Arguing with teacher Refusing to do things Saying things are "stupid" Dawdling Incompetence *(passive power)* Doing things their way Being critical of others Obstructing	Prevention	Acknowledge student quietly. Greet students Notice small things about students Show curiosity about students Lunch with students *(all of them in rotation)*
	Acknowledge the student and the needs of the situation.	Acknowledge the student's power Don't fight and don't give in. Redirect to positive power by asking for help Offer limited choices Be firm and kind State both viewpoints Schedule a conference *(with the student)* Require a "reentry" plan Let routines be the boss
	Make a graceful exit	Withdraw from conflict Leave and calm down Table the matter Remove the audience Take a teacher time out Act, don't talk Decide what you will do
	Use power positively	Class room jobs Leadership opportunities Have them tutor a younger child Ask for their ideas *(esp. privately)*

Handouts for Workshop

Chart of Classroom Interventions by Mistaken Goal continued

	Teach belonging and significance skills	Class meetings Follow through and using agreements Encourage positive power *(Leadership and contribution)*
Revenge Might look like: Saying hurtful things Damaging things Hurting kids Stealing/lying Obstructing in hurtful way	Prevention	Don't grab the bait Develop mutual respect Set a few reasonable limits Encouragement
	Acknowledge the student and the needs of the situation	Acknowledge hurt feelings Share your feelings Avoid feeling hurt Avoid punishment and retaliation Show you care Act don't talk Use reflective listening Do not protect from natural consequences
	Teach recovery skills	Teach apologies (whole class) Teach about making amends *("What can be done to fix this mistake?")*
	Teach problem solving skills	Use class meetings Positive time out until student feels better Bugs and wishes "I-messages"
Assumed Inadequacy Might look like: (This one is more of a challenge because other mistaken goals can masquerade as inadequacy) Very discouraged but with low energy Need to get it right… and be so far from the mark that it isn't worth trying.	Prevention tools	Self-initiated "cool down time" Class meetings Teach internal monitoring as a science project Build trust Use reflective listening
	Acknowledge the student and the needs of the situation	Have faith in child's abilities Break task down to small steps Stop all criticism Encourage any positive attempt Teach skills/show how, but don't do for Provide academic skills support *(tutoring)*
	Teach self-encouragement skills	Model noticing change Model making mistakes as an opportunity to learn. Model not being perfect Encourage, encourage, encourage Ask "what" and "how" questions Focus on assets Guide student to use assets to handle challenges Compliments at class meetings *(Giving and receiving)*. Class meeting brainstorm of "getting unstuck strategies" *(for everyone)* Set up opportunities for success Teach strategies for becoming "un-stuck" Outlaw "I cant's" *(with humor)*
	Prevention	Build on student's interests Don't pity Don't give up Enjoy the child Encourage, encourage, encourage

Adapted by Jody McVittie from: Nelsen, Jane. *Positive Discipline.* New York: Ballantine Books, 2006. Albert, Linda. • *Cooperative Discipline.* Circle Pines, MN: AGS Publishing, 2003. • Dreikurs, Rudolf and Vicki Stolz. *Children the Challenge.* New York: Hawthorn Books, 1964.

Positive Discipline in the Classroom – Suggested Framework for Getting Started

Developed by Sound Discipline SoundDiscipline.org

This is an outline of the basic process of implementing Positive Discipline in a classroom. The time frames are suggested. Classes may move through this more quickly or slowly. The foundation needs to be built systematically. Each teacher knows his/her classroom community and will need to use his/her own judgment about how to pace these lessons. That may mean that a given "week" may actually take a week and a half or two; OR 2 weeks might be compressed in to one week or less than one week.

Building the foundation for effective class meetings is a scaffolded process. New skills and tools are added each week, and the skills and tools taught in the previous week are still used. Page numbers for specific lessons are not given as often there are several choices and the teacher will want to pick the best match for his/her classroom.

The long-term goal is to **teach students the skills to solve problems within the context of a respectful and caring community. In the process students are also learning many life skills. Students can then use most of their energies toward successful academic engagement.**

WEEK	FOCUS	LESSONS - 15 min once or twice/day	TEACHER REFLECTION
1	*Prepare the Ground* for classroom community.	• Agreements, teaching Routines. • Develop a system for Classroom Jobs.	*How does the practice of coming back to the agreements by asking students "How are we doing?" impact your classroom?* *What are you doing to practice Encouragement?* *Which of your students are going to need it the most?*
2	Strengthen the classroom community by building skills (extra time here will save time later).	• Self-Regulation (several approaches), Positive Time Out, Communication Skills, Mutual Respect	*What are you noticing about how your students are using the Brain in the Hand?*
3	*Prepare the Ground* with more tools.	• Building Cooperation, Mistakes, Respecting Differences, Win/Win • Forming a Circle	*Notice your own mood. How does that affect your students? What happens if you stay calm when the energy in the room goes up?*
4	Begin *Essential Skills for Class Meetings*. (All class meeting activities and lessons now occur in a circle)	• Compliments, Listening Skills, "Buy-In" or variation, "We Decided." • If necessary, work on Preparing the Ground pieces again with alternate activities.	*What happens when you acknowledge a mistake out loud and ask for help in fixing it?*
5	Continue building Essential Skills, creating a community that is <u>helpful, not hurtful</u>.	• Teach Solutions, Brainstorming, Recovery from Mistakes.	*How can you help yourself move toward using more solutions than consequences?*

Handouts for Workshop

WEEK	FOCUS	LESSONS - 15 min once or twice/day	TEACHER REFLECTION
6	Problem solving skills and practice. Practice with "fake problems" and teach role playing.	• "Problem-Solving Suggestions" • Create a Solution Table or Peace Table • "Problem-Solving Suggestions" can be a poster at the table. • Additional tools include a Wheel of Choice, Bugs & Wishes, and examples of "I-messages". • In some classrooms being "solution observers" is a rotating job. The "observer" is a student who watches the students solving a problem and reminds them of the steps.	*How do you model problem solving? Are you giving students the idea that "we can solve most anything in our own classroom"?*
7	Practice class meetings with group problems only.	• Class Meeting Format. • With your class, develop a system for putting items on your agenda. • Start the week by brainstorming a list of school or classroom problems that the students can pick from to practice; • The teacher should NOT add problems.	*Are there any preparing the ground skills that the students still need to practice?* *Are you taking care of yourself? Getting enough sleep? Taking breaks where you need it?*
8	*Continue group problems.*	• Teacher does an assessment of the class community. (see notes below this chart)	*"We are after improvement not perfection." What things are going well?*
9	Class meetings in action.	• When ready, begin using Class Meeting agenda with student-generated problems using names.	*When will this class be ready to have students lead the meeting? What small steps can be taken now to get ready for this?*
10+	When basic problem-solving skills are better: When routine is established and students more skilled: After at least 3 weeks of student generated problems:	• Consider introducing separate realities. This is a longer activity. "Animal Kingdon." • Move to student-led class meetings. • Remember that your job as a teacher will ALWAYS be to keep the circle helpful, not hurtful and to participate as a member of the group, sitting in the circle. • It works to OCCASIONALLY add a teacher problem on the agenda, but NOT one that involves an individual student.	

Assessing classroom skill level & readiness for Class Meetings:
- Are the students being respectful to each other?
- Can they listen while others talk?
- Can they work on solutions (with gentle reminders)?
- Is there a feeling of emotional safety and trust?
- Is the equipment in place (notebook or box) for an agenda?
- Are they always passing an object around the circle to give compliments and brainstorm?
- With the practice problems, do they decide whether to share feelings while others listen, talk without fixing, or ask for problem solving help?

If some of these elements are missing, consider the following and take appropriate action:
- Are pieces of the *Preparing the Ground* work missing?
- Do they need more practice with one of the building blocks? Check your own modeling – from the students' perspective, does it feel like you care about them?
- Are you looking for the "belief behind the behavior?"
- Can you see misbehavior as a misguided attempt at belonging and significance?

Positive Discipline in the Classroom Leadership Tools
(Tools to Avoid Punishment, Rescuing, Controlling, Power Struggles, Revenge)

Jane Nelsen and Lynn Lott

- Ask "what" and "how" questions instead of *telling* what, how, and why. Make sure you listen to what the student says.
- Offer limited choices
- Act, don't talk
- Use few words (1-10)
- Write a post-it note
- Connect before correct
- Special time
- Use humor (respectfully)
- Mirror: "I notice _____"
- Compliments
- Kind and firm
- Encouragement instead of praise or rewards
- Emotional honesty: "I feel____, because____ and I wish____"
- Jobs for a feeling of belonging and significance
- Positive time out (or cool-down space): Let students help design it
- See mistakes as opportunities for learning
- If you say it, mean it; and if you mean it follow through with respect and dignity
- Understand the belief behind the behavior: Use perception modification instead of behavior modification
- Joint problem-solving with mutually agreeable deadlines
- Go beyond consequences – brainstorm for solutions

- Do nothing – allow natural consequences
- "You can figure it out; come back with your plan"
- Use friendly eyes/smile and nonverbal signals
- Routines
- Class meetings
- Wheel of Choice
- Decide what you will do
- Small steps
- Use nonverbal cues
- Message of caring
- Listen without talking

> For more Positive Discipline in the Classroom tools check out *Positive Discipline Tools for Teachers Cards: 52 tools for Classroom Management.* Available from www.positivediscipline.com

The Results of Rewards Handout

Lois Ingber

Teachers want their students to behave and often choose to use rewards or positive incentives as a replacement for punishment. Some teachers use both rewards and punishments. We propose that neither *rewards* nor *punishments* are helpful in teaching our students to become ethical, caring responsible adults. Why do we say this?

1. Rewards and punishments are two sides of the same coin: they both aim to *control* behavior instead of focusing on *teaching*. Rewards and punishment model the use of *power* as a means of solving problems.
2. Rewards and punishments are forms of *"doing to"* and *"doing for"* students instead of *"doing with"* students. They don't invite students to learn from within or teach cooperative problem solving, both necessary skills in today's world.
3. Rewards and punishments *distract* students from the *real* issues. The child becomes more concerned with avoiding the punishment or gaining the reward than learning the *intrinsic value* of the appropriate decision or activity itself.
4. Rewards and punishments erode our *relationships* with our students. Relationships with our students are our most important tool for *influencing* our students' development.

Rewards:

- **Eventually lose their effectiveness.** The child loses interest in "working for" the reward, or may want rewards that are more appealing (bigger, better).
- **May bring temporary "obedience,"** but never help a child develop a commitment to a task or action when there is no "payoff."
- **Teach students to be self-centered.** They learn to think, "What's in it for me?" instead of doing the activity simply because it is worth doing for its own sake.
- **Are discouraging.** They are conditioned on the successful completion of the task. *Without successful completion, the withholding of the reward turns it into a "punishment" because; from the child's perspective the child is denied something promised.*
- **Erode intrinsic motivation.** The child does not have the opportunity to develop an interest or liking in the activity on its own merits. Students are denied the opportunity to make a genuine contribution, the foundation for feeling responsible and capable (belonging and significance).
- **De-value or degrade the task or action needed,** as the "reward" is presented as more important.
- **Interfere with self-esteem.** They create dependency upon an outside person for approval rather than a conscientious evaluation by the child of her own efforts.

Instead of rewards…. focus on solutions with your students:

- Problem solve together.
- Share your enjoyment of working together in the classroom.
- Avoid making everyday tasks seem like a burden.
- Make agreements and follow through.
- Invite the student to contribute to the class by giving them a job.
- Teach and hold class meetings.

Prepared by Lois Ingber, L.C.S.W., 2008. Sources: Positive Discipline by Jane Nelsen and Lynn Lott, and Unconditional Parenting and Punished by Rewards by Alfie Kohn. Another source with excellent research is Drive by Daniel Pink.

Handouts for Workshop

Solutions: Focus on Solutions
No More Logical Consequences (At Least Hardly Ever. . .)
By Jane Nelsen from Positive Discipline Newsletter (www.positivediscipline.com)

During a class meeting, students in a fifth-grade class were asked to brainstorm logical consequences for two students who didn't hear the recess bell and were late for class. **Following is their list of "consequences:"**

- Make them write their names on the board.
- Make them stay after school that many minutes.
- Take away that many minutes from tomorrow's recess.
- No recess tomorrow.
- The teacher could yell at them.

The students were then asked to forget about consequences and brainstorm for solutions that would help the students be on time. **Following is their list of solutions:**

- Someone could tap them on the shoulder when the bell rings.
- Everyone could yell together, "Bell!"
- They could play closer to the bell.
- They could watch others to see when they are going in.
- Adjust the bell so it is louder.
- They could choose a buddy to remind them that it is time to come in.

The difference between these two lists is profound. The first looks and sounds like punishment. It focuses on the past and making kids "pay" for their mistake.

The second list looks and sounds like solutions that focus on "helping" the kids do better in the future. It focuses on seeing problems as opportunities for learning. It other words, the first list is designed to hurt, the second is designed to help.

In the first list, the kids try to disguise punishment by calling it a logical consequence. Why do they do that? Could it be that this is what they are learning from adults? The Four Rs of Logical Consequences (Related, Respectful, Reasonable, and Revealed in advance) were conceived in an attempt to stop the trend of logical consequences sounding like punishment, but they have not totally eliminated this problem.

Where did we ever get the crazy idea that in order to make children DO better first we have to make them FEEL worse? When people first hear this quote from "Positive Discipline," they usually laugh as they think about how it doesn't make sense. However, when it comes to act, it seems that parents, teachers, and students have difficulty accepting that people do better when they feel better.

For example, many teachers like Nos. 2 and 3 on the first list above, ("Make them stay after school that many minutes," and "Take away that many minutes off tomorrow's recess.") It is true that those suggestions are related, reasonable, and could be enforced respectfully and revealed in advance. However, they all focus on making the child pay for the past mistake instead of finding a solution to solve the problem in the future. In other words, they are designed to make the children feel bad in the hopes that that will motivate them to do better. Punishment often stops misbehavior, but it hardly ever motivates children to do better in the future – unless they are approval junkies. Instead, they are motivated to rebel, get revenge, or to be more careful about getting caught.

Kay Rogers, a recently retired teacher from Sharon School in North Carolina said, "After I heard about the possibility of focusing on solutions instead of consequences, it was the hardest habit for me to break. All my life I had believed that kids learned from punishment -- or at least from consequences. I can now see that my students and I both tried to disguise punishment by calling it consequences -- even though the consequences weren't as harsh as blatant punishment. I had to learn about the effectiveness of focusing on solutions right along with my students. We were all surprised by the difference it made in our classroom. The level of respect and caring for each other was raised ten-fold. Students became pleased to find their name on the agenda because they knew, as Jane Nelsen had told us, that we would have a whole room full of consultants to give them valuable suggestions. And, the solutions they found were much more effective in changing behavior than anything we had done before."

This does not mean logical consequences cannot be effective when properly understood and appropriately used.

> Solutions are Related, Respectful, Reasonable *and* HELPFUL.

Hopefully the chapter on Natural and Logical Consequences in the newly revised edition of *Positive Discipline* will help. However, logical consequences are rarely necessary and are only one possibility. Rudolph Dreikurs taught that logical consequences are effective ONLY for the mistaken goal of undue attention (and are only one option even for that goal). Too many adults look for logical consequences "to punish" every behavior. Looking for solutions is more effective in most situations.

Many teachers have switched and now teach the Three Rs and an H for Solutions: Related, Respectful, Reasonable and HELPFUL. Once students have brainstormed for solutions to a problem, it is extremely important to let the individual student choose the solution they think will be most helpful. A vote should be taken only if the problem involves the whole class.

Of course, focusing on solutions instead of consequences is also more effective in homes. One parent said, "I can't believe how many power struggles I created by trying to impose 'logical consequences'. We have so much more peace in our home now that we focus on solutions."

The chapter on logical consequences in Positive Discipline explains when and how to use effective logical consequences. However, in most cases, it is much simpler and much more helpful to focus on solutions.

Substitute Strategies: Respect and the "Guest Teacher"

Jody McVittie

Having a substitute teacher for a day can be a nightmare--for the students, for the regular teacher, and for the substitute. Several steps can make these days a much better experience.

1. Recognize what happens from the students' point of view.

- Students have a strong positive relationship with their teacher. When the teacher is not present, they can feel abandoned, betrayed, or hurt. This invites hurtful behavior that can be aimed at peers and / or the guest teacher.
- Sometimes, students behave well for their regular teacher because they are afraid of what the teacher may do "to" them, but have not internalized the socially appropriate behavior. As a result, when the teacher is absent, their behavior may change dramatically.
- Sometimes students create mischief because it is fun to collaborate with each other and working toward a common goal (though it is not helpful to the substitute) creates an engaging sense of connection.

2. Plan for guest teachers using multiple strategies.

- Whenever possible, let students know ahead of time that you will be absent, and that there will be a guest teacher.
- Let students know that you would **prefer to be in the classroom because you care about them.** You will do your best to make sure the guest teacher has the information they need.
- When you can't let the students know ahead of time, leave a short note for the guest teacher to read to your students.
- Consider having a place for students to leave notes for you in case they have messages to communicate. Commit to reading those before class starts the day you return.
- When you know which substitute works well for your classroom, have them return if possible. Students appreciate your efforts to make their day successful.

3. Develop a classroom procedure for guest teachers *with the students* ahead of time.

If you are doing class meetings, go to Role-playing and Brainstorming: Working with Guest Teachers. If you have not yet started class meetings, you can engage students by holding a discussion. Tips:

- Let students know that occasionally there will be a guest teacher.
- Reflect on what happens daily in the classroom.
- Brainstorm different ways they can bother a guest teacher (write them down), then reflect on what it might feel like to be the guest teacher. Students can then brainstorm ways to make the day better for both the substitute and the students. Role-play one or two of the suggestions.

- Ask students to imagine what it would be like to have a different teacher in the classroom for a day.
    - "What were you feeling?"
    - "What might be different?"
    - "What might be hard or what might be fun?"
    - "What would make it easier for you?"
    - "What would you like the substitute to know about you or about our class?"
- Have students imagine *being* the substitute.
    - "What might you feel walking into the classroom?"
    - "What might be hard? What might be fun?"
    - "What would make it easier for the substitute?"
- Another solution-focused prompt is: "How can we invite our guest teacher to feel welcome in our classroom?" Typical student responses to this include:
    - Make morning announcements that welcome and remind the students about guest teachers
    - Have nametags that the students wear.
    - Have a book with a list of student jobs.
    - Have a book with a list of class guidelines and procedures.
    - Have a welcoming committee. Have students get specific about the welcomer's job. (Introductions, class tour, materials, explaining routines etc.)
- Role-play one or more of these ideas to help students understand and practice.

4. Develop a plan for assessing how the day went with the guest teacher. Students will have lots of ideas:
- The class can create a reflection form for the guest teacher. (Ideas for this could be a homework project.)
- The class can create a self-reflection form for students. (Sample below.)

5. Make the plan work.
- Let the guest teacher know that the class is working on welcoming him or her.
- Inform the guest teacher about classroom routines and how your class solves problems.
- Follow through with your agreements with the class. Let them know ahead of time whenever possible, leave a letter, keep the "guest teacher" book available, have a place for notes to you, and review and discuss self-reflection forms.

Ideas from guest teachers who have been successful and enjoy their work:
- Acknowledge openly at the beginning of class that it is tough when your regular teacher is absent.
- Take time to introduce and share something about yourself.
- Allow the students to introduce and say something about themselves. Try to learn their names.
- If you believe students are playing games with names, be straight with them. ("I'm guessing from the laughter that there is some fun with names going on. I personally prefer to be known by my real name, but if you'd rather have a different identity today, it is ok with me. The really important thing is that you can learn with the name that you choose.")
- Work hard to see the students for who they are, not what they do.

"Substituting behaviors" - a true story from Elk Grove School District, contributed by Jane Nelsen:

A counselor used the issue of substitutes during a class meeting with fourth grade students by asking the kids, "What do you do to 'bug a sub?'" The kids got a kick out of sharing all the things they did such as changing names, book drops, making fun of the substitute. All their sharing was recorded on a flip chart.

The next question was, "How do you think the substitute feels when these things are being done?"

It was interesting to watch the kids think about this as though they had never thought about it before. They had heard lectures about how rude they were, but they had never been invited to think about it. They started volunteering their ideas about how the things they did must make the substitute feel angry, hurt, and sad.

The counselor then asked, "How many of you would be willing to help the substitute instead of hurting him or her?" They all raised their hand, so the counselor asked, "What could you do to help?"

Every suggestion the kids brainstormed was very respectful, such as help her feel welcome, show her where things are, give our correct names, think about her feelings, be respectful. The students followed through on their ideas. The next time there was a substitute, she left a note for the regular teacher that she had never been treated so respectfully.

Handouts for Workshop

Substitutes: Sample Guest Teacher Checklist

Kay Kummerow from *The Adlerian Resource Book*, adapted by Jody McVittie

To my students:

I'm sorry that I cannot be with you in class today. Please record your behavior and academic progress for today. (Circle yes or no, or answer with a sentence.)

- Did you smile at the guest teacher when you walked in the door? Yes No
- Did you say hello? Yes No
- What is the guest teacher's name? _____
- Have you had this teacher before in another class? Yes No
- Were you in your seat when the tardy bell rang? Yes No
- Did you help with attendance? Yes No
- Did you listen to the directions for the lessons? Yes No
- Did you understand the directions? Yes No
- Did you ask a question about the directions? Yes No
- What question did you ask?

- Were you surprised when you saw that I was absent today? Yes No
- Did you remember that I told you I would be absent today? Yes No
- Today I'm at a workshop. What do you think I want to learn about?

- Are you surprised to learn that teachers also learn? Yes No
- Would you be interested in hearing about my workshop? Yes No
- Were you a cooperative and helpful member of the class today? Yes No
- What did you do to help make this a good class today?

- Do you think that this guest teacher will want to teach our class again? Yes No
- Why or why not?

- List five (5) things you learned today.

Handouts for Workshop

Top Card Handout
Jane Nelsen

| Rejection | Criticism | Stress | Meaninglessness |

1. Label your least favorite box #1. Label your second least favorite box #2.

2. My top card is _____ (the box ranked No. 1)

3. My style is _____ (the box ranked No. 2)

4. A bumper sticker for my top card could be:
_____

5. My best assets are:

_____

_____

_____

6. My liabilities are:

_____

_____

_____

7. My top card may invite from others:

_____

_____

_____

8. Specific steps for improvement:

_____

_____

_____

Top Cards: Teaching Ups and Downs and Possibilities

Lynn Lott

Top Card	Possible Teaching Assets	Possible Teaching Liabilities	May Need to Practice
CONTROL (Eagle)	May teach children: Organizational skills. Leadership skills. Productive persistence. Assertiveness. Respect for law and order.	Rigid. Controlling. May invite rebellion and resistance or unhealthy pleasing.	Letting go. Offering choices. Asking what and how questions. Involving children in decisions. Class meetings.
PLEASING (Chameleon)	May help children learn to be friendly, considerate and non-aggressive. Peacemakers, compromisers, volunteers, and champions of the underdog.	Doormats, keep score ("now you owe me"). May invite resentment, depression, or revenge.	Have faith in children to solve their own problems. Joint problem solving. Emotional honesty. Class meetings.
COMFORT (Turtle)	Model for children benefits of being easygoing, diplomatic, predictable, and to enjoy simple pleasures.	Permissiveness, which may invite children to be spoiled and demanding. More interest in comfort than in the "needs of the situation."	Creating routines. Setting goals. Solving problems together. Teaching life skills. Allowing children to experience consequences of their choices. Class meetings.
SUPERIORITY (Lion)	Model success and achievement. Teach children to assess quality and motivate to excellence.	Lecture, preach, expect too much. Invite feelings of inadequacy and failure to "measure up." See things in terms of right and wrong instead of possibilities.	Letting go of need to be right. Getting into child's world and supporting needs and goals. Unconditional love. Enjoying the process and developing a sense of humor. Holding class meetings where all ideas are valued.

Trauma: Working with Students Exposed to Trauma

Information from Helping Traumatized Children Learn available at https://traumasensitiveschools.org/tlpi-publications/download-a-free-copy-of-helping-traumatized-children-learn/ Compiled by Jody McVittie

It is important to remember that children living in situations that are highly stressful or traumatic appropriately have brains that adapt for survival. It is not helpful to label students or to ask, "What is wrong?" but instead to see the markers of the survival response as an adaptive response to the environment the child has been exposed to. There are also tremendous variations in how human beings develop. Our job is not to label, but to think about what in the current environment can help each student thrive.

Children exposed to trauma often struggle to: accurately perceive *safety* (over perceive danger), *self-regulate* (attention, behavior, emotion), hold a *self-image* that includes the belief that they matter or *succeed academically and/or socially* at school.

What trauma can look like in the classroom (and school)

Students exposed to trauma may:

- Disrupt the ability to process verbal information and use language to communicate. (May make it difficult to follow instructions.)
- Be less skilled in using language to forge social relationships and more skilled using language to build walls between themselves and those perceived to be dangerous or threatening.
- Have limited problem-solving skills.
- Struggle with sequential ordering and therefore not be able to organize (thoughts, feelings, if-then events, multi-step tasks), which in turn results in difficulty reading, writing and with critical thinking. This interferes with a student's understanding of behavior and consequences.
- Not have internalized cause and effect relationships. This means that they cannot easily predict events, sense their power over events or make meaning of "consequences."
- Struggle to see the world from the point of view of another.
- Struggle to focus and attend to what is happening in the classroom because their brains are preoccupied with ensuring safety /warding off danger.
- Struggle to self-regulate and recognize emotions. This results in poor impulse control, trouble reading social cues, and lack of a predictable sense of self.
- Have low executive functions.
- Be slow to trust adults or peers.
- Struggle to engage with academic material effectively.

Remember to take care of yourself. Vicarious trauma is real.

The Student Intervention Team Meeting

For students who have experienced trauma

Thinking it through:

- How do you establish trust? (Who should be there? Who will be the advocate for the student? What kind of practice is necessary?)
- How do you establish safety? (What are the ground rules? How will the student be supported?)
- What are the student's strengths?
- What doable piece of the challenge needs to be addressed?
- How can the student use his/her strengths to meet the challenge?
- How do you work with family/care givers to frame things in a helpful way – to invite them to see the student's best side?
- What is a reasonable amount of change to expect? Over what time period?
- What skills will be needed for the student to be successful?
- Who is going to be responsible? And for what?
- What is the follow through going to look like? (Who, when, how, next meeting?)

Understanding Attachment and the Development of Beliefs

Penny Davis, MA, CPDT, adapted from 'Attachment Parenting' by Grossmont College Foster and Kinship Education

AROUSAL/RELAXATION CYCLE

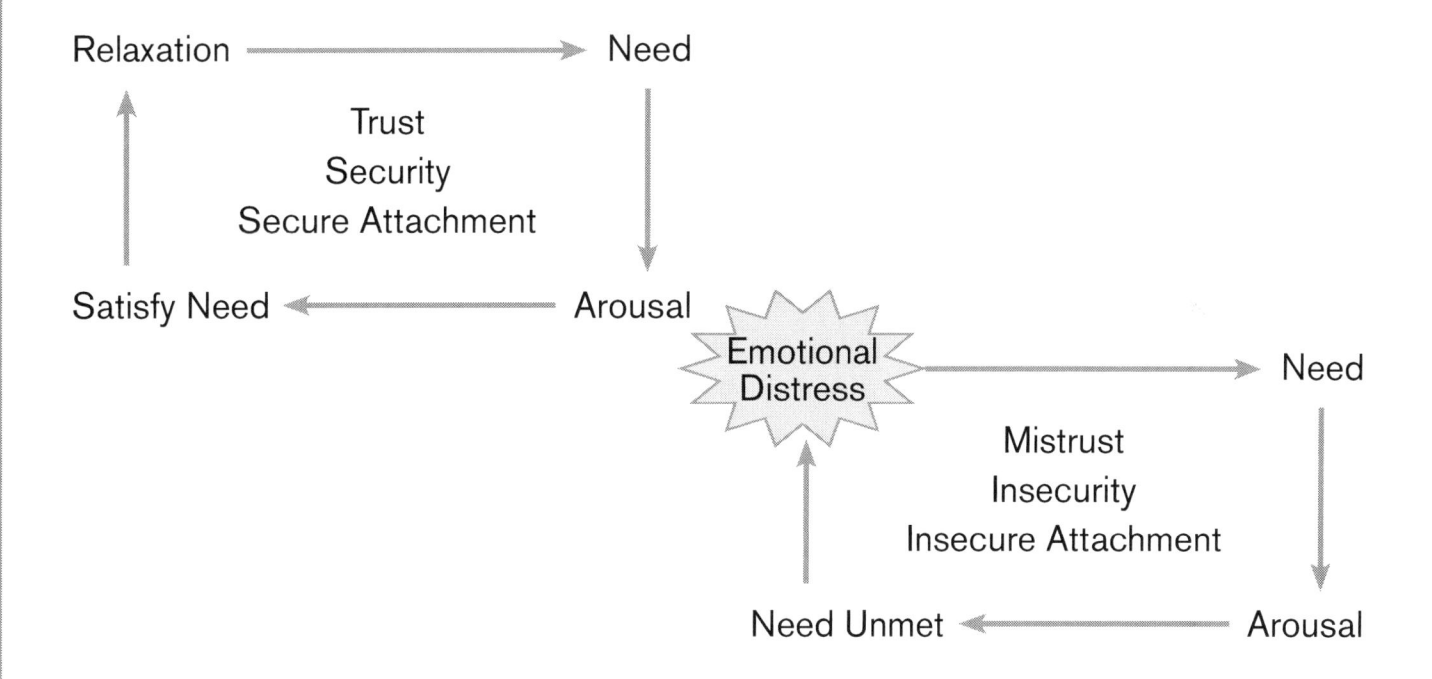

Relaxation → Need

Trust
Security
Secure Attachment

Satisfy Need ← Arousal

Emotional Distress

→ Need

Mistrust
Insecurity
Insecure Attachment

Need Unmet ← Arousal

Attachment Building Blocks

Penny Davis, MA, CPDA, adapted from 'Attachment Parenting' by Grossmont College Foster and Kinship Education

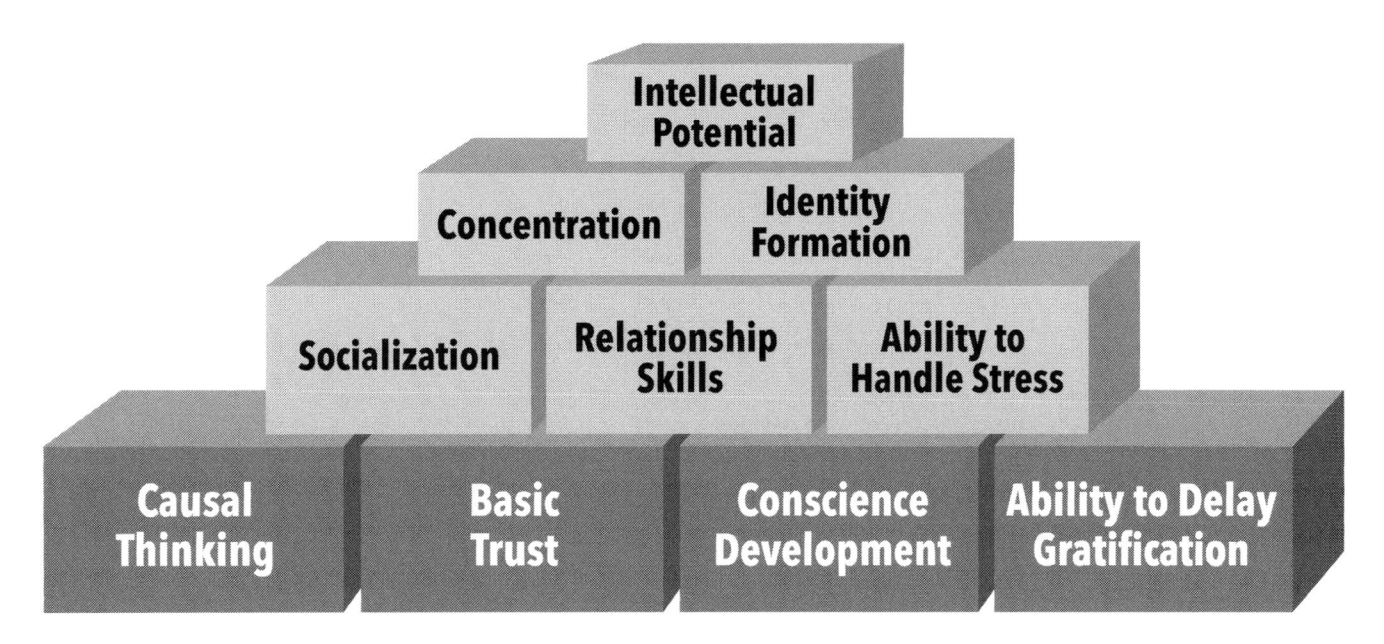

- **Intellectual Potential**
- **Concentration** | **Identity Formation**
- **Socialization** | **Relationship Skills** | **Ability to Handle Stress**
- **Causal Thinking** | **Basic Trust** | **Conscience Development** | **Ability to Delay Gratification**

Trauma: Rebuilding the Foundation for Students with Insecure Attachments or Trauma

Jody McVittie

Basic Trust
Routines (including class meetings)
Consistency and reliability in the relationship.
Relationships based on dignity and respect (firm and kind)
Listening to their story

Causal Thinking
"What" and "how" questions
Limited choices
Focusing on solutions

Conscience Development
"What" and "how" questions
Class meetings
Gradual building of empathy (being listened to, feeling felt)
Respecting differences (Activity: Animal Kingdom)

Ability to Delay Gratification
Routines
Consistency
Relationships built on dignity and respect (firm and kind)
Class meetings – working with peers
Mistakes are opportunities to learn

Identity Formation and Intellectual Potential
Classroom jobs and responsibility
Being able to contribute in meaningful ways
Using "I" statements and learning language for emotions
Opportunities to practice during play
Learning how to make amends and fix mistakes instead of "paying for them"
"It seems like you feel….. because…"

Relationship Skills and Socialization
Adult relationships based on dignity and respect (firm and kind)
Class meetings
Problem solving
Wheel of choice
Opportunities for play and practice and making mistakes
Mistakes are opportunities to learn

Ability to Handle Stress and Concentration
De-escalation tools (modeled, taught, expected)
Teaching students about their own brain (brain in the hand)
Using "I-statements"
Learning language for emotions
Space for "chilling out" (Positive Time Out or Chill Down Time – CDT)
Class meeting to be heard and validated, and to recognize that others have similar feelings
Mistakes are opportunities to learn

> *We learn best from those with whom we are in caring, mutually respectful relationships that promote independence. Such supportive relationships enable students from diverse backgrounds to feel comfortable bringing their personal experiences into the classroom, discover their common humanity and feel as though they are viewed as assets to the school community.*
>
> Learning First Alliance Every Child Learning: Safe and Supportive Schools

Teachers Helping Teachers Problem-Solving Steps
Face Sheet

A quick summary

The Teachers Helping Teachers Problem-Solving Steps process is an effective and powerful practice that allows teachers to work with peers to solve nagging classroom problems. Teachers "grow their toolbox" for effective responses and often feel encouraged and empowered by the process. In our experience, teachers using these steps as a team quickly improve their skills using the Mistaken Goal Chart and gain helpful insight into the world of their students. The process eliminates the endless analysis and the search for causes that lead to blame and excuses without helpful action.

Why the Teachers Helping Teachers Problem Solving Steps are important

- Deepens teacher's understanding of the mistaken goal chart.
- Significantly increases number and breadth of tools teachers have available for responding to misbehavior.
- Invites a sense of community when teachers understand that others have similar challenges.
- Reminds teachers that mistakes are opportunities to learn.
- Creates strong collaborative relationships for a teaching team.

In this section, you will find

- A one-page guide listing the steps of the Teachers Helping Teachers Problem Solving process.
- A longer version of the process that explains each step in more detail.

Moving it forward

The problem-solving process can be done by reading and working through the step-by-step description, however, most find that additional training is very helpful. Many Certified Positive Discipline Trainers are available to train and support school staff to effectively use this process.

▪ Tips

When using the Teachers Helping Teachers Problem Solving Steps:

- Follow the steps.
- Use very specific, first person problems.
- Stay with the specific event.
- Avoid talking about the history.
- Avoid analyzing.
- Make sure that suggestions are given to the scribe.
- Do both role-plays.

> We must realize that *we cannot build on deficiencies, only on strength.* We cannot help our children – or anyone else – to have faith in themselves as long as we have no faith in them.
>
> - Dreikurs *Social Equality: The Challenge of Today*, p. 122
> (emphasis in original)

Notes

Teachers Helping Teachers Problem-Solving Steps

Lynn Lott and Jane Nelsen

1. Explain the process (problem solving, real first-person problem, role play, solutions) and ask for a volunteer.

2. On a chart, record teacher's name, grade level, number of students in class, fictional name (for confidentiality) and age of challenging student.

3. State the problem in a one-line caption. (What would the headline be?)

4. Describe the last time the problem happened with enough detail so the group can get an idea of exactly what happened, as if describing a movie script. "What did you say and do? What did the student say and do? … Then what happened?"

5. Ask the teacher, "What were you thinking? How did you feel?" Refer to the Mistaken Goal Chart. Ask group if anyone else ever felt that way.

6. Using the teacher's feelings as the key, try to guess the belief behind the student's behavior.

7. Ask volunteer if she/he would be willing to try something more effective.

8. Set up role-play. Invite volunteer to play role of student. Ask for volunteers for other parts as needed. Role-play need not be more than 1 minute.

9. Process role-play by asking each player what they were thinking, feeling and deciding (to do) as the person they role-played.

10. Ask group to brainstorm (without discussing or analyzing) suggestions the volunteer could try. Refer to the mistaken goal chart. Record all suggestions. Volunteer just listens.

11. Ask volunteer to choose one suggestion they would be willing to try.

12. Do a second role-play using the suggestion, asking volunteer to play whichever role would be most helpful themself or the student). Process thoughts, feelings and decisions of each major role player as above. If you have a group playing other students, you can ask what they noticed.

13. Ask for a commitment from the volunteer to try the suggestion for one week and report back.

14. Ask the group to share appreciations for what they learned from the process and for the volunteer.

Teachers Helping Teachers Problem-Solving Steps – Detail

Jane Nelsen and Lynn Lott

The Teachers Helping Teachers Problem-Solving Steps process is an effective and powerful practice that allows teachers to work with peers to solve nagging classroom problems. Teachers "grow their toolbox" for effective responses and often feel encouraged and empowered by the process. In our experience, teachers using these steps as a team quickly improve their skills using the Mistaken Goal Chart and gain helpful insight into the world of their students. Going through the steps with other teachers can be fun and invite helpful collaboration. It eliminates the endless analysis and looking for causes that lead to blame and excuses without helpful action.

1. *Explain the process (problem solving, real first-person problem, role play, solutions) and ask for a volunteer.*
   - Introduce Teachers Helping Teachers Problem-Solving steps by telling the group that this is a process meant to help teachers increase their repertoire of effective responses, while receiving help with a real challenge.
   - The process involves inviting a volunteer to share a real, recent, first-person challenge (the volunteer's own challenge with a student) which has not been solved.
   - The challenge will be described and then role-played before the group works on suggesting solutions. Not only will the volunteer get help, but observers will also see something of themselves and their own students in the situation and will get helpful insights and suggestions.
   - Ask for a volunteer and then invite him or her to sit next to you. The volunteer teacher sits next to you because they are a coteacher with you in this process. This way, you can offer encouragement with your friendly energy. Also, you need to be close enough to convey in a friendly manner when you need to interrupt.

2. *Welcome the volunteer teacher.* On a flip chart write the volunteer teacher's name, teaching grade level, and number of students in class. Write the challenging student's fictitious name, and age of the student.

3. *Ask for a brief statement (a one-word or one-sentence headline) of the problem.*
   - In this step, you are looking for a general idea of the problem, not the details. Sometimes the teacher may give too much detail. Interrupt and say, "Later you will provide details. For now, if this challenge was a headline in a newspaper, what would it be?"

4. *Ask the teacher to describe the last time the problem occurred in enough detail and dialogue (like a movie script) that the group can get an idea of how to role-play the situation. If the volunteer needs help describing the situation, ask, "What did you do?" "What did the student do?" "Then what happened?" "What happened next?"*
   - At this point, you are looking for the step-by-step story of the problem the last time it occurred. Unless you focus on the specifics of the one incident, you, the teacher, and everyone involved will become overwhelmed and leave without satisfactory help.
   - One episode represents a microcosm of what occurs between this teacher and student. Focusing on and understanding the single incident will help other teachers with similar situations.
   - Ask for a description that includes details and dialogue for role-players. This helps the teacher focus on the incident instead of telling stories about background and causes. Background details are a distraction to this process. Those details could be discussed forever without focusing on solutions.
   - Sticking to the steps as outlined keeps the focus on finding a solution for a specific incident that brings clarity to the whole.

Teachers Helping Teachers Problem Solving Steps

- Specifics are important because they help you find more clues about the mistaken goal. What the teacher did and the student's response to what the teacher did provide insight into the belief behind the student's behavior (of which they may not be consciously aware). For example,
  - If the student stops the behavior for a while in response to what the teacher did but starts up again a few moments or an hour later, the belief behind the behavior is likely "I belong when I'm the center of attention" and the mistaken goal is probably undue attention.
  - If the student resists cooperation (actively or passively), the belief behind the behavior is likely "I belong when I'm the boss" and the goal is likely misguided power.

5. *Ask the teacher, "What did you think when this happened?" "When you thought that, what is one word that describes how you felt?" (If the volunteer has difficulty expressing a one-word feeling, refer them to the second column of the Mistaken Goal Chart and ask them to choose the group of feelings that fits.) Ask the group, "How many of you have ever felt that way?" (This is important so that the volunteer knows that they are not alone.)*

- Most people are not used to identifying their feelings. Explain that it takes only one word to describe a feeling.
- If the teacher is going on and on about what they think instead of what they feel, or if they come up with a vague feeling such as "frustrated," use the Mistaken Goal Chart and ask the teacher to find a feeling in the second column that comes closest to describing his/her own.
- **Ask for a show of hands of who in the group has experienced similar feelings.** It is very encouraging for the volunteer teacher to not feel alone or inadequate. Knowing others are or have been in the same boat is reassuring.

6. *Based on the feeling expressed, guess the student's belief behind behavior and mistaken goal using the Mistaken Goal Chart.*

- It is important for the teacher to express feelings, because feelings give us clues about the belief behind the student's behavior, which we call the student's mistaken goal.
- If appropriate, you can explain that the adult's feeling is the key to understanding the belief behind the behavior. For example, if the teacher feels annoyed, this is a clue that the student's belief might be "I believe I belong when I'm the center of attention" and the mistaken goal would be Undue Attention.
- Some people get this confused and think you have to know what the student feels in order to understand his/her goal.
- Don't spend a lot of time trying to figure out the belief or goal. You are just making a guess and will get more information from the role-play. Even if you never know for sure what the mistaken goal is, people will get help from role-playing and brainstorming.

7. *Ask, "Would you be willing to try something else that would be more effective?"*

- This question is important to verify, clarify, and substantiate a commitment. It is a respectful agreement to move forward.
- Once in a while a teacher might say something like, "I have already tried everything." With a friendly smile, say something like, "It can certainly seem that way sometimes. Would you like to go exploring to discover if there might be a useful idea?" If the answer is no (extremely rare), and the teacher does not show a willingness to try something else, do not go further. Thank them for sharing this much and stop the process.

8. *Set up a role-play of the scene that was described by asking for volunteers to play each part. (Remember that the role-play need not take longer than one minute to give all the information needed.)*

- Invite the teacher to play the role of the student so she/he can see the world through the eyes of the student. Ask for volunteers to play the parts of others described in the challenge. Have four to six people represent

Teachers Helping Teachers Problem Solving Steps

students in the classroom. This is important to show that even bystanders are affected by what goes on. The role-play is not meant to be improvisation. As much as possible, stick to the original script and dialogue they heard during the description of the problem.
- Some facilitators are afraid that people will object to role-playing, and some people do. The resistance won't discourage a facilitator who is confident about the value of role-playing.
- Proceed to set up the role-play with confidence. When you ask for volunteers to play roles, be quiet and wait. Someone will fill the void of silence and volunteer. You might joke with them in your own way, or say, "I feel resistance. It reminds me of my resistance before I found out how valuable this is and how much fun it can be. Okay, who are the brave souls who are going to jump in and help me show how much fun this is?" Or simply, "I can wait."
- Set up the room to represent the real situation. Are the desks in rows or groupings? Is the teacher in the front of the room or somewhere else?
- To get the role-play started, remind someone of his or her opening line or ask the volunteer teacher to remind someone of an opening line.

9. *Process the role-play by asking players to share thoughts, feelings and decisions.*
    - Stop the players as soon as you think they've had enough time to experience their thoughts, feelings and decisions (usually less than a minute).
    - Ask the person playing the adult what they were thinking, feeling, and deciding. Then ask the "student" what they were thinking, feeling, and deciding. Finally turn to the group playing other students and invite any of them to share their thoughts, feelings, and decisions.
    - This information sheds more light on the problem, and the processing serves as a debriefing for role-players who may be left with a lot of stirred-up feelings they need to express. Asking the students what they are deciding (to do) helps teachers see the long-term results of their actions instead of just the immediate result. Remember, feelings can usually be expressed in one word.

10. *Brainstorm with the group for possible solutions the teacher could try.*
    - Brainstorming allows each person to participate. It helps people accept and value how easy it can be to solve other people's problems. When it's someone else's problem, we are not emotionally involved, so we have objectivity and perspective. Once we accept this, we can appreciate the value of being consultants to each other instead of thinking we should be able to solve all our own problems—or that we are failures if we even admit we are having a problem.
    - Ask for a scribe to record all brainstormed suggestions on the flip chart. Suggestions should be written as stated. You might need to ask the person to state their suggestion concisely.
    - It is helpful to place the flip chart away from the volunteer teacher and ask that comments be directed to the scribe instead of the volunteer.
    - Tell the volunteer that they will surely hear suggestions that have been tried and to remain silent, remembering that the suggestions are really for all the teachers in the room and that putting all of the suggestions on the flip chart is helpful for everyone. *(Be sure every suggestion is written down.)*
    - This is not a time for discussion or asking questions of the volunteer teacher, nor is it time to analyze any of the suggestions with the volunteer teacher.
    - Encourage the group to think of as many alternatives as possible.
        - Ask everyone in the group to refer to the alternatives column of the "Mistaken Goal Chart" for ideas, or to make suggestions from their personal experience. You can also use the Positive Discipline tool cards to stimulate brainstorming.
        - Suggestions will improve as teachers learn more of the tools recommended in the books *Positive Discipline in the Classroom* and *Positive Discipline: A Teacher's A-Z Guide*. Do not censor negative suggestions.

11. Ask the teacher to choose a suggestion to try for one week.

- Read all the suggestions aloud, and then ask the volunteer to choose one they would be willing to try.
- Occasionally a teacher will say, "I've already tried all of them." Say something like, "Sounds like you really care and are trying everything you can think of. Would you be willing to pick one you have already tried, and we'll see what we can learn from the role-play about why it isn't working?"

12. Set up a second role-play using the suggestion, asking volunteer to play whichever role would be most helpful (them self or the student). Process thoughts, feelings, and decisions of each major role player as above. If you have a group playing students, you can ask what they were thinking, feeling, and deciding.

- Ask the teacher whether they would find practicing in the teacher or the student role more helpful. Ask them to take that role. (However, if a negative suggestion is chosen, be sure the teacher role-plays the student so that they can experience what the student might think, feel, and decide in response to that suggestion.)
- Sometimes the teacher will choose an idea that could be very effective but when they try to apply it, some old habits (such as lecturing, controlling, throwing in a little humiliation) are incorporated and then it is less effective. All this will come out in the role-play, and those watching will also gain some insight about why some of the things they do may not be working.
- If the person role-playing does start lecturing or doing something other than the chosen suggestion, it is okay to interrupt and say, "Excuse me. What did you say you were going to do?" This almost always causes laughter from the role players and others as everyone sees how easy it is to get sidetracked into old habits. That is one reason why it is so important to role-play the suggestion.
- If the chosen suggestion is a negative one, the role-play will demonstrate why it doesn't work when you process the student's thoughts, feelings, and decisions. It is important to ask all role players what they were thinking, feeling, and deciding in order to learn how a situation affects everyone. Finding out that a chosen suggestion won't work doesn't mean the time has been wasted. Everyone will learn many valuable things during the process.
- If the suggestion did not produce positive results in the role-play, ask the teacher what they learned from it. Ask if they would be willing to see what happens based on what was learned, and ask them to report back to the group next week. Many teachers find that they are able to be more creative the next time they encounter the problem because of what they learned during the Teachers Helping Teachers Problem-Solving Steps.

13. Ask for the teacher's commitment to try the suggestion for one week and report back to the group at the following meeting.

- Let the teacher know how important it is for the group to hear the results of their efforts so everyone can know how suggestions work in the real world. (We recommend regularly scheduled meetings for teachers, no less than once a month and preferably once a week while they are learning these new skills.)

14. Ask the group for appreciations for the volunteer teacher.

- Occasionally, participants want to keep teaching the volunteer. It is helpful to offer the following suggestions for appreciations:
  - This is the time to give back to the volunteer by telling them what this experience gave to you. Appreciations may sound like this: "I learned ___," "I felt___," "I have the same problem, so now I can try_____," "I know how hard it is to share____."
  - What help did you get for yourself by watching this?
  - What did you see that you appreciate about the volunteer?
  - What ideas did you see that you could use?

Teachers Helping Teachers Problem Solving Steps

Once teachers have become familiar with the expanded version, the short version provides an outline of the steps to be followed. Teachers may want to rotate the facilitator position so that everyone has an equal opportunity to have fun making mistakes while learning. The facilitator and every member of the group should have a copy of the Mistaken Goal Chart so they can refer to it when guessing the mistaken goal and when brainstorming for suggestions.

- **Extension** (to be used only if you are knowledgeable about birth order):
  - It can be fun to alert the group to some possibilities they could look for based on the birth order of the teacher and the student.
  - For example, if the teacher is the oldest sibling in the family, are perfectionism and bossiness a problem? (Joke with the teacher: "We know you don't have these characteristics, but some other firstborn teacher might.") You might ask, "Are you sometimes too hard on yourself when things don't go as well as you would like?" This often helps a firstborn person feel understood. For those who are middle born, is trying to save the world a problem? They often see all sides to every issue and get caught up in what's fair. They often work well with rebels and underdogs. For teachers born last in their family, is a lack of order a problem, or are they waiting for someone else to fix things for them? They often allow for lots of creativity. A teacher who is an only child may be similar to an oldest or youngest. Ask only-children teachers if they sometimes have difficulties with students who fight or disagree with each other or borrow items without asking permission. You can also make some guesses about the student based on birth order. Is a youngest child looking for special service, a middle child looking for a place by being different, an oldest child giving up because they can't be first, or an only child having trouble sharing? There may not be time to spend on this issue, but it is helpful if facilitators are aware of it.

Moving it Forward
Face Sheet

You have taken the Positive Discipline in the Classroom workshop and are using the tools in your classroom. As your students are becoming more skilled at class meetings, you are also noticing that they are able to keep their agreements, are more helpful to each other, classroom work time is more productive and you are growing a real community of learners. You would like to share some of what you've learned with your peers. Now what?

You might:

- Continue to model and simply answer questions from your staff and parents.
- Invite a colleague to watch your students run a class meeting.
- Have your students demonstrate a class meeting for another class.
- Lead your whole staff through some of the activities you have taught your students.
- Invite some of your staff to take the full workshop.
- Create a team to explore climate, social learning and discipline.
- Invite a certified Positive Discipline trainer to your school for a workshop.

You might be tempted to teach your staff the activities that made an impression on you in the workshop. Please limit the activities you teach your staff to a few you have taught your students or the nine we have included in this section. We ask that you become a certified trainer before you teach activities that are not in this manual.

Tips

- Keep the information simple, practical, applicable, fun, experiential and real.
- Keep in mind that you are not trying to change others. You are offering a gift – it is up to them whether they believe you that it works, or whether they choose to try a new tool.
- Recognize that you are planting seeds. Some may find fertile soil, others won't.
- Know that there will be colleagues who might be threatened by new ideas or changes, and remind them only to use what works for them in their classroom.

Some short topics that have worked to begin to introduce Positive Discipline concepts:

- Asking vs. Telling
- Do as I Say
- Do vs. Don't
- Encouragement Circles
- Listening: Effective and Ineffective
- Taking Care of Yourself
- The Two Lists
- "What" and "How" Questions
- The Wright Family

Notes

Moving it Forward

Asking vs. Telling

Inspired by *Positive Discipline Workbook Facilitators' Guide*, Jane Nelsen

OBJECTIVES:
- To explore the power of asking instead of telling
- To connect the power of asking to the development of desirable character traits.

MATERIALS:
- Sentence strips made from statements below (It is helpful to print the two sets on 2 different colors of paper)
- Character Traits poster from Two Lists Activity

COMMENT:
- This activity can be done with three volunteers: the first reads the "A" statements, the second reads the "B" statements, and the third is a student listening to the statements.

DIRECTIONS:

1. **Set up.**
   - Have 8 volunteers form a line. They will be adults.
   - Distribute statement strips with A statements on one side and B statements on the other, one to each volunteer.
   - Ask for another volunteer to be a student.

2. **Reading A statements.**
   - Ask the student to stand in front of the first person in line, ready to listen as that person reads their A statement to the student.
   - Ask the student to remain silent, pause and notice what they are thinking, feeling and deciding about the adults and themselves as they hear the words.
   - Have the student proceed down the rest of the line in the same manner, listening to each A statement.

3. **Process.** Ask the student:
   - "What are you feeling?"
   - "What are you thinking or deciding about the adults?"
   - "What are you thinking or deciding about yourself?"
   - Referring to the character traits or skills of the Two Lists activity, ask the student which character traits or skills are being developed by the statements.

4. **Reading B statements.**
   - Have the student stand in front of the line again and this time the volunteers read their B statements.
   - Repeat the rest of the steps in #2 and #3 above.

5. **Reflection:**
   - Invite comments from the volunteers about what they noticed and learned; especially about the character traits they want to develop in students.
   - Invite others in the room to share what they noticed.

Moving it Forward

Asking vs. Telling Statements (Primary)

"A" Statements
1. You should have your homework ready before you come to class!
2. Stop bothering your classmates!
3. Don't forget to take your coat with you for recess and be sure to put it on...it's cold outside!
4. If you don't get your work done in class, you will stay in from recess and get it done then!
5. Stay in your seat!
6. Put your papers away, books back on the shelf and clean up before you leave the classroom!
7. Stop whining and complaining!
8. You shouldn't treat your friends that way.

"B" Statements
1. What do you need to bring with you to be prepared for class?
2. What can you and your classmate do to solve this problem?
3. What do you need to take with you if want to be warm outside at recess?
4. What is your plan for getting your work done before class is over?
5. How does your walking around the room affect your classmates?
6. What do you need to do to clean up your space before you leave this classroom?
7. How can you speak to me so I can hear, what you are saying?
8. What do you think will happen if you continue to treat your friends that way?

Asking vs. Telling Statements (Secondary)

"A" Statements
1. Stop bothering Michael!
2. Bring your materials to class next time!
3. Put your cell phone away.
4. You shouldn't treat your friends that way.
5. You need to apologize for that.
6. Stay in your seat!
7. Turn your project in by Friday or I can't give you credit for this semester.

"B" Statements
1. What can you and Michael do to solve this problem?
2. What system can you create so your materials show up to class with you?
3. What is our agreement about cell phone use during this time?
4. What do you think will happen if you continue to treat your friends that way?
5. How can you fix your mistake?
6. How does your walking around the room affect your classmates?
7. What's your plan for completing your project by Friday so I can give you credit?

Asking vs. Telling Statements (Early Childhood)

"A" Statements
1. Pick up your plate.
2. Push in your chair.
3. Put on your coat.
4. Be quiet.
5. Go lay on your cot.
6. Sit down at the table.
7. Put the toys away.

"B" Statements
1. Where does your plate belong?
2. What can you do with your chair?
3. What do you need before you can go outside?
4. What kind of voice would help us all hear each other?
5. Remind me of what it is time to do now?
6. What did we agree about eating time?
7. What is your job at clean-up time?

Do as I Say
Ruben Castaneda

OBJECTIVE:
- To demonstrate to teachers how some students' actions are based on behavior learned from adults around them.
- To introduce mirror neurons.

MATERIALS:
- None

COMMENT:
- This is a lovely set-up for understanding the power of modeling and mirror neurons.

DIRECTIONS:

1. **Gather the group's attention.** Model and ask the group:
   - To put their eyes on you.
   - To put both feet flat on the floor (you may be standing, but they will probably be sitting).
   - To place both hands on their knees and to take a deep breath and exhale.

2. **Begin and model intentional action.** Ask the group to make a circle with their index finger and thumb.

3. **Continue action with words that do not match.** Do this with confidence as if nothing is abnormal.
   - State, "Now place the circle on your chin", while at the same time you place *your circle on your cheek.*
   - Observe the group: most of them will have followed what you *did*. Watch for those who catch themselves and try to adjust.

4. **Reflection.** Keeping your hand on your cheek, ask the group,
   - "Where did you put your hand?" (Many will have followed your actions, not your words.)
   - "Why did that happen?"
   - "Why do you have it on your cheek?"
   - "What are we learning in terms of teaching/modeling for children?"
   - "What are some behaviors they may have noticed their student picked up from them?"
   - "What do they need to do if they expect a different behavior from their student in the future?"

Extension

Introduce mirror neurons. If you don't know much about mirror neurons watch http://video.pbs.org/video/1615173073/

- We are hardwired to learn by watching.
- When watching an intentional action, our brain gets ready to do the same thing.
- This is present from birth. (When you stick your tongue out to an alert newborn 3 times, the baby will copy you. When you see someone yawn, you may find yourself repressing your own yawn.)
- Mirror neurons work for emotions too. By engaging the emotional parts of our brain through our mirror neurons, we are actually able feel other people's emotions. It is part of our brain's natural empathy system.

Do vs. Don't

Kelly Pfeiffer

OBJECTIVE:
- To understand the power of telling students what to do instead of what not to do.
- To become more aware that the language we use has profound impacts.

MATERIALS:
- Flip chart, markers
- Cue cards for your instructions (following page)

COMMENTS:
- This activity stands alone or can be used to complement and enhance other practices.
- Punishment focuses on what not to do instead of what to do. Children often experience "don't" as punishment.
- Routines help students know what to do.
- The Wheel of Choice offers ideas for what to do.
- Bugs and Wishes teaches students to ask for what they want (helping the other student know what to do.)

DIRECTIONS:

1. **Introduce activity.**
   - Ask participants to simply follow the instructions.
   - There will be two rounds.

2. **Round 1.**
   - Give the commands/instructions pausing briefly after each.
   - After all of the instructions, say, "That was the end of round 1. Now we will do round 2."

3. **Round 2.** Give the commands for round two.

4. **Reflection.**
   - Ask participants "What was different between round 1 and round 2?"
   - Record responses which will look like:

   Round 1: Harder, required more thinking, I wasn't sure what to do, confusing, slower.

   Round 2: Easier, I knew what to do, faster, clear, simple to process.
   - "What did you learn from this about instructions?"

5. **Moving it forward.**
   - Divide a fresh sheet of paper into two columns. Label the left column "Don't" and the right, "Do."
   - Ask participants to share things for which they hear themselves and others saying, "Don't" (Scribe in left column.) e.g. Don't hit, Don't run, Don't yell, etc.
   - Invite the group to brainstorm "Do" statements that correspond to each "Don't" statement.
   - "What did you learn/notice from this?"

Cue cards for your instructions

Statements for Round 1:
Don't sit down
Don't put your hands by your sides
Don't close your mouth
Don't open your mouth
Don't look at me
Don't stand still
Don't stand up

Statements for Round 2:
Stand up
Raise your hands
Open your mouth
Close your mouth
Look at another person
Walk around the room
Sit down

Encouragement Circles

Jane Nelsen and Cheryl Erwin

OBJECTIVE:
To enhance awareness of the power of and need for encouragement for the adults in the school community.

MATERIALS:
- Flip Chart
- Markers

COMMENTS:
- Having someone whisper into your ear or touch you from behind can be uncomfortable. Advise your group to be aware and respectful.
- There are two reasons the directions indicate that the encourager should give a statement that they themselves would like to hear.
  ○ It removes the responsibility of finding the "right" comment.
  ○ Personally speaking the statement is also a form of self-encouragement.

DIRECTIONS:

1. **Preparing the group.** As a group, brainstorm things that would be helpful/encouraging to hear after having a stressful day. Scribe them on the flip chart. Examples might include:
   - I'm glad you are my co-worker.
   - I saw you working with [student's name] today and it made a difference.
   - You make a difference.
   - I can tell you've had a tough day.
   - When I watch you work with your students I can tell you really care about them.
   - I appreciate the effort you have put in today.

2. **Set up the circle.**
   - Count the number of people participating. Arrange ½ that many chairs in a circle facing inward.
   - Invite ½ of the participants to sit in the chairs.
   - The other participants each stand behind a seated person.

3. **Sharing encouragement, round 1.**
   - The standing participants whisper one of the encouraging statements that they personally would like to hear to the person in front of them (not what they think the person would like to hear).
   - The sitting participants remain quiet and just receive the statement.
   - Then everyone rotates to the right.
   - Repeat this process about 5-10 times (This process can be very encouraging. Consider completing the circle if time permits.)

4. **Sharing encouragement, round 2.** Have the participants switch places. Repeat step 3.

5. **Reflection.** When both sets of participants have received and given, invite them to process.
   - "What did you notice?"
   - "How did it feel to give encouragement?"
   - "How did it feel to receive encouragement?"
   - "Anything else?"

6. **Moving it forward.** Invite a discussion about how what they learned here might be used in a school to encourage each other. School staff need encouragement from each other.

Positive Discipline in the School and Classroom Manual
by Jane Nelsen, Lynn Lott, Teresa LaSala, Jody McVittie, and Suzanne Smitha

Listening: Effective and Ineffective

Lynn Lott and Jane Nelsen

OBJECTIVE:
- To experience the difference between effective and ineffective listening.

MATERIALS:
- Flip chart paper, prepared with statements
- Markers

COMMENTS:
- The sense of "feeling felt" helps a person regain self-control.
- The sense of "being heard" is so powerful it alone can help us move toward solutions.
- Acknowledging feelings in the "It seems like you feel" statements is a powerful form of connection.

DIRECTIONS:

1. **Set up:**
   - Have audience divide into partners, "A" and "B."
   - Have everyone think of something that they could complain about for 30 seconds. It could be a student's misbehavior or something else that went wrong recently.

2. **First role play:** Give advice
   - Post sentence prompt: "I think you should have…."
   - Ask A to complain or rant to B for about 30 seconds.
   - B responds with advice beginning with: "I think you should have…."

3. **Second role play:** Criticize
   - Post sentence prompt: "I can't believe you….!"
   - Switch roles. Have B rant to A about something for 30 seconds.
   - A responds with criticism beginning with: "I can't believe you…!"

4. **Third role play:** Validate
   - Post sentence prompt: "It seems like you feel _____ because _____ and you wish _____."
   - Maintain the same roles as the second role-play.
   - B will tell the same "rant" again.
   - A responds with effective listening beginning with "It seems like you feel __because __and you wish __." A is then to listen and use only non-verbal communication, regardless of how tempting it is to speak.
   - Explain that the "you wish" part could be funny or serious. Examples:
     - "It *seems like you feel* angry *because* John is bugging you *and you wish* at least for today, he lived on the other side of the moon!"
     - "It *seems like you feel* angry *because* John is bugging you and you *wish* he would stop."

5. **Reflection**
   - This activity can be processed after each role-play, or in the interest of time, only after the third role-play.
   - Ask participants what they were feeling, thinking and deciding in each of the different role-plays.
   - Which style helps them move toward solutions?
   - If it hasn't come up, invite participants to notice that it can feel awkward to criticize other adults, but criticizing children comes more easily.

Moving it Forward

Taking Care of Yourself

Lynn Lott and Jane Nelsen

OBJECTIVE:
- To recognize that failure to care for ourselves is hurtful to ourselves and others.
- To recognize the cumulative impact of the stress of daily events.
- To generate and focus on ideas for self-care practices.

MATERIALS:
- Sticky notes (2 per participant)
- Flip chart
- Markers

COMMENTS:
- Taking care of ourselves is essential if we are to do our best with young people.
- We teach better when we feel better.
- It is important to model self-care skills so the young people in our lives can learn them.
- Preview the video referenced below if you plan on including the reference to Steven Covey's rock activity.

DIRECTIONS:

1. **Set up.**
   - Give each participant 2 sticky notes.
   - Draw a large pot on the flip chart. Make it only big enough to hold about 2/3rds of the sticky notes from participants.

2. **What makes you angry?**
   - Ask participants to write one thing that makes them angry on each note.
   - You can offer humorous examples such as: people who blink their lights at me when I am going the speed limit, my mother in law inviting herself to visit when I have other plans.

3. **Filling the pot.**
   - Ask participants to put their sticky note in the pot when they are done writing.
   - Invite participants to share as they walk up or you can read several aloud after some have accumulated.
   - The pot will start to get very full. When participants look for a spot to put their sticky note you might comment, "What happens when a pot gets overfilled?"

4. **The results of our cumulative stress.**
   - Point to the pot of sticky notes and ask, "Is this what your day looks like?"
   - "When these things fill our day and then a student does something really annoying, how are we likely to react?" (Participants usually recognize that the child gets a reaction out of proportion to the incident.)
   - "Do you do your best job as a teacher when you've had a day like this?"

5. **Taking care of yourself.**
   - "What kind of things do you do to take care of yourself?" You will get responses like: exercise, talk to friends, walk pets, listen to music, read, pray, take a hot bath etc.
   - If you did not hear suggestions that include things that can be done during the school day, ask for additional suggestions.
   - Each time you get a response, move one of the sticky notes from inside the pot to the outside of the pot. Write the response inside the pot where that sticky note was.

Positive Discipline in the School and Classroom Manual
by Jane Nelsen, Lynn Lott, Teresa LaSala, Jody McVittie, and Suzanne Smitha

Moving it Forward

- Gradually instead of a pot filled with sticky notes, you have a pot filled with suggestions of how to take care of yourself. The sticky notes are now stuck on top of each other at the margins of the flip chart and make a powerful visual.

6. **Reflection**
   - What did you learn from this?
   - How do children learn self-care?
   - What are small steps you could take to improve your self-care?
   - Time permitting, have participants write down 2 things they will do this week or pair up and share commitments with a partner.

7. **The big rocks (optional).**
   - Talk about Steven Covey's demonstration of the rocks in the jar. If you take a jar of rocks…all kinds of rocks, big and little and dump them out you will have a pile of rocks. If you then put in all the small rocks, then the medium rocks, and then try to get the big rocks in, what happens? (The big rocks don't fit.)
   - Ask, "Is taking care of yourself a big rock or a little rock?" "What does that mean for planning your day?"

The Two Lists: Where Are We and Where Do We Want to Go?

OBJECTIVES:
- Recognize the importance of social skills for our students.
- Identify skills needed for long-term success.
- Acknowledge common challenges and goals.
- Develop awareness of the importance of practice and role modeling when teaching social skills.

MATERIALS:
- Flip chart and markers

COMMENTS:
- This exercise is very effective at the beginning of any introductory talk. It helps participants get in touch with how Positive Discipline will be relevant to them and/or their community.
- Connection to real problems invites buy-in.
- It is helpful to explore and understand what behaviors challenge teachers.
- The list of qualities and gifts is a constant reminder of the long-term goals.
- Some schools post them in the faculty lounge.
- Both lists are a good reference in other activities.

DIRECTIONS:

1. **Brainstorm.** Ask participants to brainstorm a list of student challenges and/or behaviors that "push their buttons." Make sure that there is a wide range of challenges and problems listed.
   - Include "smaller" ones like whining, talking back, not listening and "bigger" ones like violence, drugs, depression, cutting, or anorexia.
   - Be sure to add some of the bigger ones if the group has not named them.

2. **Tape the list to the wall.**

3. **Brainstorm again.** Start the second list by asking the participants, "What characteristics and lifeskills would you want your students to have as they reach adulthood?" (The list will include things like: self-esteem, responsibility, kindness, compassion, faith, problem-solving skills, sense of humor, resilience, love, honesty, ability to form relationships, setting goals, learning from mistakes, communication skills, etc.)
   - Be sure to add any you think are missing (e.g. sense of humor).
   - Point out that this second list rarely includes academic skills.
   - Notice that these qualities are what we want in a good neighbor.

4. **Tape the list to the wall.**

5. **Compare the lists.** Ask the group to look at the two lists, and with curiosity ask, "How do children learn?" Accept answers until you get one that is "by watching", or "from modeling", or by "doing what you do."

6. **Explore.** "What do we do when a student does something from the first list?
   - "Do we model patience, problem solving skills, or a sense of humor?"
   - "Or do we lose it, punish them, or send them out of the classroom?"
   - "What do we do with a student who is missing academic skills (offer support/training), compared to what we do with a student who is missing social skills (exclusion/consequences)?"
   - "How would students learn how to respond appropriately to items on the first list if they didn't see adults modeling appropriate responses?" (The "problems" are opportunities to teach.)

7. **Introduce mirror neurons** by doing the "Do as I Say" activity.
8. **Moving it Forward.** This gives us our compass for this work.
    - The Positive Discipline curriculum is designed to teach students the skills needed to move from the first list to the second list.
    - Our students will learn best from us when we can model what we want from them, even under stress.

"What" and "How" Questions
Suzanne Smitha

OBJECTIVES:
- To introduce the concept of "what" and "how" questions.
- To help teachers "feel" the different loci of control when "what" and "how" questions are used (external vs. internal).
- To strengthen students' abilities to use their internal locus of control.
- To establish an environment for more effective problem solving.

MATERIALS:
- None needed

DIRECTIONS:

1. **Set up.**
Ask the audience or a volunteer to put their hands together and interlace their fingers.

2. **Learn from a volunteer.** Ask one volunteer:
   - "What did you do with your hands?"
   - "How did you do it?"
   - "Why did you do that with your hands?" (The person will answer the "Why" question differently with something like, "Because you told me to.")

3. **Learn from the group.** Ask the group:
   - "What did you notice?"
   - "How are the 'What and How' answers different from the 'Why' answer?"
   - "Where was the locus of control with each question?" (external/internal)

4. **Invite discussion** about what students are learning. Bring forward how shifting from why questions to what and how questions helps:
   - Students assume responsibility for their actions.
   - The process for effective problem solving.
   - Open dialogue.
   - Remove the sense of judgment.

Moving it Forward

The Wright Family

There are many variations of this activity online. The original source is unknown. It has been adapted for the Positive Discipline Curriculum by Cheryl Forse, Deb Pysno, Catherine Bronnert, and Dori Keiper

OBJECTIVE:
- Enhance awareness of how stress impacts one's ability to process information.
- Increase awareness of the kinds of stressors students experience and the impact this has on learning.

MATERIALS:
- 1 to 3 small objects for each participant. (coins, buttons, stones, candy, etc.)
- The Life with the Wright Family Story (attached below)

COMMENTS:
- We are naturally wired to seek belonging and significance. Students who do not have an inherent sense of belonging and significance experience stress as they move toward finding their place and sense of value.
- When stress is increased due to academic, social or behavioral challenges, a student's ability to attend to content is significantly compromised.
- Even when the instruction to listen to the story is repeated several times and the instruction to pass the object left and right is only given once, participants focus on passing and are not able to hear the content of the story. When their brain is stressed, students also focus on the actions and lose their ability to focus on intellectual content.

DIRECTIONS:
1. **Set-up.**
   - Invite all participants to form a circle: each standing close enough to reach the hand of the persons beside them.
   - Distribute up to 3 objects to each person.
   - Ask them to listen to the story you are about to read. (Make an effort to mention this 2 or 3 times).
   - When they hear the word "right," they are to pass an object to the person on their right. When they hear the word "left", they pass an object to the person on their left.

2. **Read the Wright Family Story.**
   - Read the complete story at a steady normal pace.
   - Continue even if there is chaos, confusion and participants are dropping objects.
   - When done reading, ask participants to "freeze" and hold onto any object/s in their hand.

3. **Ask curiosity questions.**
   - Ask the questions listed below the story.

4. **Reflection on activity.**
   - "What happened?"
   - "What were you thinking and feeling?"
   - "What decisions did you make during the process?"
   - "What did you notice?"
   - "What did you learn?"

5. **Connection to the classroom.**
   - How does this relate to learning in a classroom? (When we shift our focus from one thing to another, we are less efficient learners.)
   - What kinds of stressors impact students' ability to process and integrate information? (Belonging and significance, family, peers, safety, etc.)

Extension/Variation

- Prior to starting this activity, ask the group to brainstorm a list of "life stressors." (Morning rush, busy schedules, paying bills, relationships, jobs/responsibilities, etc.)
- Begin the activity as in step one.

Moving it Forward

- After giving each participant their small object/s, ask them to reflect for a moment, making a connection between their held object/s and their own personal life stressors.
- Continue with directions above.
- In addition to the questions and reflection above, make a connection to how we all have life stressors, yet how we carry and handle these may be different.
  - "Who gave all their object/s and stressors away? Who held onto their object/s and stressors?"
  - "Who gave up on the process and didn't want to deal with their object/s and stressors?"
  - "Who gave all their focus to the object/s and stressors?"

Life with the Wright Family Story*

One day the Wright family decided to take a vacation. The first thing they had to decide was who would be left at home, since there was not enough room in the Wright family car for all of them. Mr. Wright decided that Aunt Linda Wright would be the one left at home. Of course, this made Aunt Linda Wright so mad that she left the house immediately, yelling, "It will be a right cold day before I return!"

The Wright family now bundled up the children – Tommy Wright, Susan Wright, Timmy Wright and Shelly Wright, and got into the car and left. Unfortunately, as they turned out of the driveway, someone had left a trashcan in the street, so they had to turn right around and stop the car. They told Timmy Wright to get out of the car and move the trash can so they could get going. Timmy took so long that they almost left him in the street. Once the Wright family got on the road, Father Wright wondered if he had left the stove on. Mother Wright told him not to worry, as she had checked the stove and he had not left it on. As they turned right at the corner, everyone started to think about other things that they might have left undone.

No need to worry now, they were off on a right fine vacation. When they arrived at the gas station, Mother Wright put gas in the car and then discovered that she had left her wallet at home. So, Tommy Wright ran home to get the money that was left behind. After Tommy left, Susan Wright started to feel sick. She left the car, saying that she had to throw up. This, of course, got Father Wright's attention and he left the car in a hurry. Shelly Wright wanted to watch Susan get sick, so she left the car, too. Mother Wright was left with Timmy Wright, who was playing a game in the backseat.

With all of this going on, Father Wright decided that this was not the right time to take a vacation, so he gathered up all of the family and left the gas station as quickly as he could. When he arrived home, he turned left into the driveway and said, "I wish the Wright family had never left home today!"

Questions:

1. "Why was Aunt Linda Wright unable to come on the trip?" (Not enough room in the car)
2. "How many children did the Wright family have?" (4)
3. "Who moved the trashcan?" (Timmy)
4. "What did Mr. Wright worry about at home?" (The stove)
5. "Why did Susan leave the car?" (She started to feel sick)
6. "Who went back home to get Mother Wright's wallet?" (Tommy)
7. "Where was Timmy at the gas station?" (In the backseat of the car)

---

* This story is available from multiple sources on the Internet. The original source is not clear.

Positive Discipline in the School and Classroom Manual by Jane Nelsen, Lynn Lott, Teresa LaSala, Jody McVittie, and Suzanne Smitha

About the Authors

Teresa LaSala, a Certified Positive Discipline Lead Trainer, provides parent workshops and trainings, as well as whole school training, consultation and ongoing supportive services in public, private, charter and parochial schools throughout the United States and internationally. She facilitates workshops drawing school leaders from around the world. Teresa is also a Whole Child Faculty Member - Regional Specialist for ASCD (an educational leadership organization). She serves as a School Culture and Climate Specialist with The School Culture and Climate Initiative based at the Center for Human and Social Development at the College of Saint Elizabeth in Convent Station, NJ; and has received an award from the NJ State Department of Education, as part of a team, for implementing a "Role Model SEL and Character Education Curriculum Program" (based on the Positive Discipline Whole School Model).

She has been a member of the Positive Discipline Association for 20 years and served 8 years on the International Board of Directors. Teresa is a licensed nurse with 23 years of experience in the areas of Family and Pediatric Care, Child Development, and Complimentary Medicine. She resides in Denville, NJ with her husband Jim and has 2 daughters, Meaghan and Lauren, who have been her greatest joy and teachers.

Jody McVittie is a Certified Positive Discipline Lead Trainer who has been teaching Positive Discipline in the Classroom since 1994. She has consulted for dozens of schools: public, independent, early childhood, elementary, and secondary. Her work with schools includes trainings in Spanish (Nicaragua) for First Nations Communities (in northern British Columbia) and for a school for the deaf. She is the Executive Director of Sound Discipline, a Seattle non-profit committed to using Positive Discipline to advance equity and empower student voice in schools.

Jody received her medical degree from Case Western University and completed a family medicine residency and a fellowship in Modesto California before returning to the Pacific Northwest to practice medicine. Twenty years ago, she shifted her focus to broader community issues that impact health outcomes including parenting, education, trauma and the impact of intra-family violence. In 2012, she was honored by the Center for Ethical Leadership with the Bill Grace Legacy award. Jody lives in Seattle, Washington and is the mother of three young adults who have been some of her best teachers.

Suzanne Smitha McPherson is a Certified Positive Discipline Lead Trainer who has used Positive Discipline with schools and families since 1991. She earned an M.S. degree from the University of Tennessee and continued advanced studies in North Carolina where she now lives. She served as a licensed school psychologist in a large urban school district for over 35 years, providing psychological, counseling and social work services before retiring in 2009. Currently working as an educational consultant, she provides consultation and training for staffs of public, private, charter and parochial schools as well as parenting education classes in her community and the southeast. Suzanne enjoys travel, especially when it is to be with her adult daughters and their families. She served for many years on the board of the Positive Discipline Association and currently volunteers with community agencies and boards.

Jane Nelsen is the author of the Positive Discipline Series and co-founder of a worldwide movement, through the Positive Discipline Association, that has certified thousands of Positive Discipline Facilitators in over 60 countries. The original Positive Discipline book, written in 1981, was the product of Jane's deep gratitude for the changes she was able to make as a parent of 7 children after learning the work of Alfred Adler and Rudolf Dreikurs in her college class in Child Development and Family Relations. Since that time, Jane has authored or co-authored many books, tool cards, and several training manuals. Enthusiasm continues to grow from interest on the part of parents, teachers, couples and business leaders who have experienced stronger relationships as a result of training in Positive Discipline.

As an Elementary School Counselor for 10 years, Jane was the director of Project ACCEPT (Adlerian Counseling Concepts for Encouraging Parents and Teachers) a federally funded project that included two experimental schools and a control school that resulted in positive child behavior change.

Lynn Lott is a distinguished and popular trainer of Adlerian Psychology. She holds two master's degrees in counseling and psychology, and works as a therapist and trainer. Lynn has authored and coauthored over 20 books and manuals and is the founder of Encouragement Consulting Workshops. She trains family therapists, parent educators and teachers around the world, and worked for years as an associate professor at Sonoma State University. Lynn is recognized as a Diplomat in Adlerian Psychology, the highest level of professional accomplishment offered by The North American Society of Adlerian Psychology (NASAP) – based upon her demonstration of professional accomplishment in and contribution to the field of Adlerian Psychology.

Resources

All website resources were retrieved during November, 2018

Adverse Child Experience (ACE) Study. Retrieved from https://www.cdc.gov/violenceprevention/acestudy/index.html

Albert, Linda (2003). *Cooperative discipline: How to manage your classroom and promote self-esteem.* Circle Pines, MN: American Guidance Service.

Bireda, Martha R. (2010). *Cultures in conflict: Eliminating racial profiling*, (5th ed). Lanham, MD: Rowman and Littlefield Education.

Bettner, Betty Lou, Ed. (1989). *An Adlerian resource book.* Chicago, IL: North American Society for Adlerian Psychology.

Blum, R.W. & Rinehart P.M. (1997). *Reducing the risk: Connections that make a difference in the lives of youth.* Retrieved from https://eric.ed.gov

Borba, Michele. (2018). Nine competencies for teaching empathy. *Educational Leadership,* 76 (2), 22-28.

Bronson, Po. (2007, August 3). *How not to talk to your kids: The inverse power of praise.* New York News & Politics. Retrieved from https://nymag.com/news/features/27840/

Carstarphan, Meria Joel & Graff, Ed. (2018). Seeding SEL across schools: strategies for leaders. *Educational Leadership,* 76 (2), 30-35.

Cole, Susan F., O'Brien, Jessica G., Gadd, M. Geron, Ristuccia, Joel, Wallace, D. Luray, & Gregory, Michael. (2005). *Massachusetts Advocates for Children: Helping Traumatized Children Learn.* Retrieved from www.traumasensitiveschools.org

College of Education, The Ohio State University. (2003). Classroom management in a diverse society. *Theory into Practice,* 42 (4)

Davies, Anne, Cameron, C., Politano, C., & Gregory, K. (1992). Together is Better: *Collaborative assessment, evaluation and reporting.* Winnipeg, Canada: Peguis.

Davis, Penny G. The impact of abuse and neglect on attachment, brain development, learning and behavior. DVD available from www.respectful-relationships2.com

Deiro, J. (2003). Do your students know you care? *Educational Leadership* 60(6), 60-63.

Dreikurs, Rudolf. (1964). *Children: The challenge.* New York, NY: Hawthorn Books, Inc.

Dreikurs, Rudolf. (1971). *Social equality: The challenge of today.* Chicago, IL: Contemporary Books, Inc.

Durlak, Joseph A., Weissberg, R. P., Dymnicki, A. B., Taylor, R. D., & Schellinger, K. B. (2011) The impact of enhancing students' social and emotional learning: A meta-analysis of school based universal interventions. *Child Development,* 82 (1), 405-432. Retrieved from https://www.casel.org/wp-content/uploads/2016/01/meta-analysis-child-development-1.pdf

Dweck, Carol S. (2006). *Mindset: The new psychology of success.* New York, NY: Random House.

Elias, Maurice J. (2001) adapted from prior versions in: Elias, M. J., Zins, J. E., Weissberg, R. P., Frey, K., Greenberg, M., Haynes, N., Kessler, R., Schwab-Stone, M., & Shriver, T. (1997). *Promoting social and emotional learning: Guidelines for educators.* Alexandria, VA: Association for Supervision and Curriculum Development and Elias, M. J., & Clabby, J. F. (1992). Building social problem-solving skills: Guidelines from a school-based program. San Francisco: Jossey-Bass.

Elias, Maurice J. (2006). The connection between academic and social emotional learning. In Elias, Maurice J. & Arnold, Harriett, *The Educator's guide to emotional intelligence and academic achievement.* Thousand Oaks, CA: Corwin Press.

Evans, T. (1996). Encouragement: The key to reforming classrooms. *Educational Leadership* 54(1), 81-85.

Felitti, Vincent J. (2002). *The relationship of adverse childhood experiences to adult health: Turning gold into lead.* (English translation from: Felitti VJ. Belastungen in der Kindheit und Gesundheit im Erwachsenenalter: die Verwandlung von Gold in Blei. Z *psychsom* Med *Psychother* 2002; 48(4): 359-369). Retrieved from https://www.memoiretraumatique.org/assets/files/v1/Documents-pdf/2002-ACE-Gold_into_Lead-%20felitti.pdf

Forbes, Heather. (2012). *Help for Billy: A beyond consequences approach to helping challenging children in the classroom.* Boulder, CO: Beyond Consequences Institute, LLC.

Glenn, H. Stephen, & Nelsen, Jane. (2000). *Raising self-reliant children in a self-indulgent world.* New York, NY: Harmony Books.

Goertz, Donna Bryant. (2001). *Children who are not yet peaceful: Preventing exclusion in the early elementary classroom.* Berkley, CA: Frog Ltd.

Greene, Ross. (2008). *Lost at school: Why our kids with behavioral challenges are falling through the cracks and how we can help them.* New York, NY: Scribner.

Greenwald O'Brien, Jessica P., & Burnett, Laurie, Editors. (2008). *Teachers' Strategies guide for working with children exposed to trauma* (2nd ed.). Framingham, MA: Framingham Public Schools.

Hammond, Zaretta. (2015). *Culturally responsive teaching and the brain.* Thousand Oaks, CA: Corwin.

Ingber, L., & McVittie, J. (2007). *BRIDGES: Building relationships for improved discipline, academic gains and effective schools.* Self-Published.

Inlay, L. (2003). Values: The implicit curriculum. *Educational Leadership,* 60(6), 69-71.

Institute for American Values. (2003). *Hardwired to connect: The new scientific case for authoritative communities.* Executive Summary retrieved from www.americanvalues.org/search/item.php?id=17

Jung, Lee Ann & Smith, D. (2018) Tear down your behavior chart! *Educational Leadership,* 76 (1), 12-18.

Kohn, Alfie. (2018). *Punished by rewards: Twenty-fifth anniversary edition: The trouble with gold stars, incentive plans, A's, praise, and other bribes.* New York, NY: Houghton Mifflin Harcourt.

Kohn, Alfie. (2018, October 28). Science confirms it: People are not pets. New York edition of *The New York Times,* p. SR10. Retrieved from https://www.nytimes.com/2018/10/27/opinion/Sunday/science-rewards-behavior.html

Krakovsky, Marina. (2007). The effort effect (Stanford). (2015, July 2). Retrieved from www.marinakrakovsky.com/the-effort-effect-stanford-marchapril-2007

Learning First Alliance. (2001). *Every child learning: Safe and supportive schools.* Association for Supervision and Curriculum Development. Retrieved from https://learningfirst.org/sites/learningfirst/files/assets/LFASafeSupportiveSchoolsReport.pdf

Lott, Lynn, & Mendenhall, Barbara. (2015). *Do-it-yourself therapy: How to think, feel, and act like a new person in just 8 weeks.* United States: Empowering People, Inc.

Lott, Lynn, & Nelsen, Jane. (1998). *Teaching parenting the positive discipline way: A step-by-step approach to starting and leading parenting classes* (5th ed.). United States: Empowering People.

Lott, Lynn, & Nelsen, Jane. (2017). *Teaching parenting the positive discipline way: A step-by-step approach to starting and leading parenting classes* (7th ed.). United States: Empowering People.

McKay, Gary, McKay, Joyce, Eckstein, Daniel, Maybell, Steven. (2001). *Raising respectful kids in a rude world.* Roseville, CA: Prima Publishing.

Medea, Andrea. (2004). *Conflict unraveled: Fixing problems at work and in families.* Chicago: PivotPoint Press.

National Center for Education Statistics. (2017). Dropout rates in the United States 2017. Washington, DC: U.S. Department of Education, Offices of Educational Research and Improvement.

Nelsen, Jane. (2006). *Positive discipline.* New York, NY: Ballantine Books.

Nelsen, Jane. (1999). *Positive time out and over 50 ways to avoid power struggles in the home and the classroom.* Rocklin, CA: Prima Publishing.

Nelsen, Jane, Duffy, R., Escobar, L. Ortalano, K. and Owen-Sohocki, D. (2001). *Positive discipline: A teacher's A-Z guide* (2nd ed.). Roseville, CA: Prima Publishing.

Nelsen, Jane, & Erwin, Cheryl. *Positive discipline for single parents: Facilitator's guide.* United States: Empowering People.

Nelsen, Jane, Erwin, C., & Foster, S. (2018). *Positive discipline for early childhood educators.* United States: Positive Discipline Association.

Nelsen, Jane, Foster, S., & Raphael, A. (2011). *Positive discipline for children with special needs.* New York, NY: Three Rivers Press.

Nelsen, Jane, & Gfroerer, Kelly. (2017). *Positive discipline tools for teachers: Effective classroom management for social, emotional, and academic success.* New York, NY: Harmony Books.

Nelsen, Jane, & Gfroerer, Kelly. (2016). *Positive discipline tools for teachers cards: 52 tools for classroom management.* Available from www.positivediscipline.com

Nelsen, Jane, & Lott, Lynn. (1992). *Positive discipline in the classroom teacher's guide: A step-by-step approach to bring positive discipline to the classroom and to help teachers of all grade levels implement classroom meetings.* Orem, UT: Empowering People Books.

Nelsen, Jane, & Lott, Lynn. (1997). *Positive discipline in the classroom teacher's guide: A step-by-step approach to bring positive discipline to the classroom and to help teachers of all grade levels implement classroom meetings* (Revised Edition). United States: Empowering People.

Nelsen, Jane, Lott, Lynn, & Glenn, H. Stephen. (2013). *Positive discipline in the classroom: Developing mutual respect, cooperation, and responsibility in your classroom* (4th ed.). New York, NY: Three Rivers Press.

Resources

Nickerson, Amanda B. (2018). Can SEL reduce school violence? *Educational Leadership,* 76 (2), 46-50.

Nova Science Now. (1.25.05). Mirror Neurons. Retrieved from https://www.youtube.com/watch?v=Xmx1qPyo8Ks

Perry, Bruce D. (2000). Consequences of emotional neglect in childhood, adapted in part from: *Maltreated children: Experience, brain development and the next generation.* New York, NY: W.W. Norton & Company.

Perry, Bruce. (2009) Examining child maltreatment through a neurodevelopmental lens: Clinical applications of the neurosequential model of therapeutics. *Journal of Loss and Trauma,* 14, 240-255.

Perry, Bruce & Szalavitz, Maia. (2006). *The boy who was raised as a dog and other stories from a child psychiatrist's notebook.* New York, NY: Basic Books.

Pew, William L. & Terner, Janet. (1978). *Courage to be imperfect.* New York, NY: Hawthorn Books.

Pink, Daniel H. (2009). TED: The science of motivation. Retrieved from http://www.ted.com/talks/dan_pink_on_motivation.html

Pink, Daniel H. (2009). *Drive: The surprising truth about what motivates us.* New York, NY: Riverhead Books.

Pink, Daniel H. (2010) RSA: Drive. Retrieved from http://www.youtube.com/watch?v=u6XAPnuFjJc

Resnick, M.D., et. al (1997). Protecting adolescents from harm: Findings from the national longitudinal study on adolescent health. *Journal of the American Medical Association,* 278 (10), 823 – 832. Retrieved from https://pdfs.semanticscholar.org/6994/963fcb809762927eeb8c422f4be82f9efaaa.pdf

Rightmyer, Elizabeth Campbell. (2003). Democratic discipline: Children creating solutions. *Young Children,* July, 38-45.

Saphier, Jon, Haley-Speca, Mary Ann, & Grower, Robert. (2008). *The skillful teacher* (6th ed.). Acton, MA: Research for Better Teaching.

Schaps, E. (2003). Creating a school community. *Educational Leadership,* 60 (6), 31-33.

Siegel, Daniel J. (2015). *Brainstorm: The power and purpose of the teenage brain.* New York, NY: Jeremy P. Tarcher/Penguin.

Siegel, Daniel J. (2010). Dr. Daniel Siegel presenting a hand model of the brain. Retrieved from https://www.youtube.com/watch?v=gm9clJ74Oxw

Siegel, Daniel J., & Bryson, Tina Payne. (2011). *The whole-brain child: 12 revolutionary strategies to nurture your child's developing mind.* New York, NY: Delacorte Press.

Siegel, Daniel J., & Hartzell, Mary. (2003). *Parenting from the inside out: How a deeper self-understanding can help you raise children who thrive.* New York, NY: Jeremy P. Tarcher: Putnam.

Sound Discipline (Producer). (2015). *Building resilience: Working with students exposed to trauma* (DVD). Available from www.SoundDiscipline.org

Sound Discipline (Producer). (2015). *Building classroom community: Classroom meetings and self-regulation* (DVD). Available from www.SoundDiscipline.org and www.positivediscipline.com

Sugai, G, Sprague, J.R, Horner, R.H., Walker, H.M. (2000). Preventing school violence: The use of office discipline referrals to assess and monitor school-wide discipline interventions. *Journal of Emotional and Behavioral Disorders,* 8 (2), 94 – 101.

Taylor, John F. (1984). *Person to person: Awareness techniques for counselors, group leaders, and parent educators.* Saratoga, California: R & E Publishers.

Tough, Paul. (2012). *How children succeed: Grit, curiosity and the hidden power of character.* New York, NY: Houghton Mifflin.

Wang, M. C., Haertel, G. D., & Walberg, H. J. (1997). Toward a knowledge base for school learning. *Review of Educational Research,* 63, 249–294.

www.positivediscipline.com for free online newsletter from Jane Nelsen as well as all Positive Discipline books, manuals, materials and workshops.

www.positivediscipline.org Website of the Positive Discipline Association. A 501 C 3 non-profit supporting respectful relationships in homes, schools and communities. Resources include webinars, workshops, approved continuing education credit, and newsletters

www.SoundDiscipline.org Website for Newsletter for the 501 C 3 non-profit Sound Discipline.